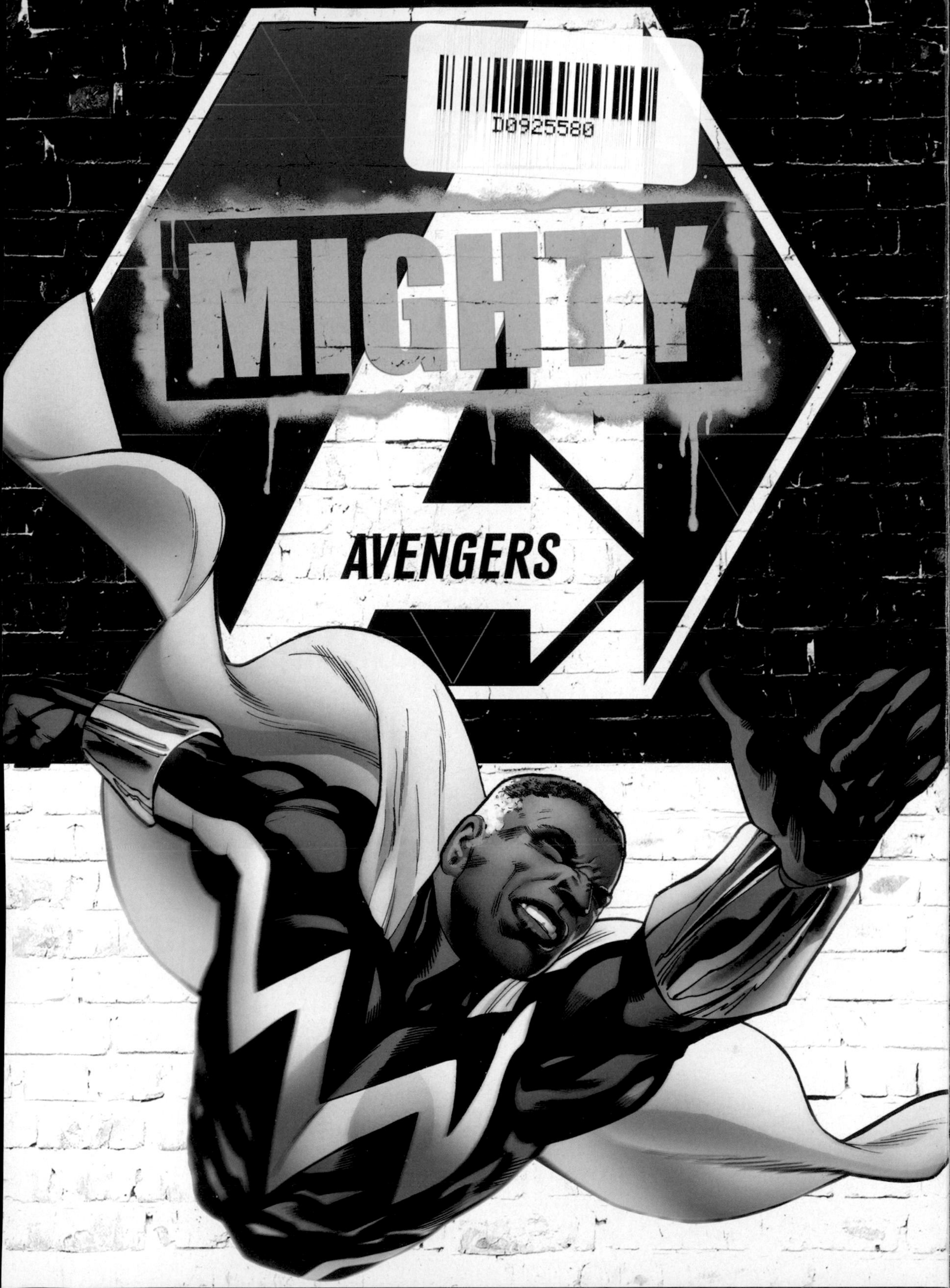
MIGHTY
AVENGERS

MIGHTY AVENGERS

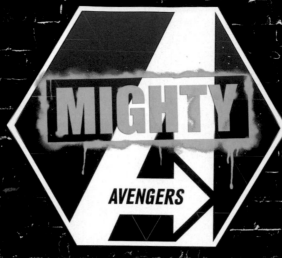

FAMILY BONDING

WRITER
AL EWING

PENCILERS
VALERIO SCHITI (#6-8) & GREG LAND (#9-10)

INKER
JAY LEISTEN (#9-10)

COLORIST
FRANK D'ARMATA WITH EDGAR DELGADO (#9)

LETTERER
VC'S CORY PETIT

COVER ART
GREG LAND & FRANK D'ARMATA (#6 & 10)
GREG LAND, JAY LEISTEN & FRANK D'ARMATA (#7-9)

ASSISTANT EDITOR: **JAKE THOMAS**
EDITORS: **TOM BREVOORT** WITH **WIL MOSS**

COLLECTION EDITOR: **SARAH BRUNSTAD** ASSOCIATE MANAGING EDITOR: **ALEX STARBUCK**
EDITORS, SPECIAL PROJECTS: **JENNIFER GRÜNWALD** & **MARK D. BEAZLEY**
SENIOR EDITOR, SPECIAL PROJECTS: **JEFF YOUNGQUIST**
SVP PRINT, SALES & MARKETING: **DAVID GABRIEL**
BOOK DESIGNER: **RODOLFO MURAGUCHI**

EDITOR IN CHIEF: **AXEL ALONSO** CHIEF CREATIVE OFFICER: **JOE QUESADA**
PUBLISHER: **DAN BUCKLEY** EXECUTIVE PRODUCER: **ALAN FINE**

MIGHTY AVENGERS VOL. 2: FAMILY BONDING. Contains material originally published in magazine form as MIGHTY AVENGERS #6-10. First printing 2014. ISBN# 978-0-7851-8875-9. Published by MARVEL WORLDWIDE, INC., a subsidiary of MARVEL ENTERTAINMENT, LLC. OFFICE OF PUBLICATION: 135 West 50th Street, New York, NY 10020. **Printed in Canada**. ALAN FINE, EVP - Office of the President, Marvel Worldwide, Inc. and EVP & CMO Marvel Characters B.V.; DAN BUCKLEY, Publisher & President - Print, Animation & Digital Divisions; JOE QUESADA, Chief Creative Officer; TOM BREVOORT, SVP of Publishing; DAVID BOGART, SVP of Operations & Procurement, Publishing; C.B. CEBULSKI, SVP of Creator & Content Development; DAVID GABRIEL, SVP Print, Sales & Marketing; JIM O'KEEFE, VP of Operations & Logistics; DAN CARR, Executive Director of Publishing Technology; SUSAN CRESPI, Editorial Operations Manager; ALEX MORALES, Publishing Operations Manager; STAN LEE, Chairman Emeritus. For information regarding advertising in Marvel Comics or on Marvel.com, please contact Niza Disla, Director of Marvel Partnerships, at ndisla@marvel.com. For Marvel subscription inquiries, please call 800-217-9158. **Manufactured between 6/6/2014 and 7/14/2014 by SOLISCO PRINTERS, SCOTT, QC, CANADA.**

10 9 8 7 6 5 4 3 2 1

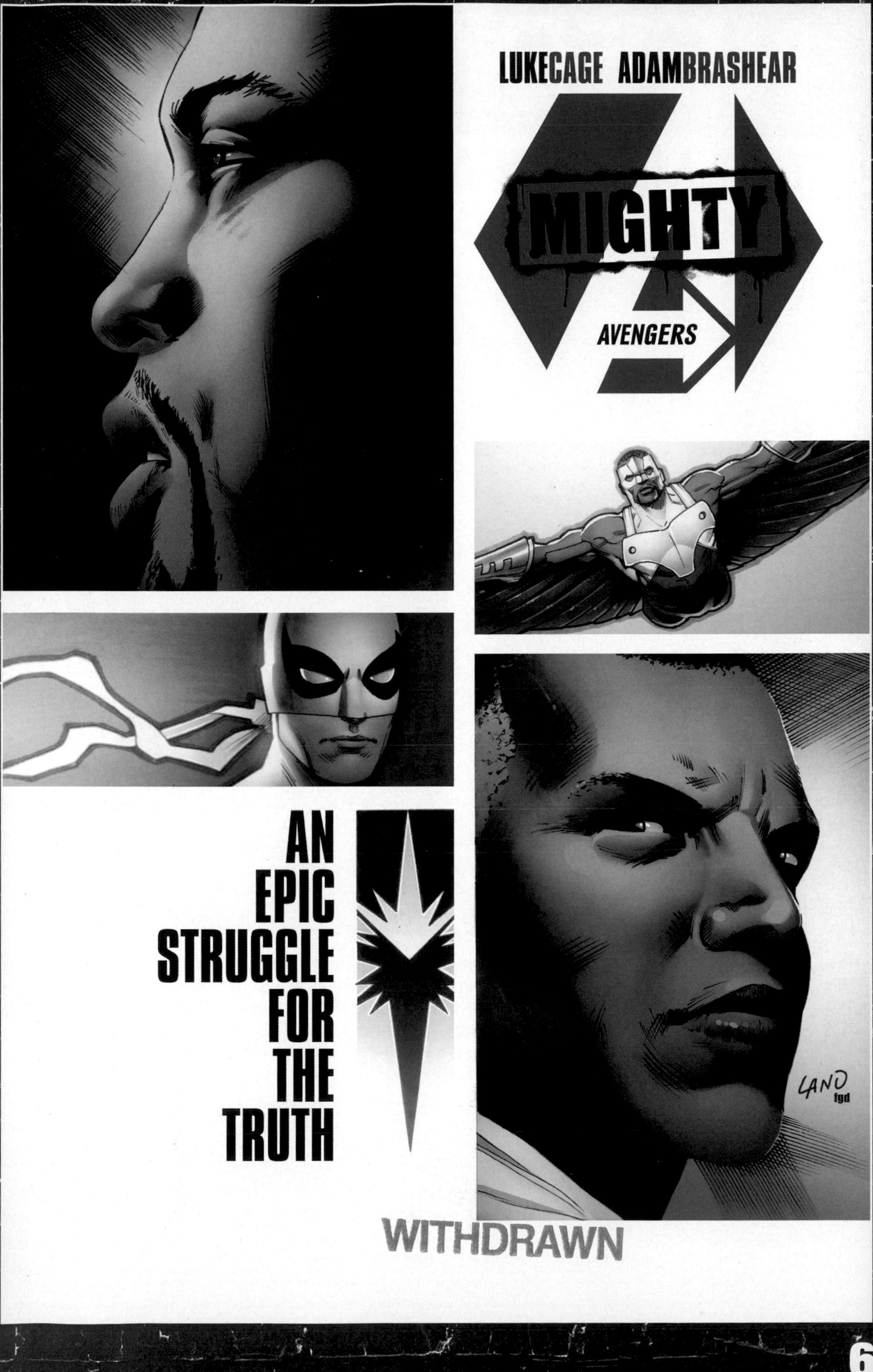

LUKECAGE ADAMBRASHEAR
MIGHTY
AVENGERS
AN EPIC STRUGGLE FOR THE TRUTH
LANO fgd
WITHDRAWN

NEED HELP?

THE MIGHTY AVENGERS ARE NOW OPEN FOR BUSINESS!

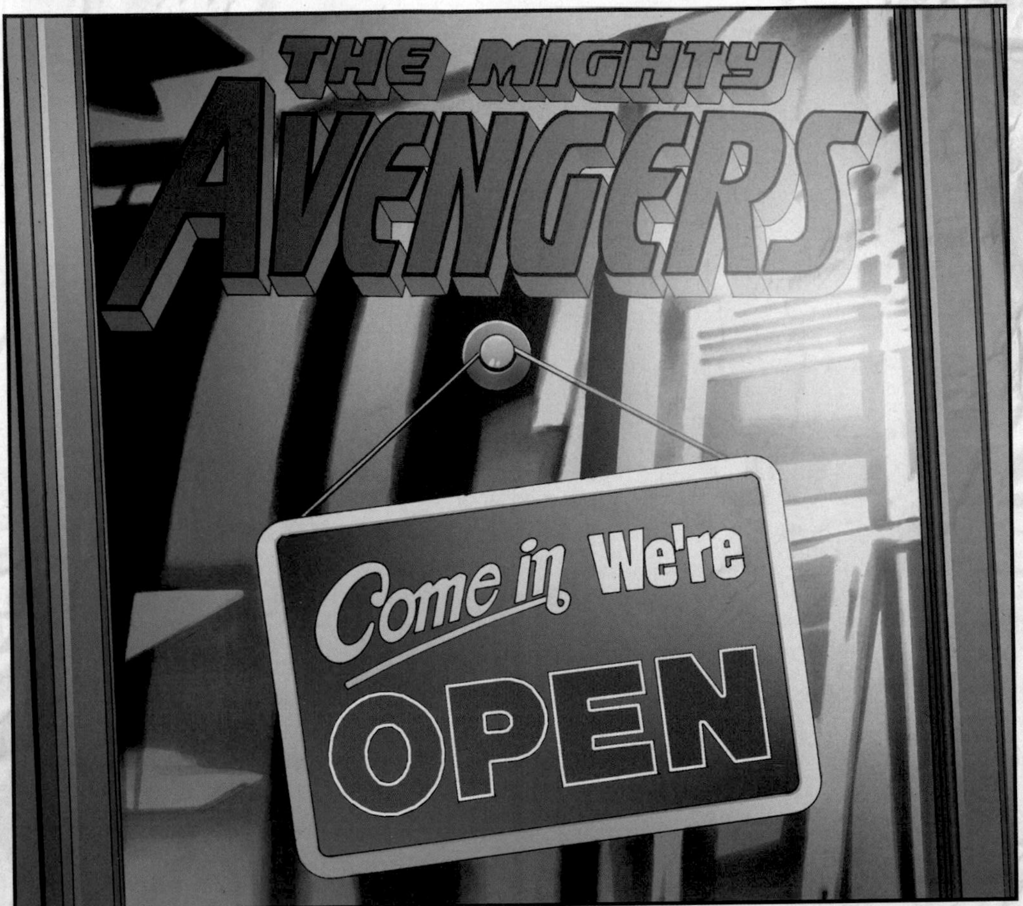
THE MIGHTY
AVENGERS
Come in We're
OPEN

Hey, I'm Luke Cage. I've been an Avenger, I've been a Hero for Hire, I've been what some people might call a super hero, fighting monstrous villains and saving the globe. But now I'm looking to save the neighborhood. Along with my associates Blue Marvel, Falcon, Spectrum, She-Hulk, Ronin, White Tiger and Power Man, I'm here to help. It can be a hard, scary world out there. Making it on your own can seem daunting. But together, we can do anything. Together, we are MIGHTY.

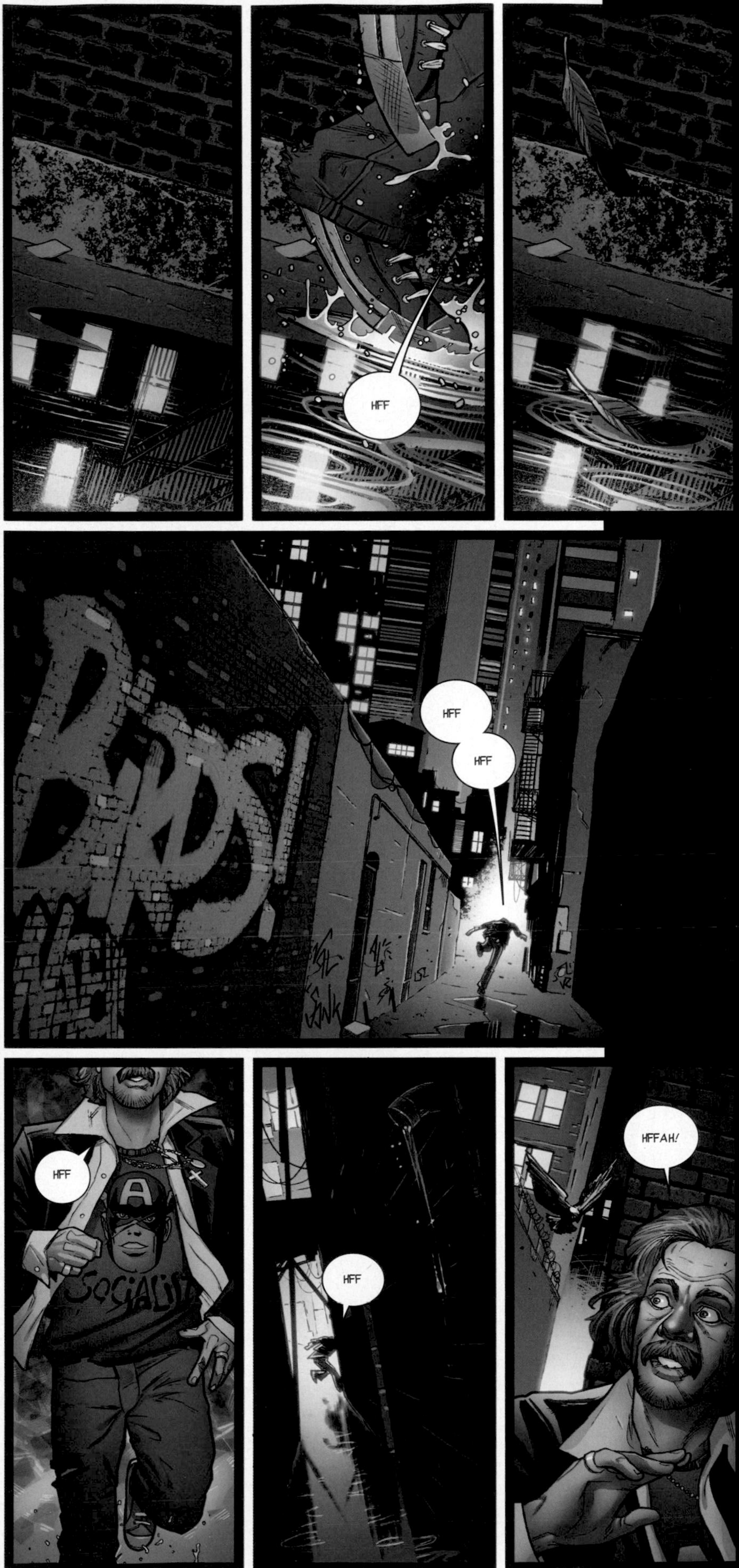
HFF
HFF
HFF
HFF
HFF
HFFAH!

Kenny Driscoll had been running since Houston Street.

He didn't know why.

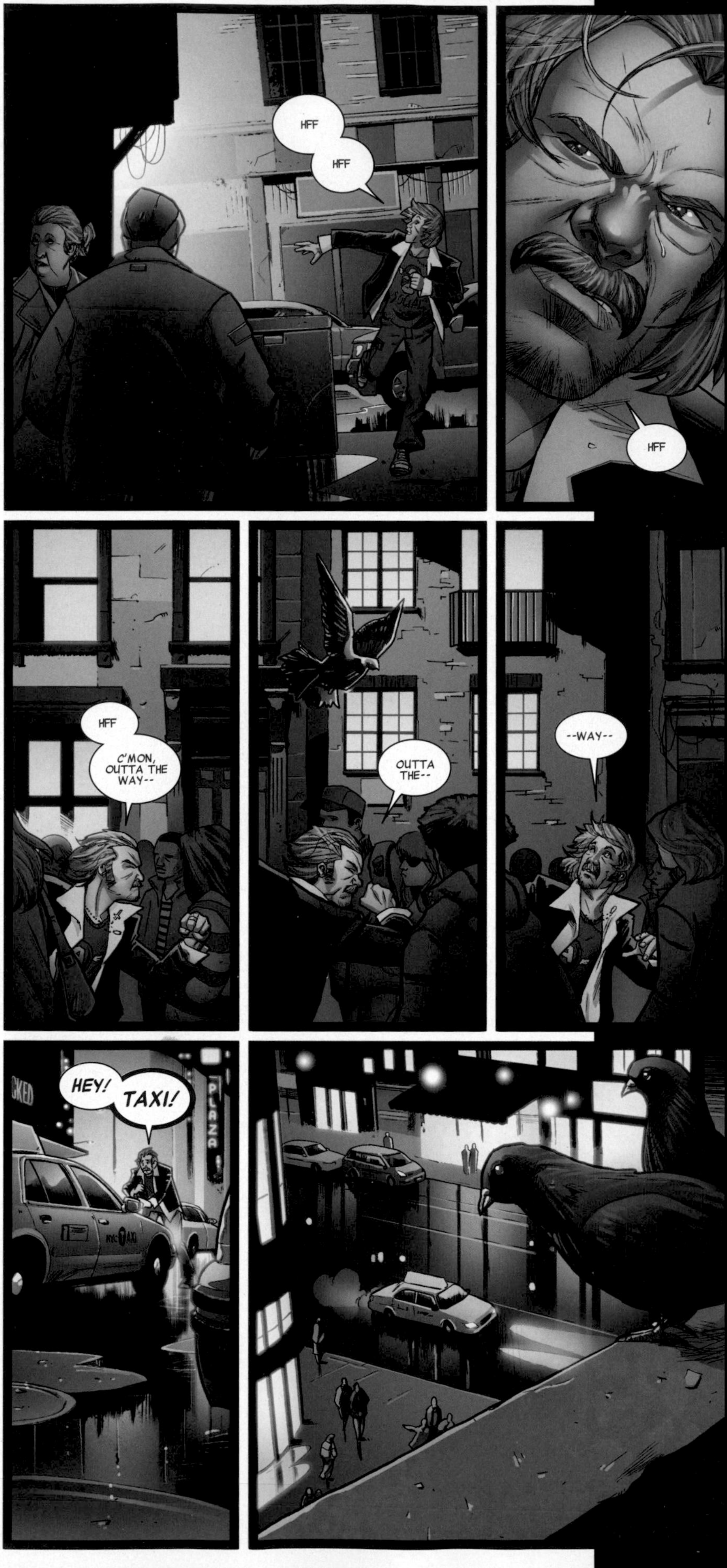
HFF
HFF
HFF
HFF
C'MON, OUTTA THE WAY--
OUTTA THE--
--WAY--
HEY!
TAXI!
PLAZA

It wasn't guilt,
he knew that.

The bookstore had it coming. It was propaganda, floor to ceiling--anti-capitalist, anti-family. Stooges for the Marxist New World Order.

Like the boss said, it had to go.

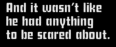

And it wasn't like he had anything to be scared about.

He wouldn't get caught. There was nothing at the scene to connect him to it.

And he'd gone around back to pour the gasoline--no cameras there, nobody watching. No witnesses at all.

Nobody there but the pigeons.

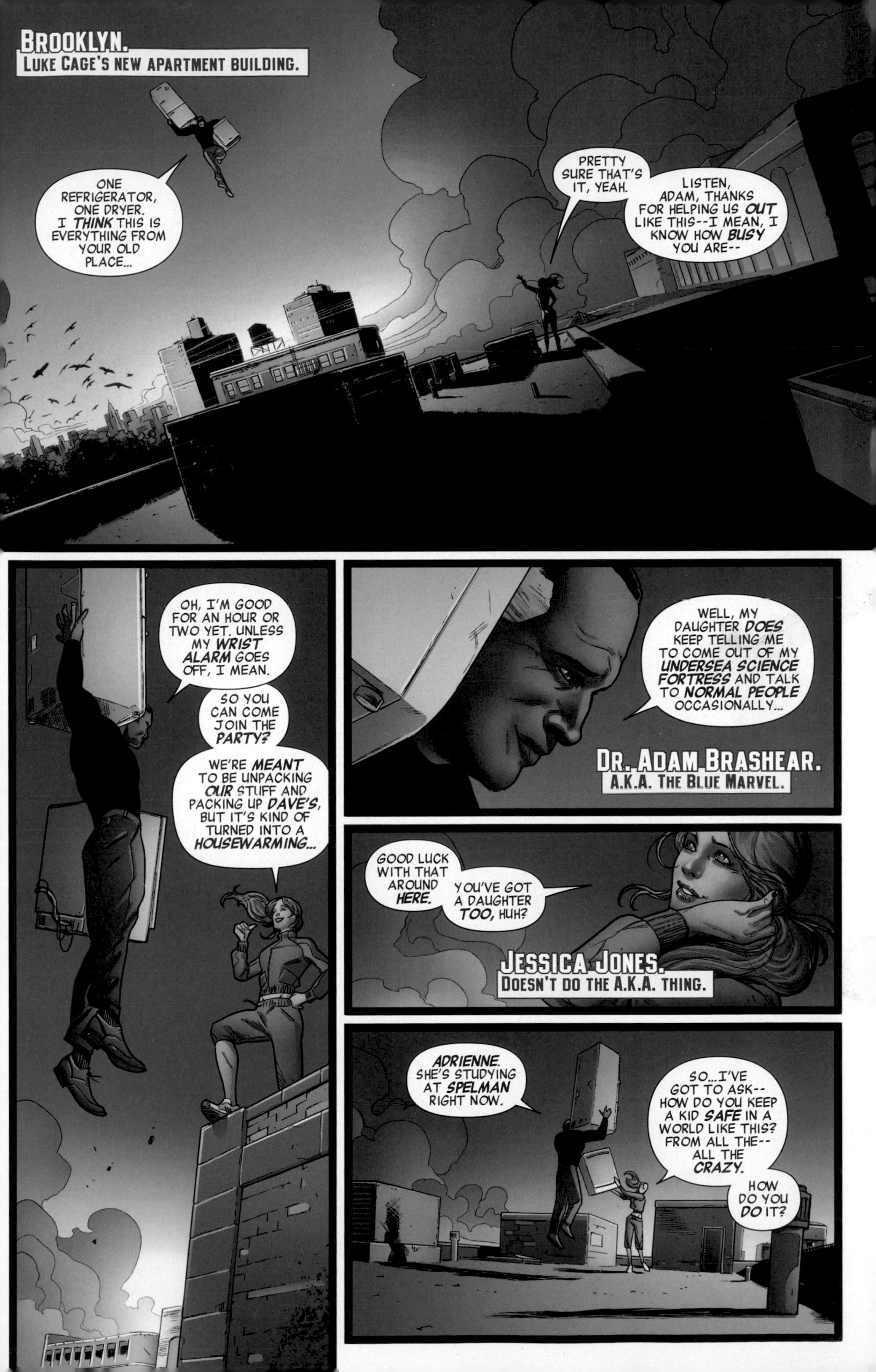

BROOKLYN.
LUKE CAGE'S NEW APARTMENT BUILDING.
ONE REFRIGERATOR, ONE DRYER. I THINK THIS IS EVERYTHING FROM YOUR OLD PLACE...
PRETTY SURE THAT'S IT, YEAH.
LISTEN, ADAM, THANKS FOR HELPING US OUT LIKE THIS--I MEAN, I KNOW HOW BUSY YOU ARE--
OH, I'M GOOD FOR AN HOUR OR TWO YET. UNLESS MY WRIST ALARM GOES OFF, I MEAN.
SO YOU CAN COME JOIN THE PARTY?
WE'RE MEANT TO BE UNPACKING OUR STUFF AND PACKING UP DAVE'S, BUT IT'S KIND OF TURNED INTO A HOUSEWARMING...
WELL, MY DAUGHTER DOES KEEP TELLING ME TO COME OUT OF MY UNDERSEA SCIENCE FORTRESS AND TALK TO NORMAL PEOPLE OCCASIONALLY...
DR. ADAM BRASHEAR.
A.K.A. THE BLUE MARVEL.
GOOD LUCK WITH THAT AROUND HERE.
YOU'VE GOT A DAUGHTER TOO, HUH?
JESSICA JONES.
DOESN'T DO THE A.K.A. THING.
ADRIENNE. SHE'S STUDYING AT SPELMAN RIGHT NOW.
SO...I'VE GOT TO ASK--HOW DO YOU KEEP A KID SAFE IN A WORLD LIKE THIS? FROM ALL THE--ALL THE CRAZY.
HOW DO YOU DO IT?

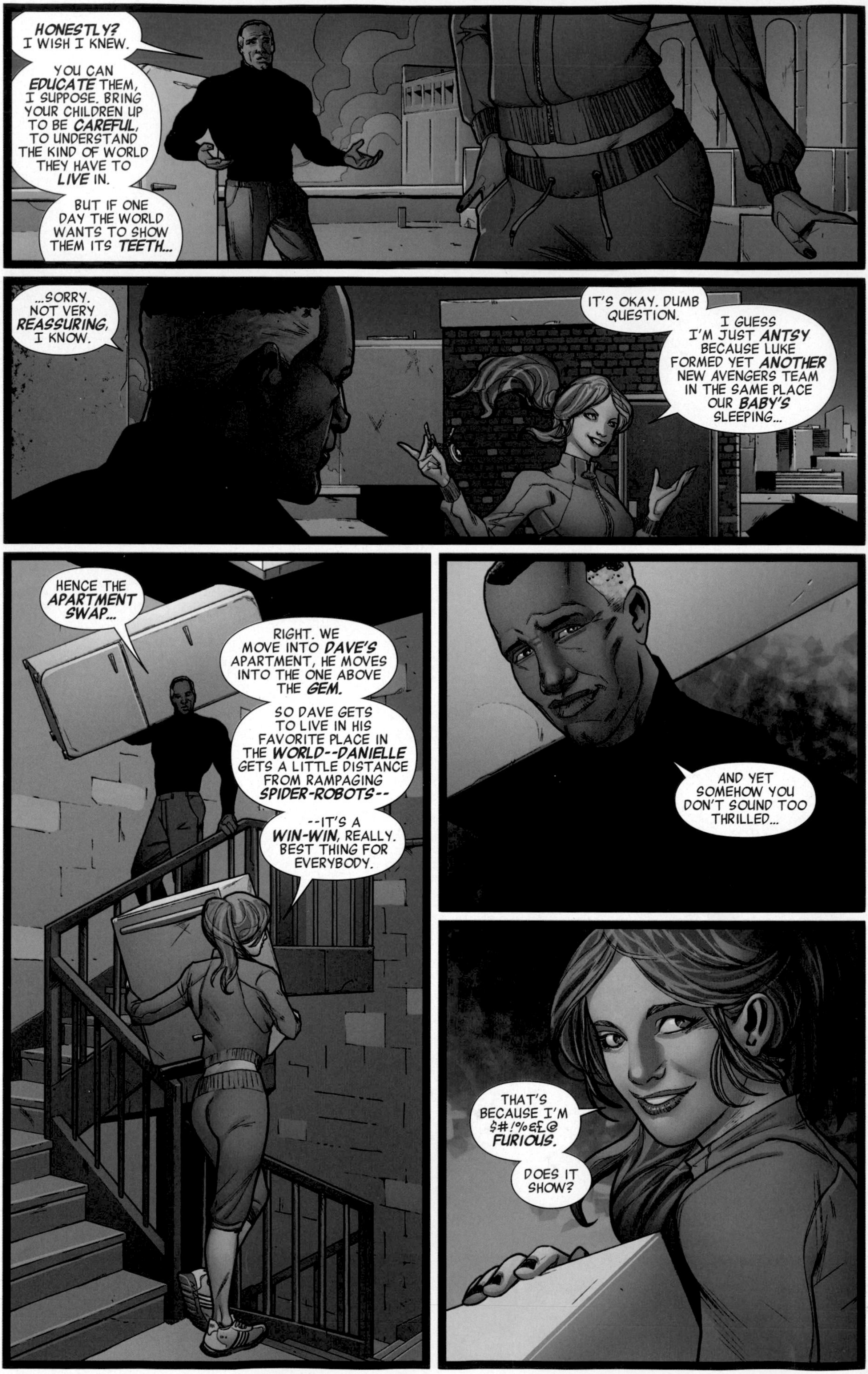
HONESTLY? I WISH I KNEW.
YOU CAN EDUCATE THEM, I SUPPOSE. BRING YOUR CHILDREN UP TO BE CAREFUL, TO UNDERSTAND THE KIND OF WORLD THEY HAVE TO LIVE IN.
BUT IF ONE DAY THE WORLD WANTS TO SHOW THEM ITS TEETH...
...SORRY. NOT VERY REASSURING, I KNOW.
IT'S OKAY. DUMB QUESTION.
I GUESS I'M JUST ANTSY BECAUSE LUKE FORMED YET ANOTHER NEW AVENGERS TEAM IN THE SAME PLACE OUR BABY'S SLEEPING...
HENCE THE APARTMENT SWAP...
RIGHT. WE MOVE INTO DAVE'S APARTMENT, HE MOVES INTO THE ONE ABOVE THE GEM.
SO DAVE GETS TO LIVE IN HIS FAVORITE PLACE IN THE WORLD--DANIELLE GETS A LITTLE DISTANCE FROM RAMPAGING SPIDER-ROBOTS--
--IT'S A WIN-WIN, REALLY. BEST THING FOR EVERYBODY.
AND YET SOMEHOW YOU DON'T SOUND TOO THRILLED...
THAT'S BECAUSE I'M $#!%&£@ FURIOUS.
DOES IT SHOW?

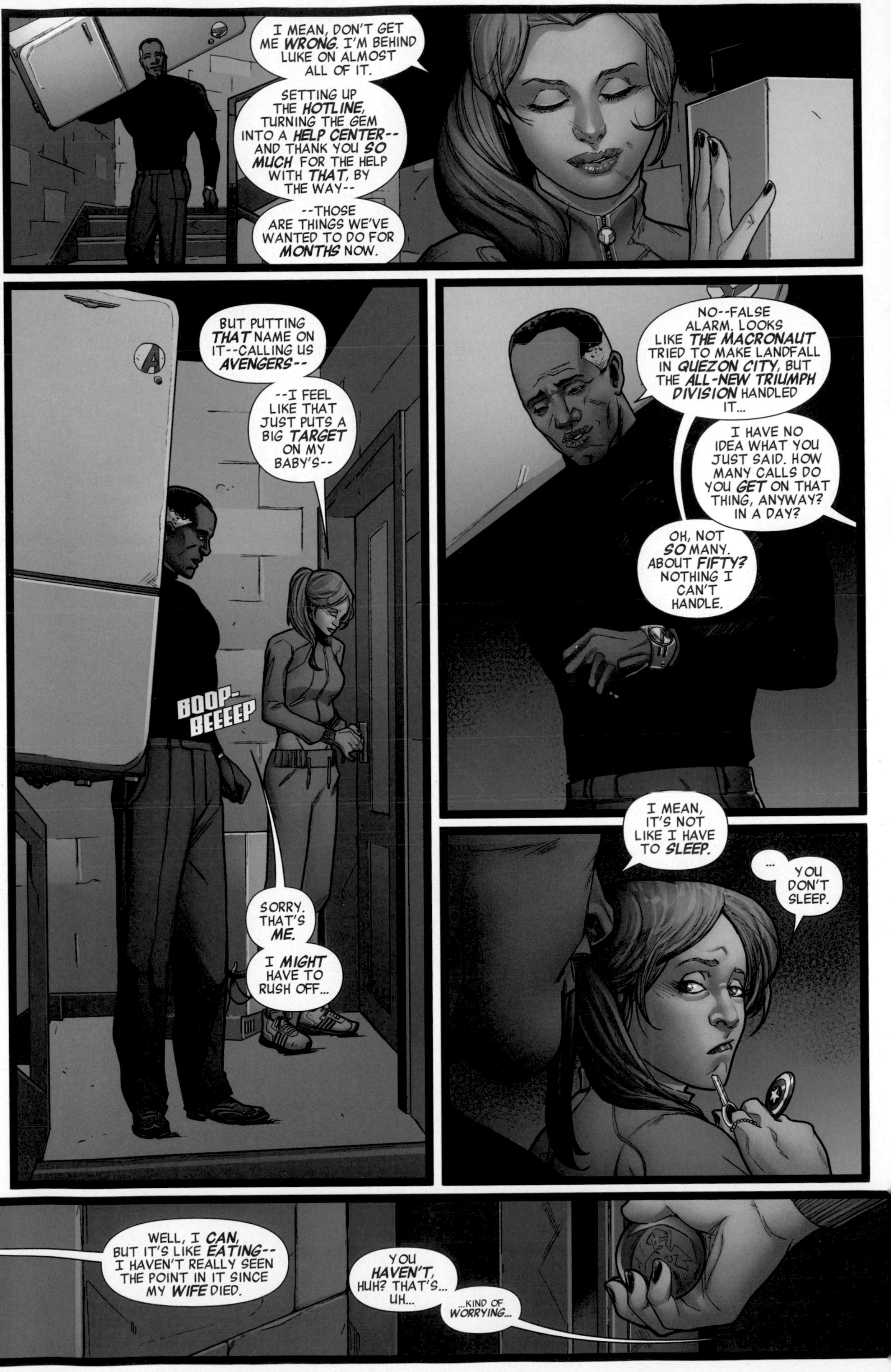

I MEAN, DON'T GET ME WRONG. I'M BEHIND LUKE ON ALMOST ALL OF IT.
SETTING UP THE HOTLINE, TURNING THE GEM INTO A HELP CENTER-- AND THANK YOU SO MUCH FOR THE HELP WITH THAT, BY THE WAY--
--THOSE ARE THINGS WE'VE WANTED TO DO FOR MONTHS NOW.
BUT PUTTING THAT NAME ON IT--CALLING US AVENGERS--
--I FEEL LIKE THAT JUST PUTS A BIG TARGET ON MY BABY'S--
BOOP-BEEEEP
SORRY. THAT'S ME.
I MIGHT HAVE TO RUSH OFF...
NO--FALSE ALARM. LOOKS LIKE THE MACRONAUT TRIED TO MAKE LANDFALL IN QUEZON CITY, BUT THE ALL-NEW TRIUMPH DIVISION HANDLED IT...
I HAVE NO IDEA WHAT YOU JUST SAID. HOW MANY CALLS DO YOU GET ON THAT THING, ANYWAY? IN A DAY?
OH, NOT SO MANY. ABOUT FIFTY? NOTHING I CAN'T HANDLE.
I MEAN, IT'S NOT LIKE I HAVE TO SLEEP.
... YOU DON'T SLEEP.
WELL, I CAN, BUT IT'S LIKE EATING-- I HAVEN'T REALLY SEEN THE POINT IN IT SINCE MY WIFE DIED.
YOU HAVEN'T, HUH? THAT'S... UH...
...KIND OF WORRYING...

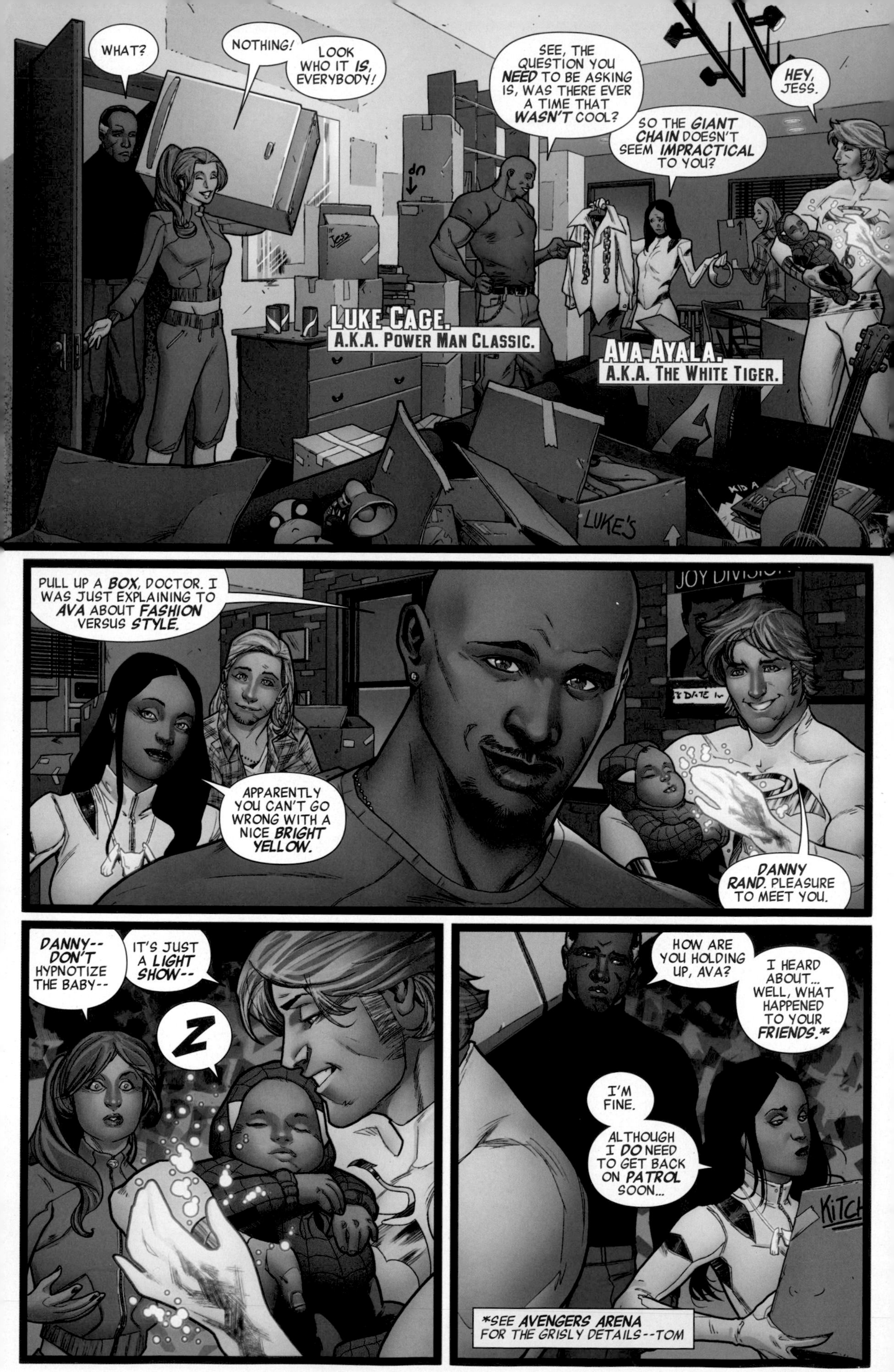

WHAT?
NOTHING!
LOOK WHO IT IS, EVERYBODY!
SEE, THE QUESTION YOU NEED TO BE ASKING IS, WAS THERE EVER A TIME THAT WASN'T COOL?
SO THE GIANT CHAIN DOESN'T SEEM IMPRACTICAL TO YOU?
HEY, JESS.
LUKE CAGE.
A.K.A. POWER MAN CLASSIC.
AVA AYALA.
A.K.A. THE WHITE TIGER.
LUKE'S
KID A
PULL UP A BOX, DOCTOR. I WAS JUST EXPLAINING TO AVA ABOUT FASHION VERSUS STYLE.
JOY DIVISIO
APPARENTLY YOU CAN'T GO WRONG WITH A NICE BRIGHT YELLOW.
DANNY RAND. PLEASURE TO MEET YOU.
DANNY-- DON'T HYPNOTIZE THE BABY--
IT'S JUST A LIGHT SHOW--
Z
HOW ARE YOU HOLDING UP, AVA?
I HEARD ABOUT... WELL, WHAT HAPPENED TO YOUR FRIENDS.*
I'M FINE.
ALTHOUGH I DO NEED TO GET BACK ON PATROL SOON...
KITCH
*SEE AVENGERS ARENA FOR THE GRISLY DETAILS--TOM

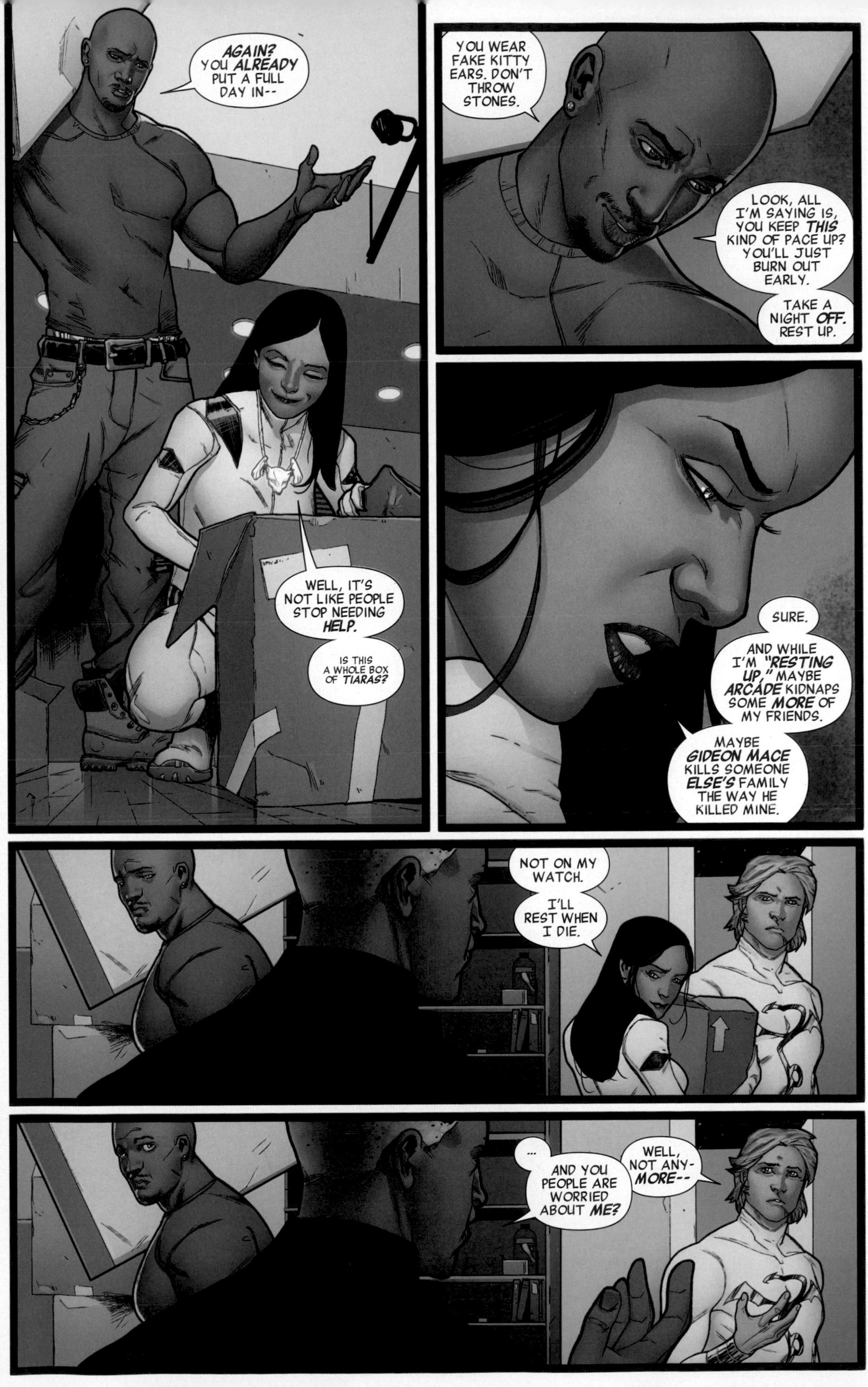
AGAIN? YOU ALREADY PUT A FULL DAY IN--
WELL, IT'S NOT LIKE PEOPLE STOP NEEDING HELP.
IS THIS A WHOLE BOX OF TIARAS?
YOU WEAR FAKE KITTY EARS. DON'T THROW STONES.
LOOK, ALL I'M SAYING IS, YOU KEEP THIS KIND OF PACE UP? YOU'LL JUST BURN OUT EARLY.
TAKE A NIGHT OFF. REST UP.
SURE.
AND WHILE I'M "RESTING UP," MAYBE ARCADE KIDNAPS SOME MORE OF MY FRIENDS.
MAYBE GIDEON MACE KILLS SOMEONE ELSE'S FAMILY THE WAY HE KILLED MINE.
NOT ON MY WATCH.
I'LL REST WHEN I DIE.
...
AND YOU PEOPLE ARE WORRIED ABOUT ME?
WELL, NOT ANY-MORE--

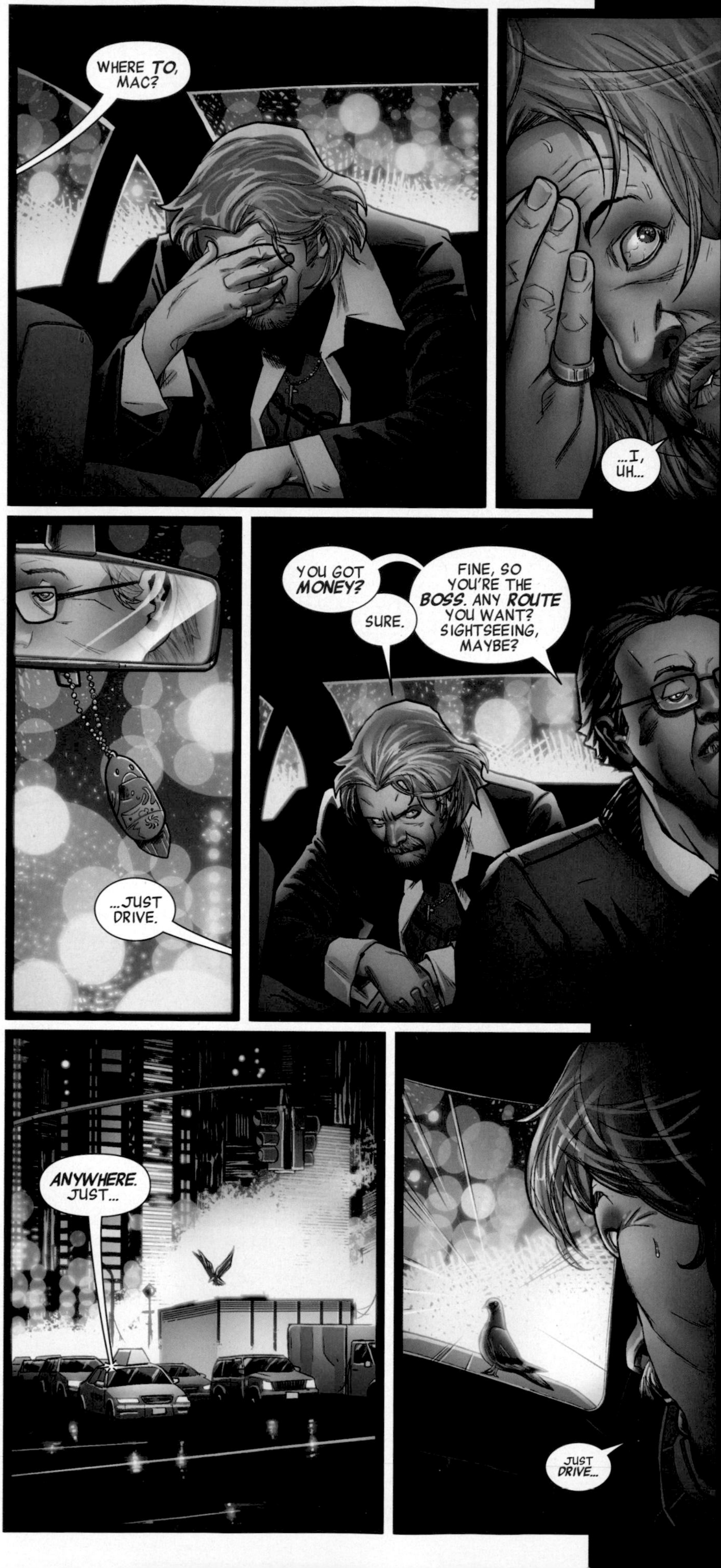
WHERE TO, MAC?
...I, UH...
YOU GOT MONEY?
SURE.
FINE, SO YOU'RE THE BOSS. ANY ROUTE YOU WANT? SIGHTSEEING, MAYBE?
...JUST DRIVE.
ANYWHERE. JUST...
JUST DRIVE...

Kenny Driscoll told himself he wasn't worried.

He was off the street now, after all.

He was safe. Hidden.

Riding in the back of one more New York taxi, one of hundreds, all barely distinguishable from one another.

All the same bright, ugly yellow.

"Canary yellow," Kenny Driscoll thought.

And shuddered.

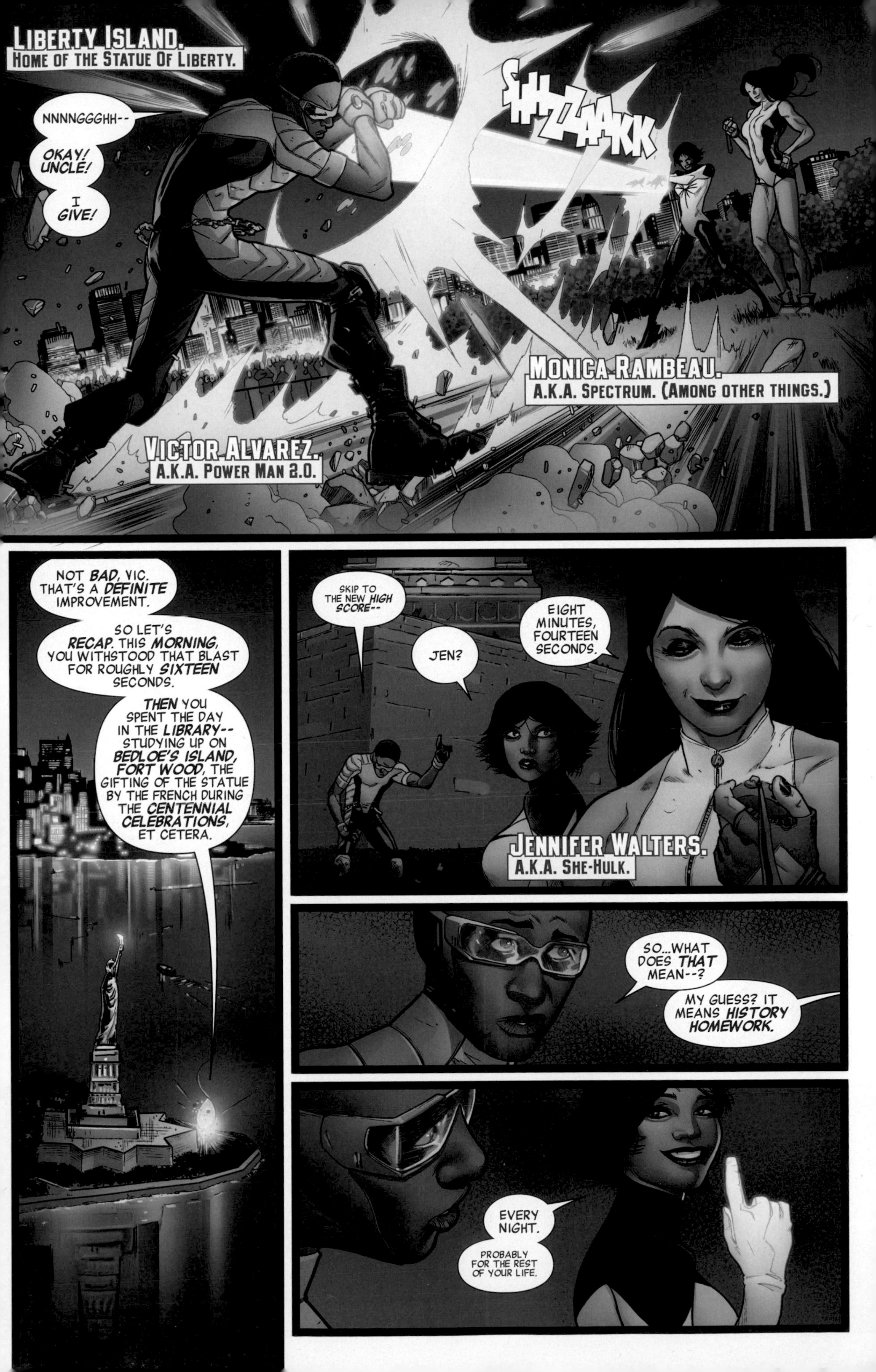
LIBERTY ISLAND.
HOME OF THE STATUE OF LIBERTY.
NNNNGGGHH--
OKAY! UNCLE!
I GIVE!
SHHZZAAKK
MONICA RAMBEAU.
A.K.A. SPECTRUM. (AMONG OTHER THINGS.)
VICTOR ALVAREZ.
A.K.A. POWER MAN 2.0.
NOT BAD, VIC. THAT'S A DEFINITE IMPROVEMENT.
SO LET'S RECAP. THIS MORNING, YOU WITHSTOOD THAT BLAST FOR ROUGHLY SIXTEEN SECONDS.
THEN YOU SPENT THE DAY IN THE LIBRARY-- STUDYING UP ON BEDLOE'S ISLAND, FORT WOOD, THE GIFTING OF THE STATUE BY THE FRENCH DURING THE CENTENNIAL CELEBRATIONS, ET CETERA.
SKIP TO THE NEW HIGH SCORE--
JEN?
EIGHT MINUTES, FOURTEEN SECONDS.
JENNIFER WALTERS.
A.K.A. SHE-HULK.
SO...WHAT DOES THAT MEAN--?
MY GUESS? IT MEANS HISTORY HOMEWORK.
EVERY NIGHT.
PROBABLY FOR THE REST OF YOUR LIFE.

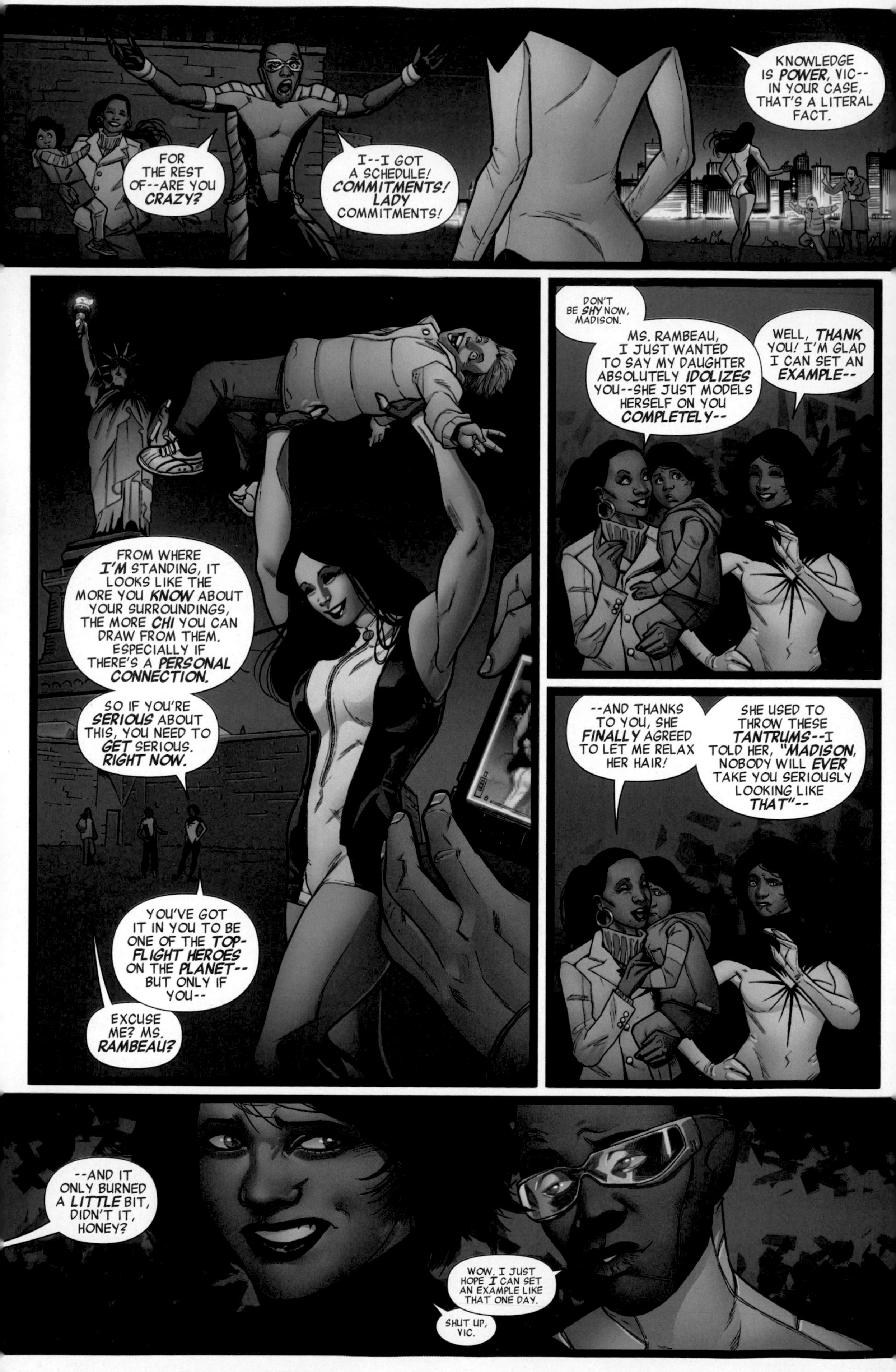

FOR THE REST OF--ARE YOU CRAZY?
I--I GOT A SCHEDULE! COMMITMENTS! LADY COMMITMENTS!
KNOWLEDGE IS POWER, VIC-- IN YOUR CASE, THAT'S A LITERAL FACT.
FROM WHERE I'M STANDING, IT LOOKS LIKE THE MORE YOU KNOW ABOUT YOUR SURROUNDINGS, THE MORE CHI YOU CAN DRAW FROM THEM. ESPECIALLY IF THERE'S A PERSONAL CONNECTION.
SO IF YOU'RE SERIOUS ABOUT THIS, YOU NEED TO GET SERIOUS. RIGHT NOW.
YOU'VE GOT IT IN YOU TO BE ONE OF THE TOP-FLIGHT HEROES ON THE PLANET--BUT ONLY IF YOU--
EXCUSE ME? MS. RAMBEAU?
DON'T BE SHY NOW, MADISON.
MS. RAMBEAU, I JUST WANTED TO SAY MY DAUGHTER ABSOLUTELY IDOLIZES YOU--SHE JUST MODELS HERSELF ON YOU COMPLETELY--
WELL, THANK YOU! I'M GLAD I CAN SET AN EXAMPLE--
--AND THANKS TO YOU, SHE FINALLY AGREED TO LET ME RELAX HER HAIR!
SHE USED TO THROW THESE TANTRUMS--I TOLD HER, "MADISON, NOBODY WILL EVER TAKE YOU SERIOUSLY LOOKING LIKE THAT"--
--AND IT ONLY BURNED A LITTLE BIT, DIDN'T IT, HONEY?
WOW. I JUST HOPE I CAN SET AN EXAMPLE LIKE THAT ONE DAY.
SHUT UP, VIC.

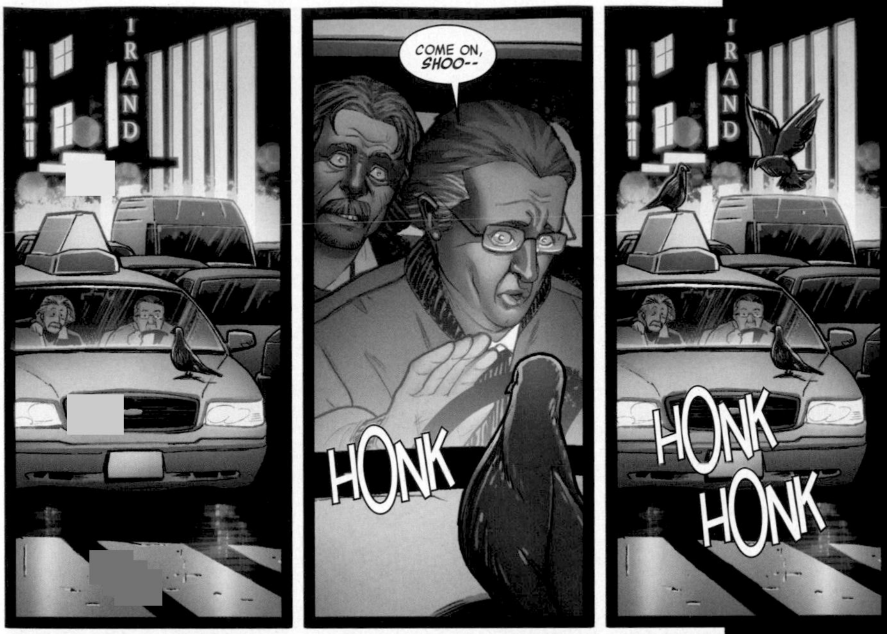
COME ON, SHOO--
HONK
HONK
HONK

Once, when Kenny Driscoll was only nine, before he even knew who Marx was, he'd snuck down from his bedroom to watch the late movie.

Hitchcock knew how to make 'em. Kenny Driscoll had nightmares for weeks.

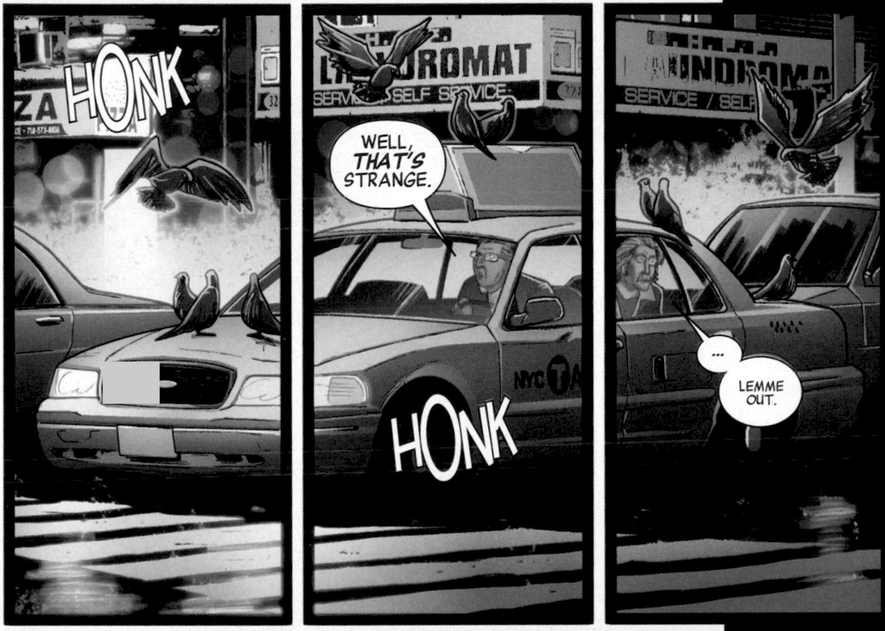
HONK
WELL, THAT'S STRANGE.
HONK
...
LEMME OUT.

Now, against all reason, he felt that old forgotten fear crawl from his stomach up his throat, to seize his mind in its cold fist.

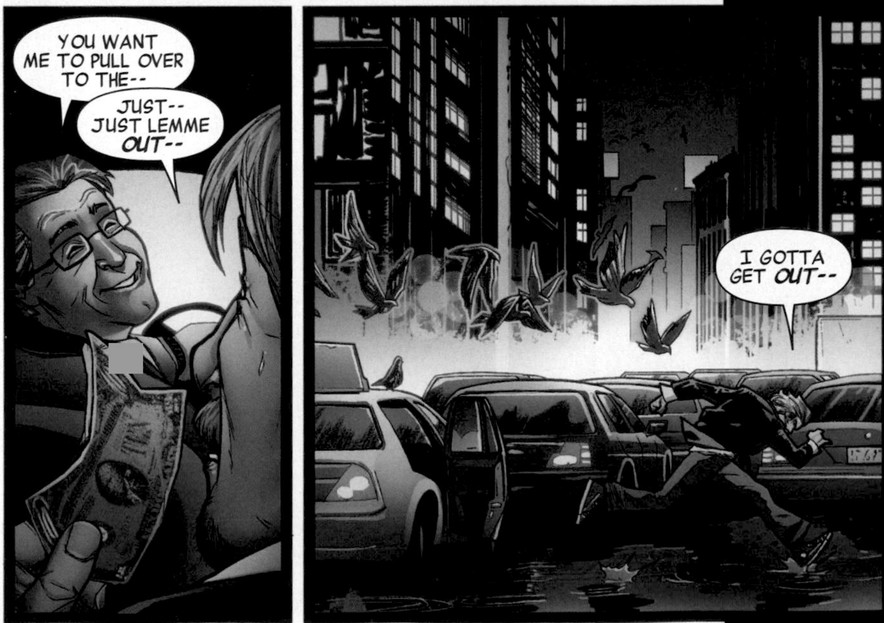
YOU WANT ME TO PULL OVER TO THE--
JUST-- JUST LEMME OUT--
I GOTTA GET OUT--

Kenny Driscoll ran.

And the birds followed.

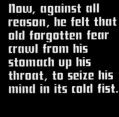

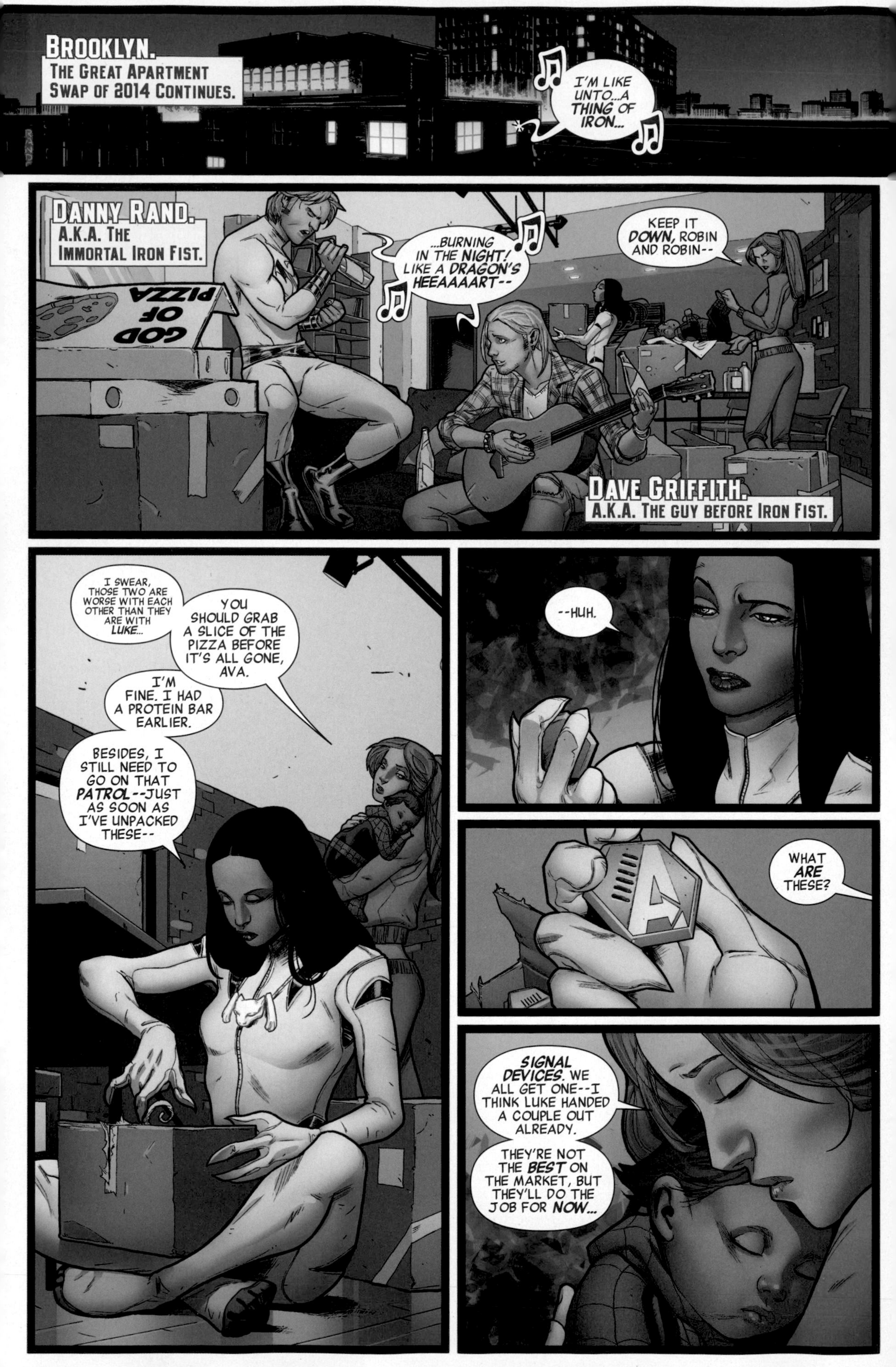
BROOKLYN.
THE GREAT APARTMENT SWAP OF 2014 CONTINUES.
I'M LIKE UNTO...A THING OF IRON...
DANNY RAND.
A.K.A. THE IMMORTAL IRON FIST.
GOD OF PIZZA
...BURNING IN THE NIGHT! LIKE A DRAGON'S HEEAAAART--
KEEP IT DOWN, ROBIN AND ROBIN--
DAVE GRIFFITH.
A.K.A. THE GUY BEFORE IRON FIST.
I SWEAR, THOSE TWO ARE WORSE WITH EACH OTHER THAN THEY ARE WITH LUKE...
YOU SHOULD GRAB A SLICE OF THE PIZZA BEFORE IT'S ALL GONE, AVA.
I'M FINE. I HAD A PROTEIN BAR EARLIER.
BESIDES, I STILL NEED TO GO ON THAT PATROL--JUST AS SOON AS I'VE UNPACKED THESE--
--HUH.
WHAT ARE THESE?
SIGNAL DEVICES. WE ALL GET ONE--I THINK LUKE HANDED A COUPLE OUT ALREADY.
THEY'RE NOT THE BEST ON THE MARKET, BUT THEY'LL DO THE JOB FOR NOW...

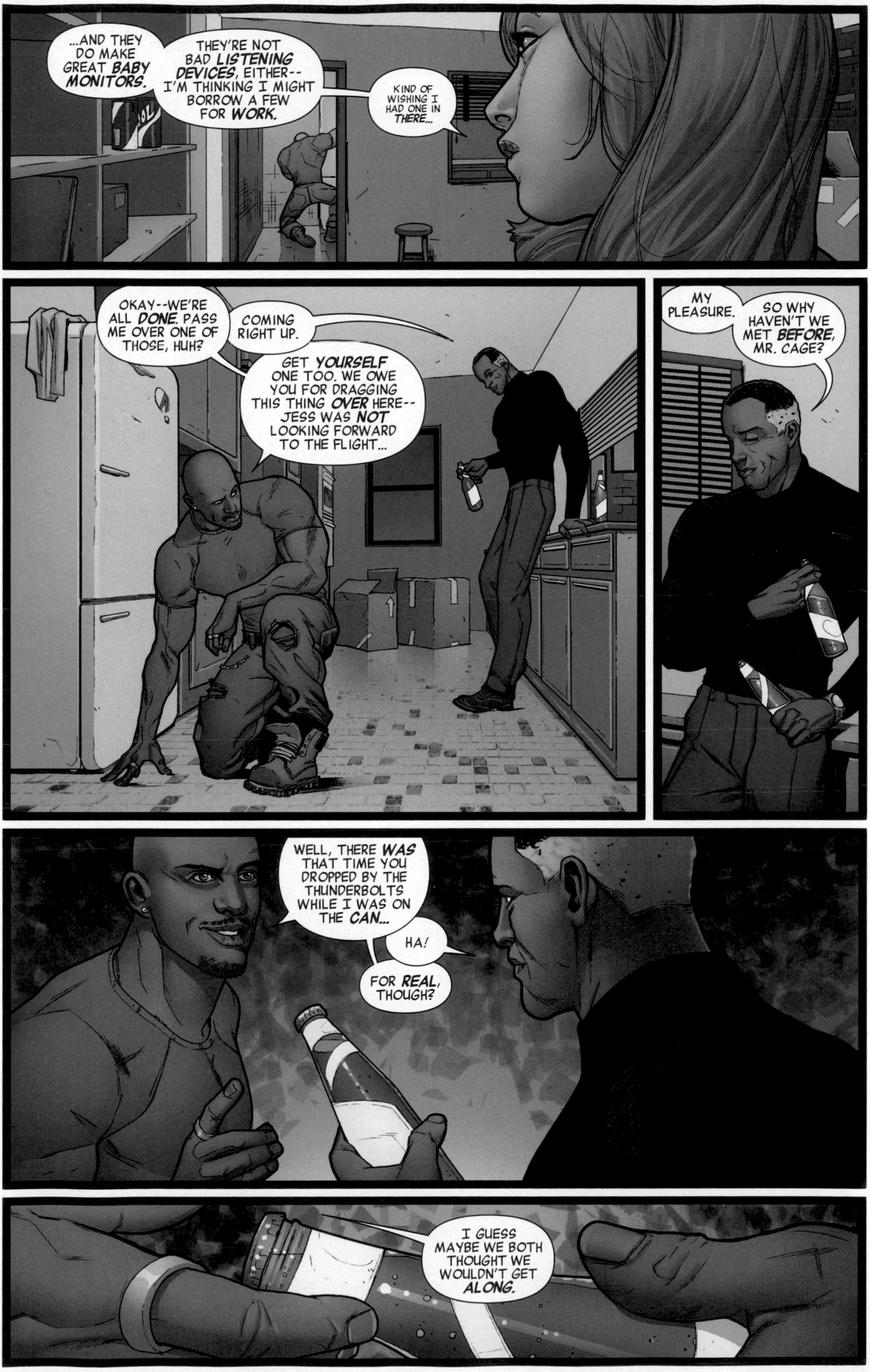
...AND THEY DO MAKE GREAT BABY MONITORS.
THEY'RE NOT BAD LISTENING DEVICES, EITHER-- I'M THINKING I MIGHT BORROW A FEW FOR WORK.
KIND OF WISHING I HAD ONE IN THERE...
OKAY--WE'RE ALL DONE. PASS ME OVER ONE OF THOSE, HUH?
COMING RIGHT UP.
GET YOURSELF ONE TOO. WE OWE YOU FOR DRAGGING THIS THING OVER HERE-- JESS WAS NOT LOOKING FORWARD TO THE FLIGHT...
MY PLEASURE.
SO WHY HAVEN'T WE MET BEFORE, MR. CAGE?
WELL, THERE WAS THAT TIME YOU DROPPED BY THE THUNDERBOLTS WHILE I WAS ON THE CAN...
HA!
FOR REAL, THOUGH?
I GUESS MAYBE WE BOTH THOUGHT WE WOULDN'T GET ALONG.

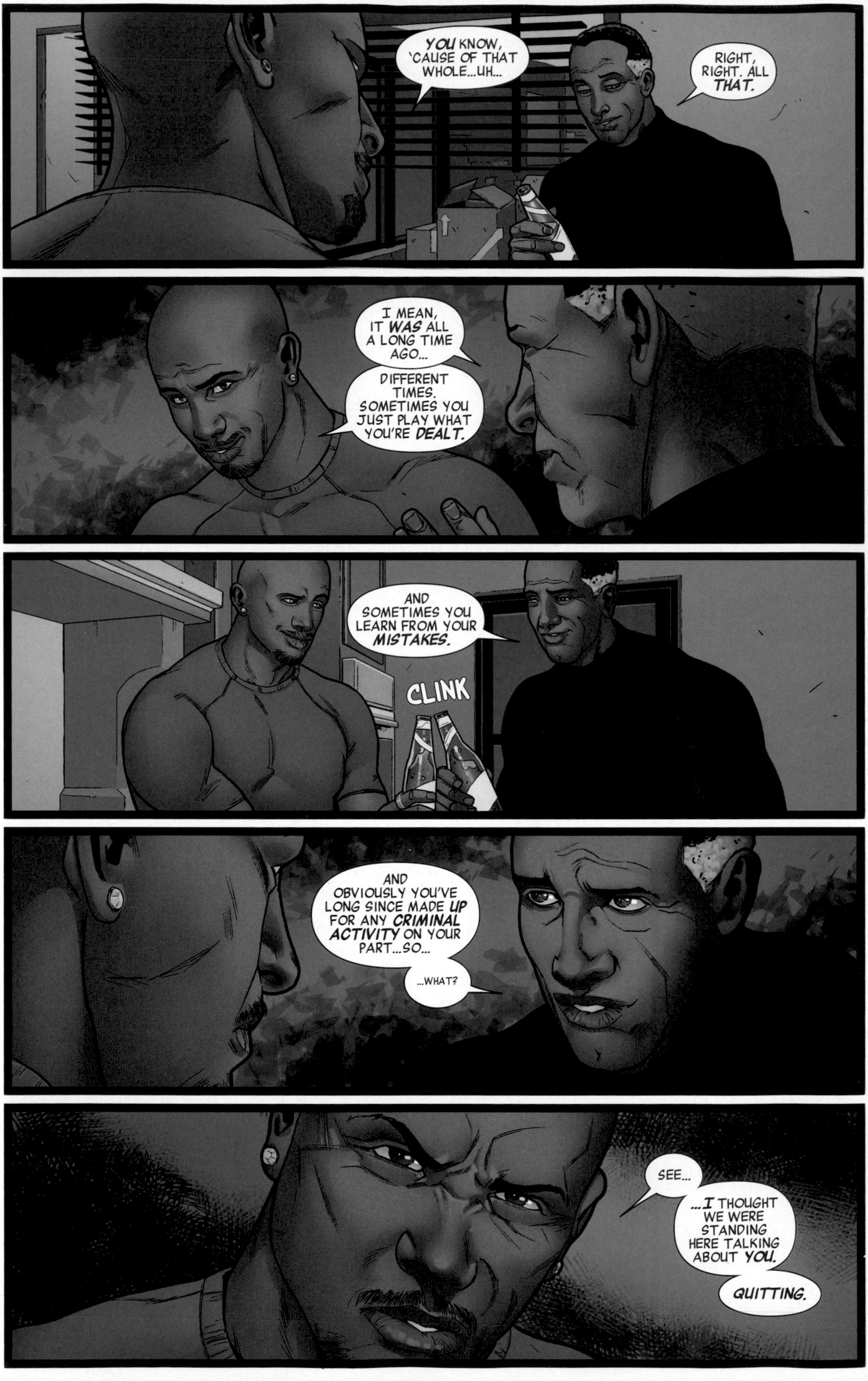
YOU KNOW, 'CAUSE OF THAT WHOLE...UH...
RIGHT, RIGHT. ALL THAT.
I MEAN, IT WAS ALL A LONG TIME AGO...
DIFFERENT TIMES. SOMETIMES YOU JUST PLAY WHAT YOU'RE DEALT.
AND SOMETIMES YOU LEARN FROM YOUR MISTAKES.
CLINK
AND OBVIOUSLY YOU'VE LONG SINCE MADE UP FOR ANY CRIMINAL ACTIVITY ON YOUR PART...SO...
...WHAT?
SEE...
...I THOUGHT WE WERE STANDING HERE TALKING ABOUT YOU.
QUITTING.

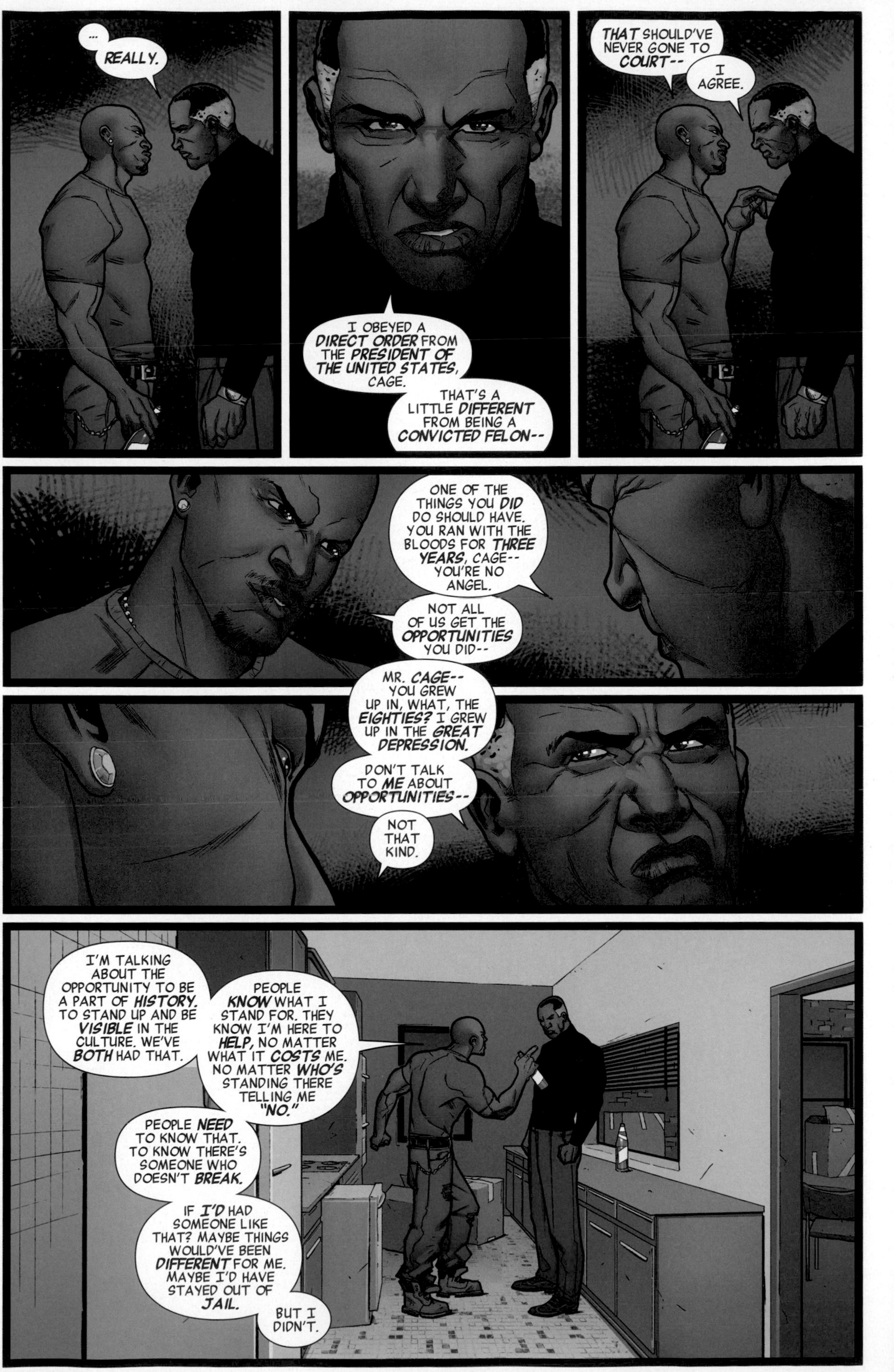
... REALLY.
I OBEYED A DIRECT ORDER FROM THE PRESIDENT OF THE UNITED STATES, CAGE.
THAT'S A LITTLE DIFFERENT FROM BEING A CONVICTED FELON--
THAT SHOULD'VE NEVER GONE TO COURT--
I AGREE.
ONE OF THE THINGS YOU DID DO SHOULD HAVE. YOU RAN WITH THE BLOODS FOR THREE YEARS, CAGE-- YOU'RE NO ANGEL.
NOT ALL OF US GET THE OPPORTUNITIES YOU DID--
MR. CAGE-- YOU GREW UP IN, WHAT, THE EIGHTIES? I GREW UP IN THE GREAT DEPRESSION.
DON'T TALK TO ME ABOUT OPPORTUNITIES--
NOT THAT KIND.
I'M TALKING ABOUT THE OPPORTUNITY TO BE A PART OF HISTORY. TO STAND UP AND BE VISIBLE IN THE CULTURE. WE'VE BOTH HAD THAT.
PEOPLE KNOW WHAT I STAND FOR. THEY KNOW I'M HERE TO HELP, NO MATTER WHAT IT COSTS ME. NO MATTER WHO'S STANDING THERE TELLING ME "NO."
PEOPLE NEED TO KNOW THAT. TO KNOW THERE'S SOMEONE WHO DOESN'T BREAK.
IF I'D HAD SOMEONE LIKE THAT? MAYBE THINGS WOULD'VE BEEN DIFFERENT FOR ME. MAYBE I'D HAVE STAYED OUT OF JAIL.
BUT I DIDN'T.

YOU HAD BETTER THINGS TO DO.

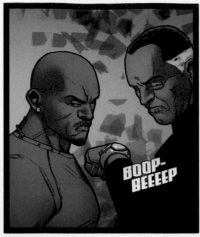

BOOP-BEEEEEP

YOU KNOW SOMETHING?

YOU REMIND ME OF YOUR FATHER.

HE MADE A SPEECH LIKE THAT ONCE...

WAIT-- HOLD UP, ARE YOU SAYING--?

ANYWAY, I'M NEEDED IN TAIWAN, SO...

...WE'LL HAVE TO FILE THIS ONE UNDER "TO BE CONTINUED."

SO WHAT HAPPENED TO ADAM?

HE... I...

DID YOU DO YOUR "I-DON'T-BREAK" SPEECH?

...PART OF IT.

I LOVE THAT ONE.

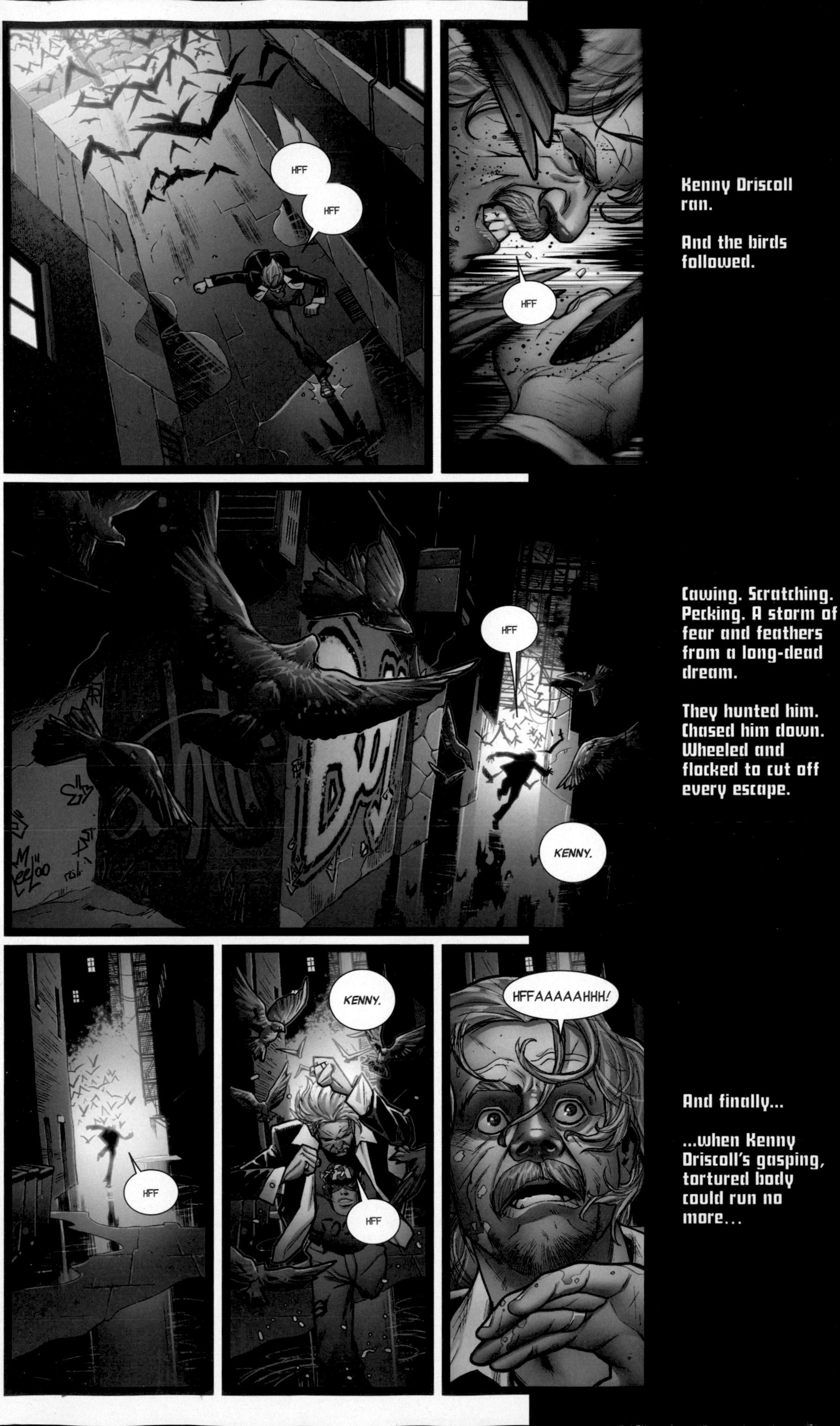

HFF
HFF
HFF
HFF
KENNY.
HFF
KENNY.
HFF
HFFAAAAAHHH!

Kenny Driscoll ran.

And the birds followed.

Cawing. Scratching. Pecking. A storm of fear and feathers from a long-dead dream.

They hunted him. Chased him down. Wheeled and flocked to cut off every escape.

And finally...

...when Kenny Driscoll's gasping, tortured body could run no more...

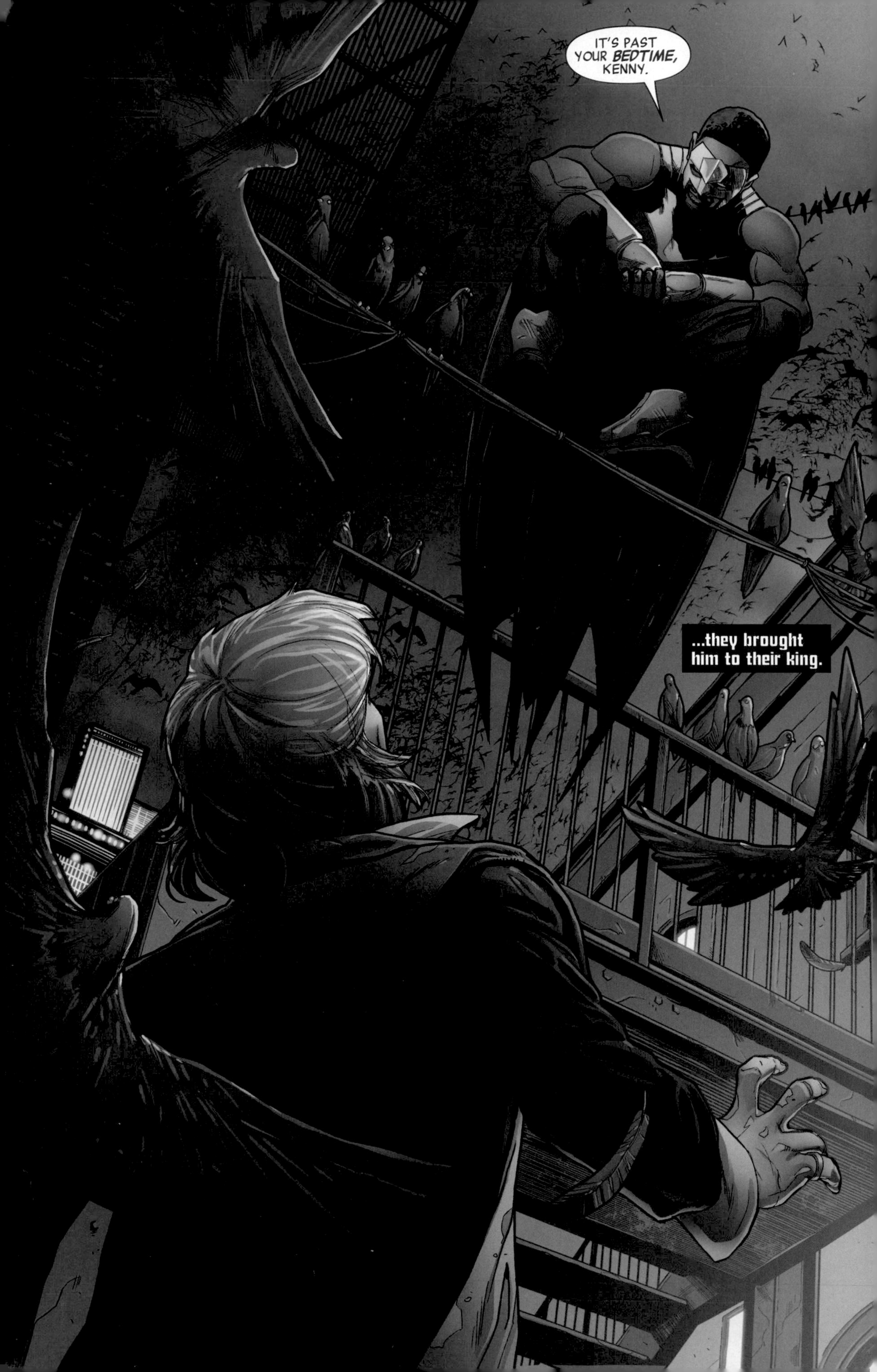
IT'S PAST YOUR BEDTIME, KENNY.
...they brought him to their king.

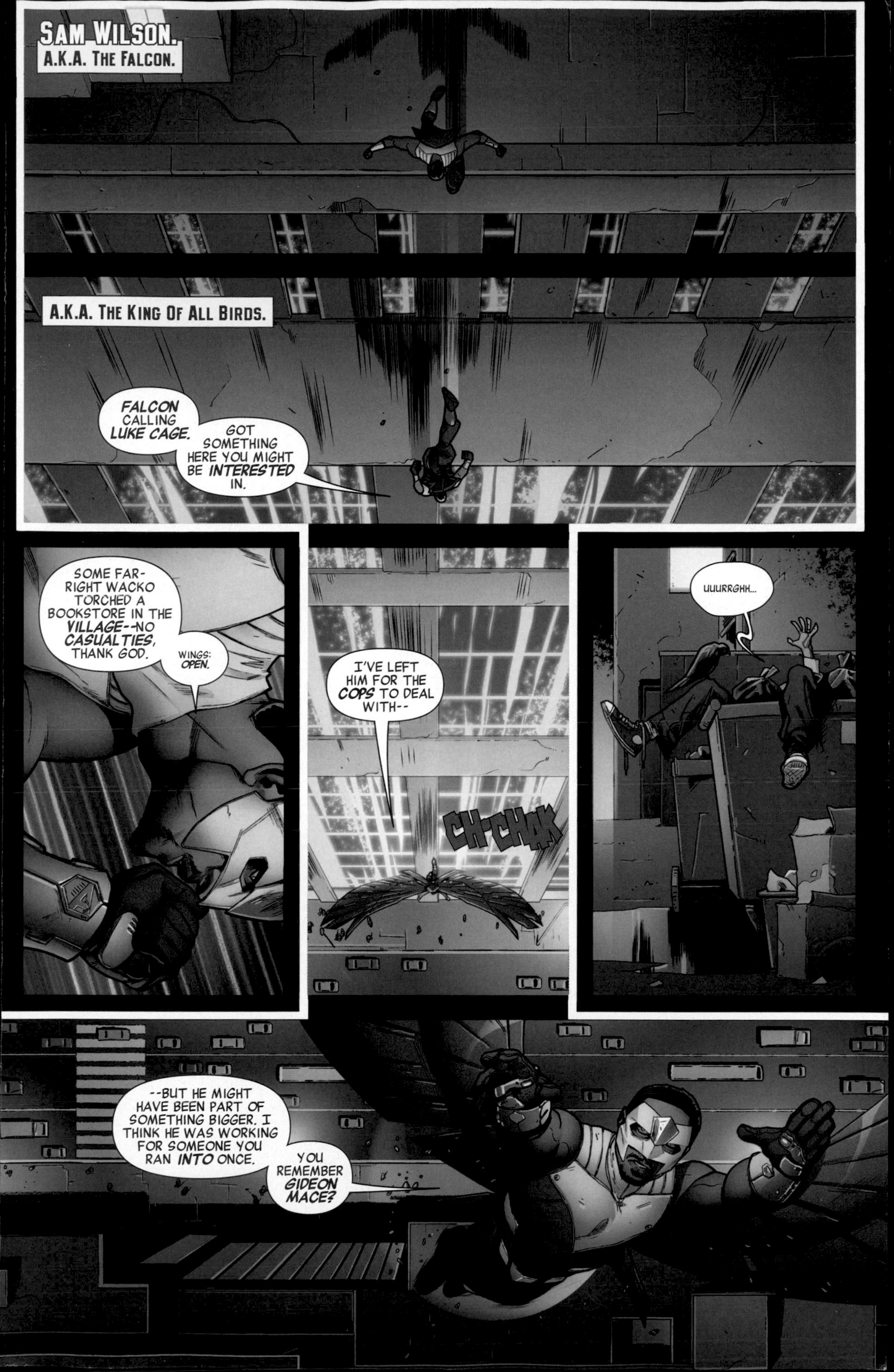

SAM WILSON.
A.K.A. THE FALCON.
A.K.A. THE KING OF ALL BIRDS.
FALCON CALLING LUKE CAGE.
GOT SOMETHING HERE YOU MIGHT BE INTERESTED IN.
SOME FAR-RIGHT WACKO TORCHED A BOOKSTORE IN THE VILLAGE--NO CASUALTIES, THANK GOD.
WINGS: OPEN.
I'VE LEFT HIM FOR THE COPS TO DEAL WITH--
CH-CHAK
UUURRGHH...
--BUT HE MIGHT HAVE BEEN PART OF SOMETHING BIGGER. I THINK HE WAS WORKING FOR SOMEONE YOU RAN INTO ONCE.
YOU REMEMBER GIDEON MACE?

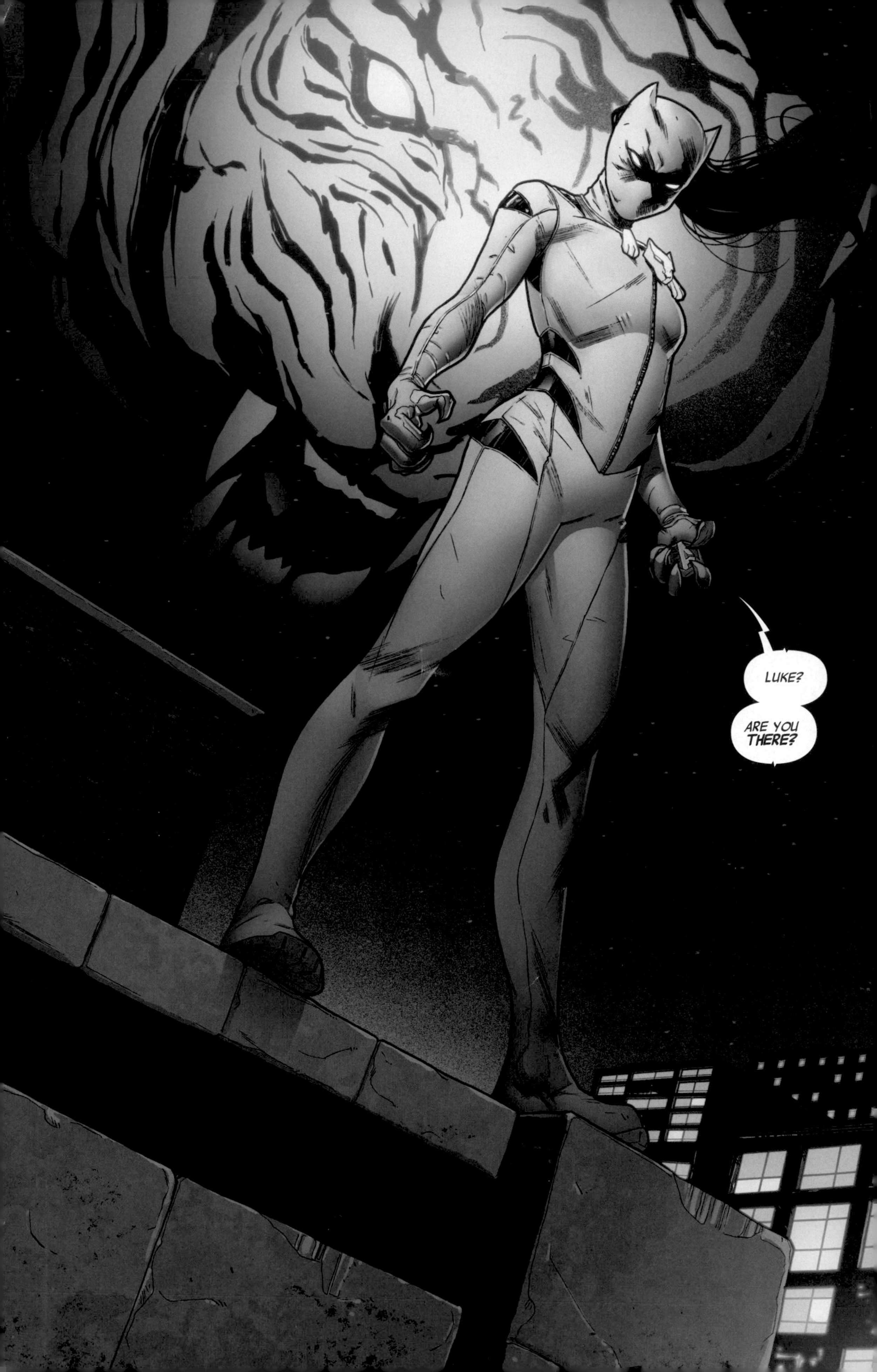
LUKE?
ARE YOU THERE?

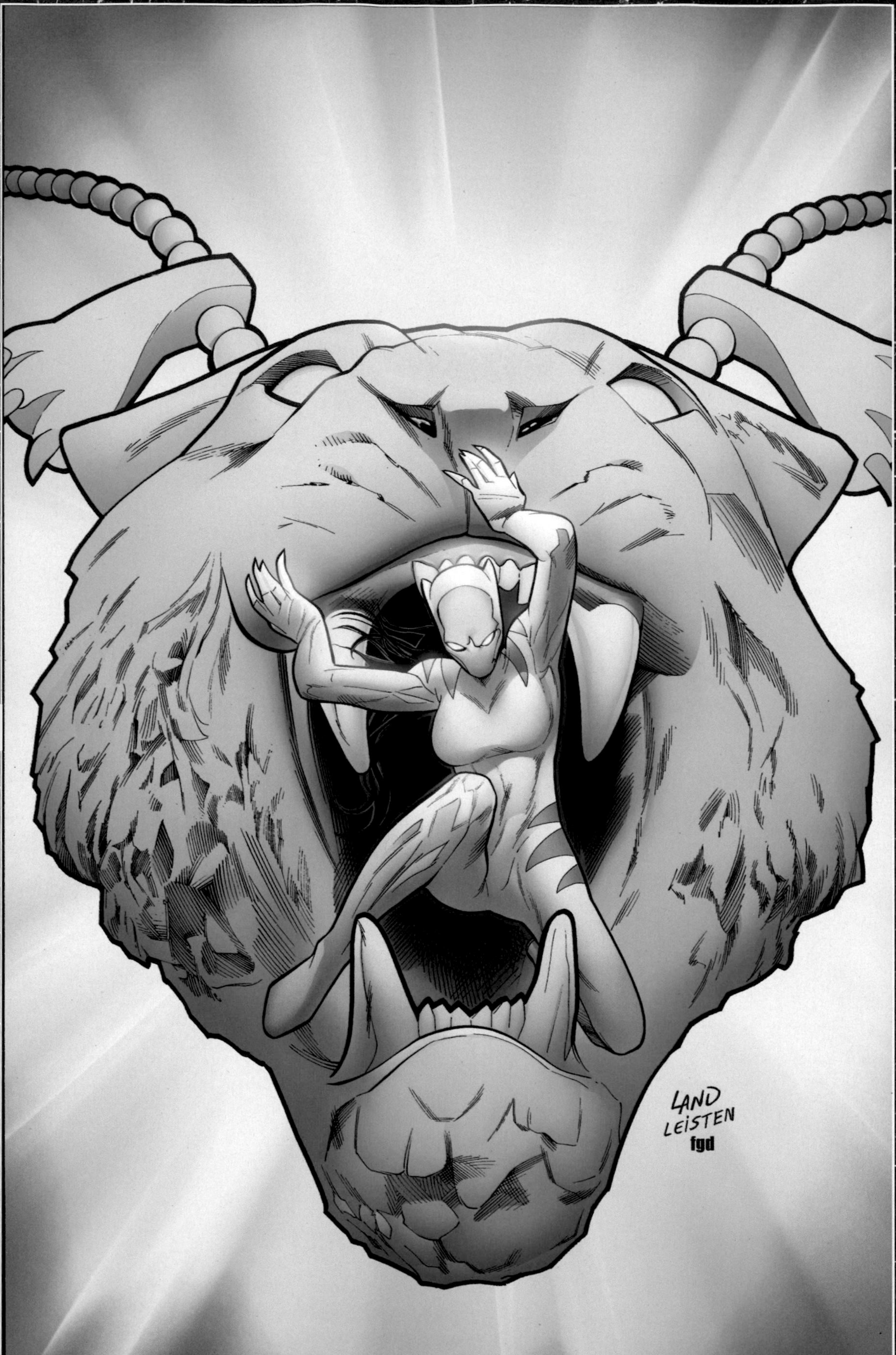
LAND
LEISTEN
fgd

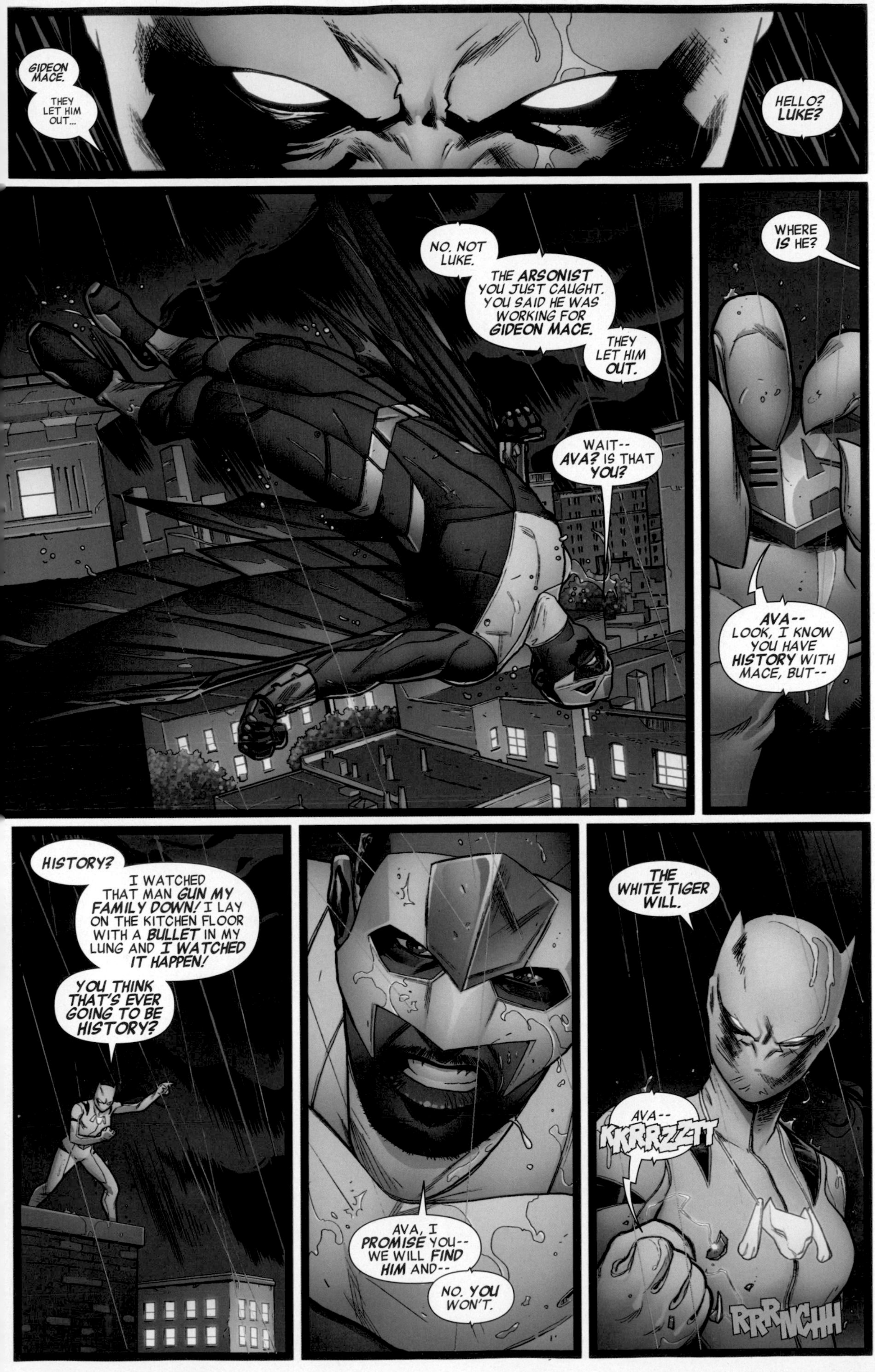
GIDEON MACE.
THEY LET HIM OUT...
HELLO? LUKE?
NO. NOT LUKE.
THE ARSONIST YOU JUST CAUGHT. YOU SAID HE WAS WORKING FOR GIDEON MACE.
THEY LET HIM OUT.
WAIT-- AVA? IS THAT YOU?
WHERE IS HE?
AVA-- LOOK, I KNOW YOU HAVE HISTORY WITH MACE, BUT--
HISTORY?
I WATCHED THAT MAN GUN MY FAMILY DOWN! I LAY ON THE KITCHEN FLOOR WITH A BULLET IN MY LUNG AND I WATCHED IT HAPPEN!
YOU THINK THAT'S EVER GOING TO BE HISTORY?
AVA, I PROMISE YOU-- WE WILL FIND HIM AND--
NO. YOU WON'T.
THE WHITE TIGER WILL.
AVA--
KKRRZZTT
RRRNCHH

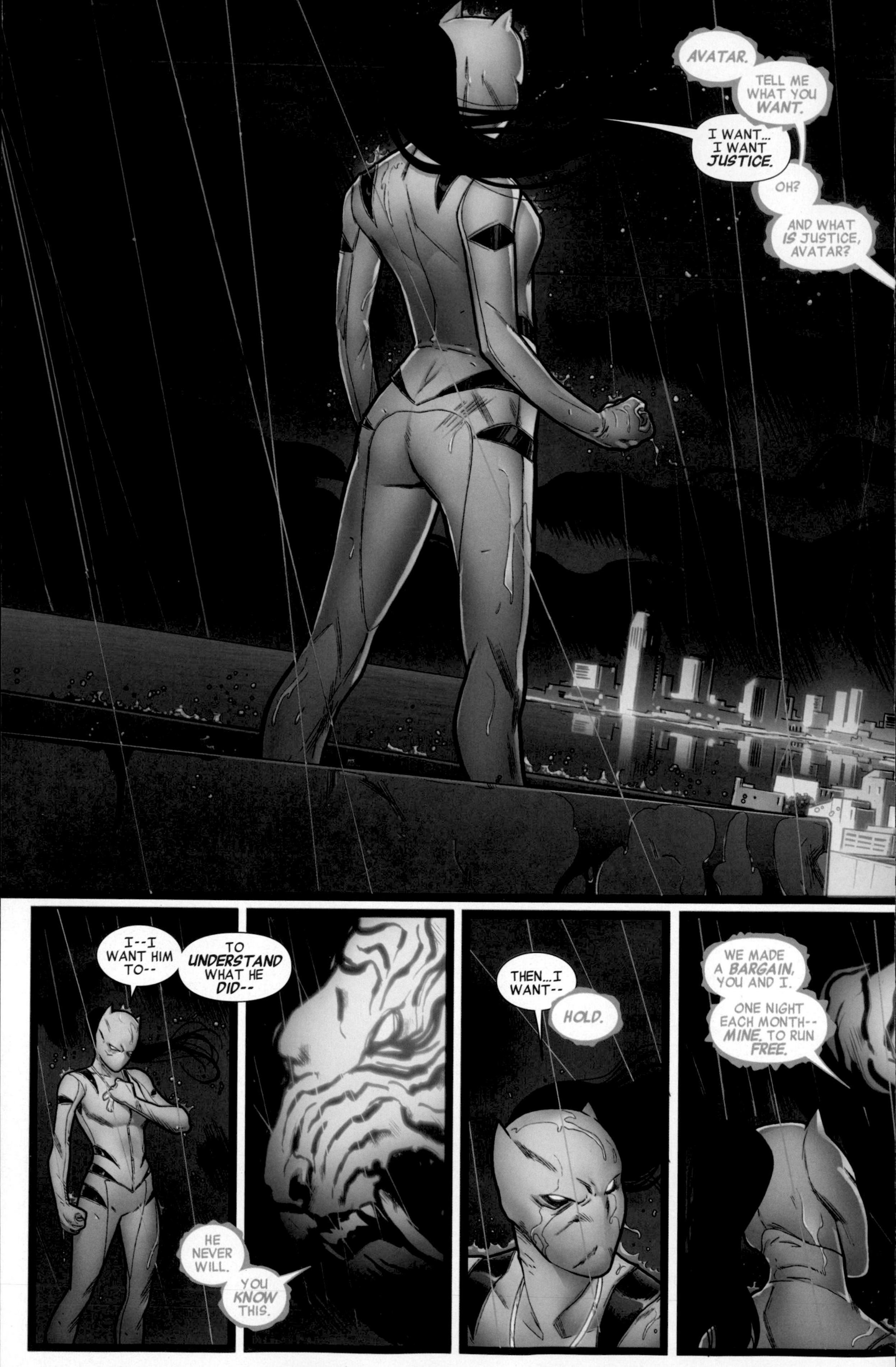

AVATAR.
TELL ME WHAT YOU WANT.
I WANT... I WANT JUSTICE.
OH?
AND WHAT IS JUSTICE, AVATAR?
I--I WANT HIM TO--
TO UNDERSTAND WHAT HE DID--
HE NEVER WILL.
YOU KNOW THIS.
THEN...I WANT--
HOLD.
WE MADE A BARGAIN, YOU AND I.
ONE NIGHT EACH MONTH-- MINE, TO RUN FREE.

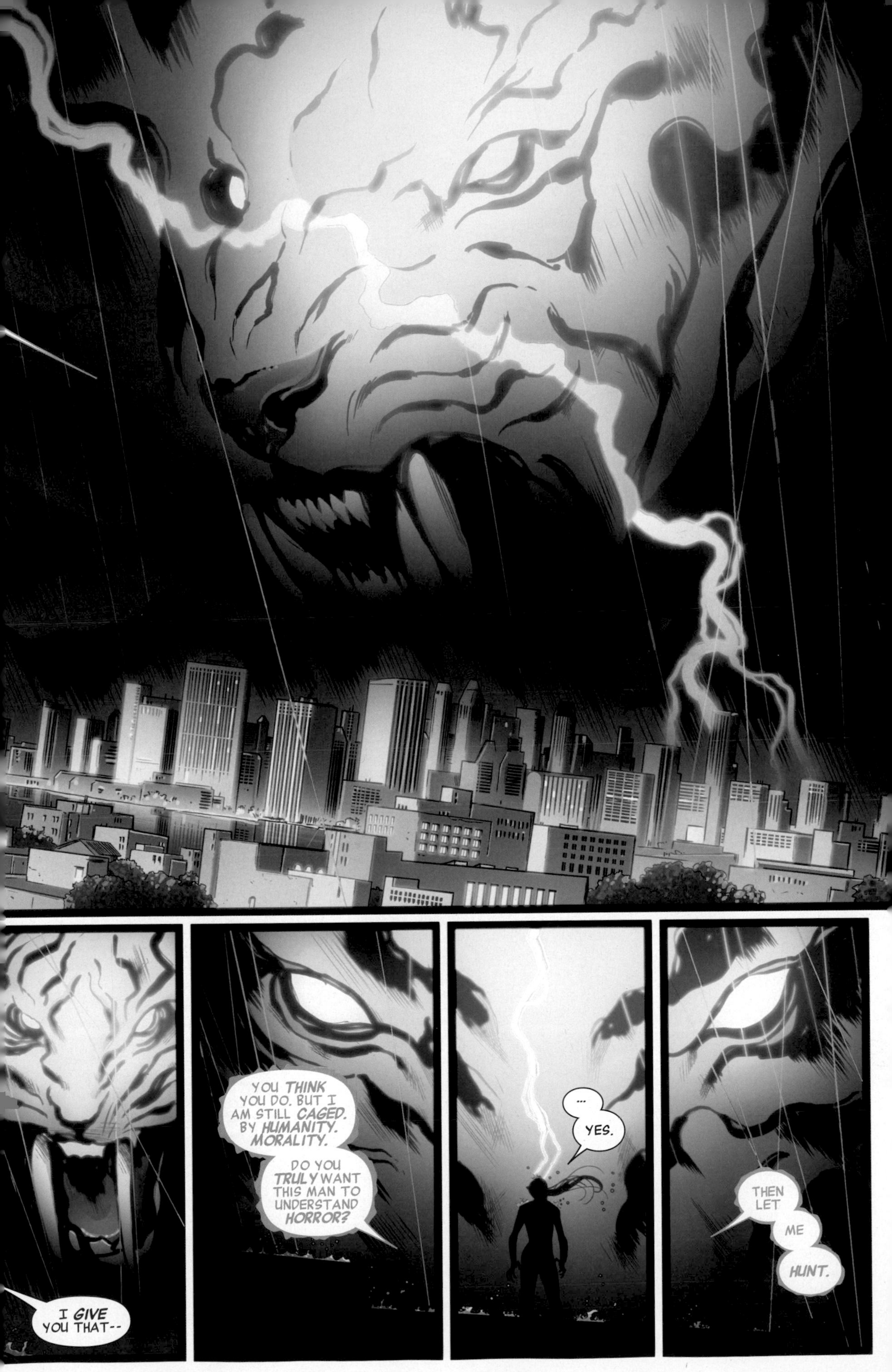
I GIVE YOU THAT--
YOU THINK YOU DO. BUT I AM STILL CAGED. BY HUMANITY. MORALITY.
DO YOU TRULY WANT THIS MAN TO UNDERSTAND HORROR?
...
YES.
THEN LET
ME
HUNT.

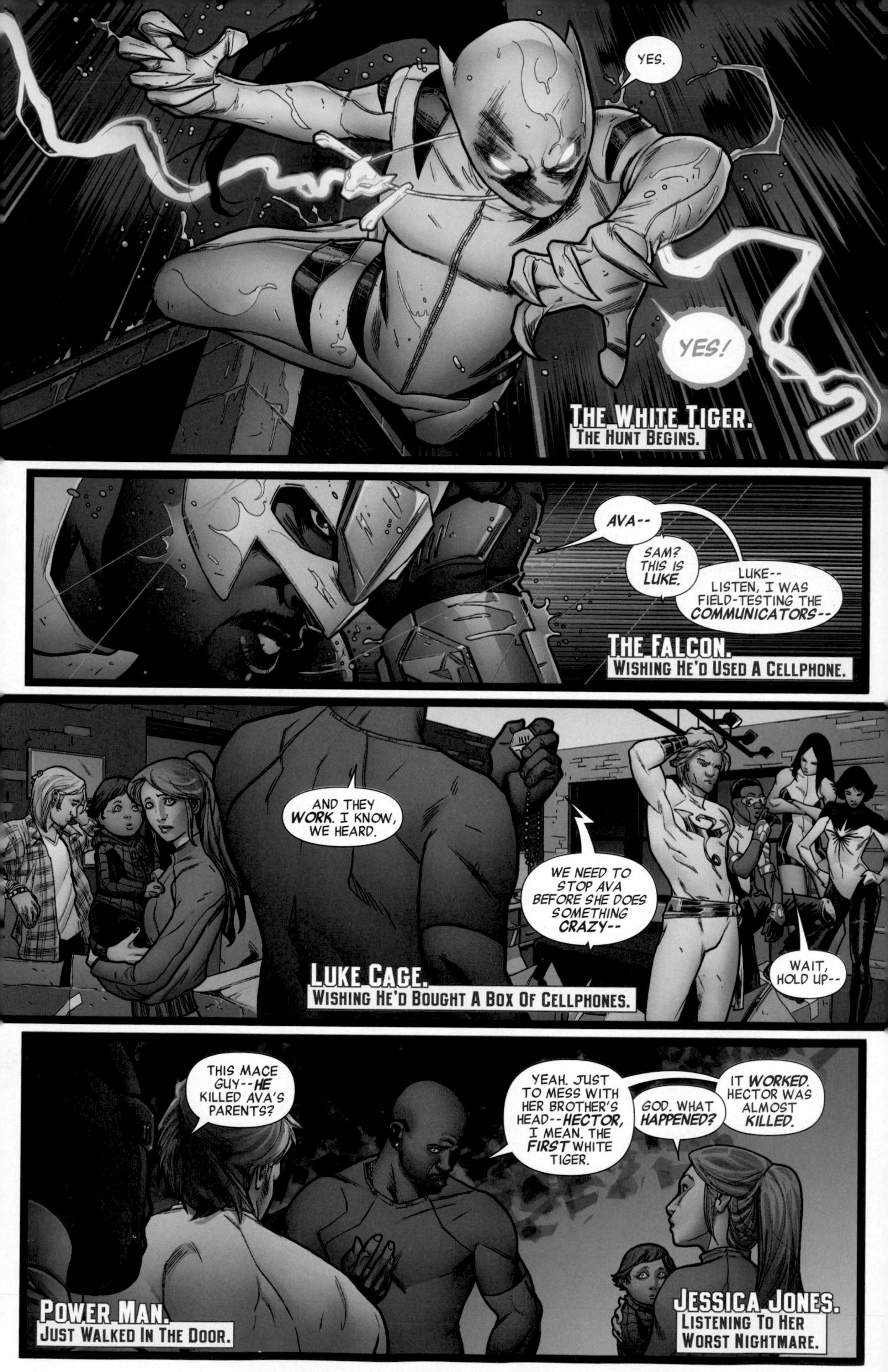
YES.
YES!
THE WHITE TIGER.
THE HUNT BEGINS.
AVA--
SAM? THIS IS LUKE.
LUKE-- LISTEN, I WAS FIELD-TESTING THE COMMUNICATORS--
THE FALCON.
WISHING HE'D USED A CELLPHONE.
AND THEY WORK. I KNOW, WE HEARD.
WE NEED TO STOP AVA BEFORE SHE DOES SOMETHING CRAZY--
LUKE CAGE.
WISHING HE'D BOUGHT A BOX OF CELLPHONES.
WAIT, HOLD UP--
THIS MACE GUY--HE KILLED AVA'S PARENTS?
YEAH. JUST TO MESS WITH HER BROTHER'S HEAD--HECTOR, I MEAN. THE FIRST WHITE TIGER.
GOD. WHAT HAPPENED?
IT WORKED. HECTOR WAS ALMOST KILLED.
POWER MAN.
JUST WALKED IN THE DOOR.
JESSICA JONES.
LISTENING TO HER WORST NIGHTMARE.

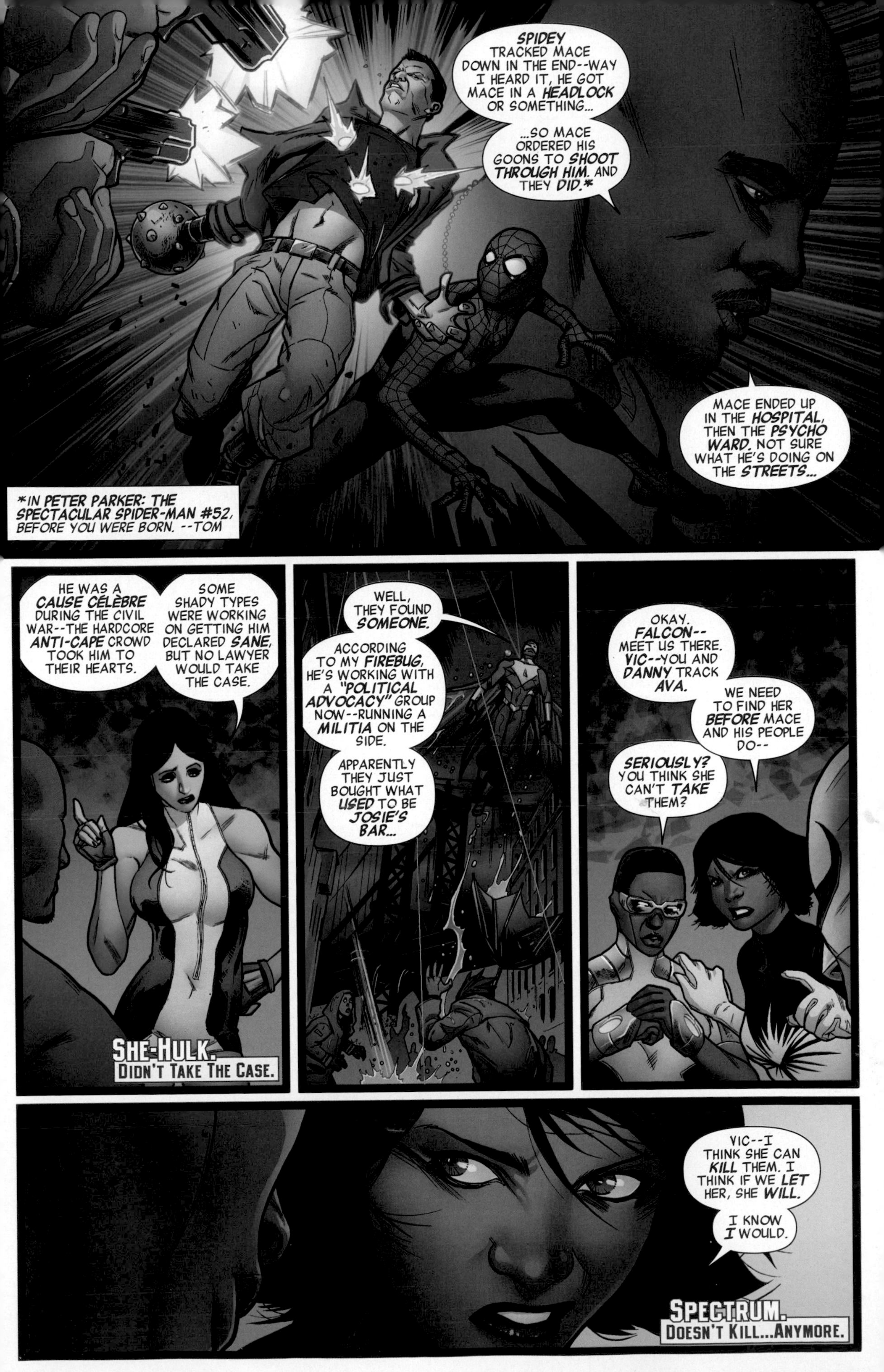
SPIDEY TRACKED MACE DOWN IN THE END--WAY I HEARD IT, HE GOT MACE IN A HEADLOCK OR SOMETHING...
...SO MACE ORDERED HIS GOONS TO SHOOT THROUGH HIM. AND THEY DID.*
MACE ENDED UP IN THE HOSPITAL, THEN THE PSYCHO WARD. NOT SURE WHAT HE'S DOING ON THE STREETS...
*IN PETER PARKER: THE SPECTACULAR SPIDER-MAN #52, BEFORE YOU WERE BORN. --TOM
HE WAS A CAUSE CÉLÈBRE DURING THE CIVIL WAR--THE HARDCORE ANTI-CAPE CROWD TOOK HIM TO THEIR HEARTS.
SOME SHADY TYPES WERE WORKING ON GETTING HIM DECLARED SANE, BUT NO LAWYER WOULD TAKE THE CASE.
SHE-HULK.
DIDN'T TAKE THE CASE.
WELL, THEY FOUND SOMEONE.
ACCORDING TO MY FIREBUG, HE'S WORKING WITH A "POLITICAL ADVOCACY" GROUP NOW--RUNNING A MILITIA ON THE SIDE.
APPARENTLY THEY JUST BOUGHT WHAT USED TO BE JOSIE'S BAR...
OKAY. FALCON--MEET US THERE. VIC--YOU AND DANNY TRACK AVA.
WE NEED TO FIND HER BEFORE MACE AND HIS PEOPLE DO--
SERIOUSLY? YOU THINK SHE CAN'T TAKE THEM?
VIC--I THINK SHE CAN KILL THEM. I THINK IF WE LET HER, SHE WILL.
I KNOW I WOULD.
SPECTRUM.
DOESN'T KILL...ANYMORE.

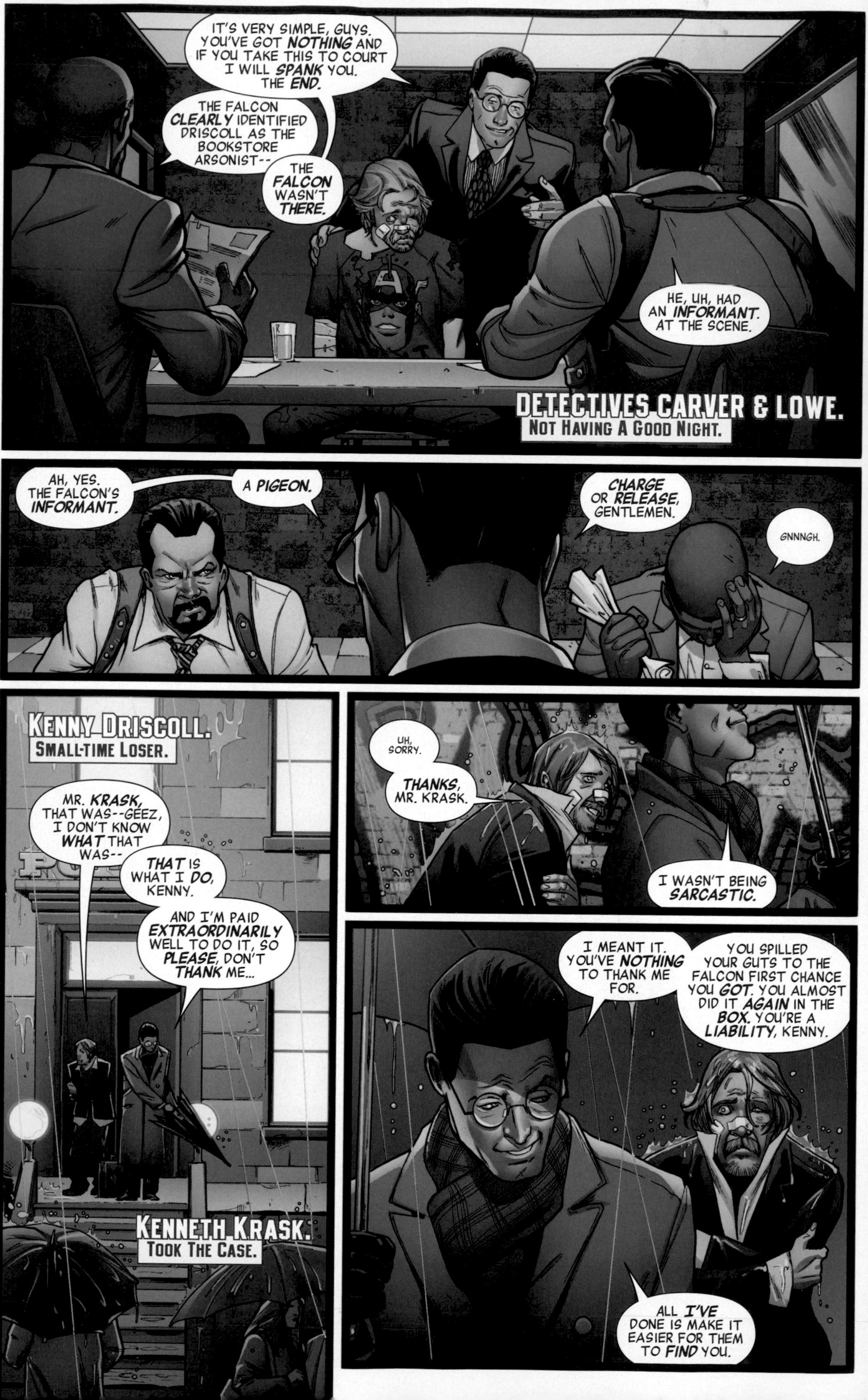
IT'S VERY SIMPLE, GUYS. YOU'VE GOT NOTHING AND IF YOU TAKE THIS TO COURT I WILL SPANK YOU. THE END.
THE FALCON CLEARLY IDENTIFIED DRISCOLL AS THE BOOKSTORE ARSONIST--
THE FALCON WASN'T THERE.
HE, UH, HAD AN INFORMANT AT THE SCENE.
DETECTIVES CARVER & LOWE.
NOT HAVING A GOOD NIGHT.
AH, YES. THE FALCON'S INFORMANT.
A PIGEON.
CHARGE OR RELEASE, GENTLEMEN.
GNNNGH.
KENNY DRISCOLL.
SMALL-TIME LOSER.
MR. KRASK, THAT WAS--GEEZ, I DON'T KNOW WHAT THAT WAS--
THAT IS WHAT I DO, KENNY.
AND I'M PAID EXTRAORDINARILY WELL TO DO IT, SO PLEASE, DON'T THANK ME...
KENNETH KRASK.
TOOK THE CASE.
UH, SORRY.
THANKS, MR. KRASK.
I WASN'T BEING SARCASTIC.
I MEANT IT. YOU'VE NOTHING TO THANK ME FOR.
YOU SPILLED YOUR GUTS TO THE FALCON FIRST CHANCE YOU GOT. YOU ALMOST DID IT AGAIN IN THE BOX. YOU'RE A LIABILITY, KENNY.
ALL I'VE DONE IS MAKE IT EASIER FOR THEM TO FIND YOU.

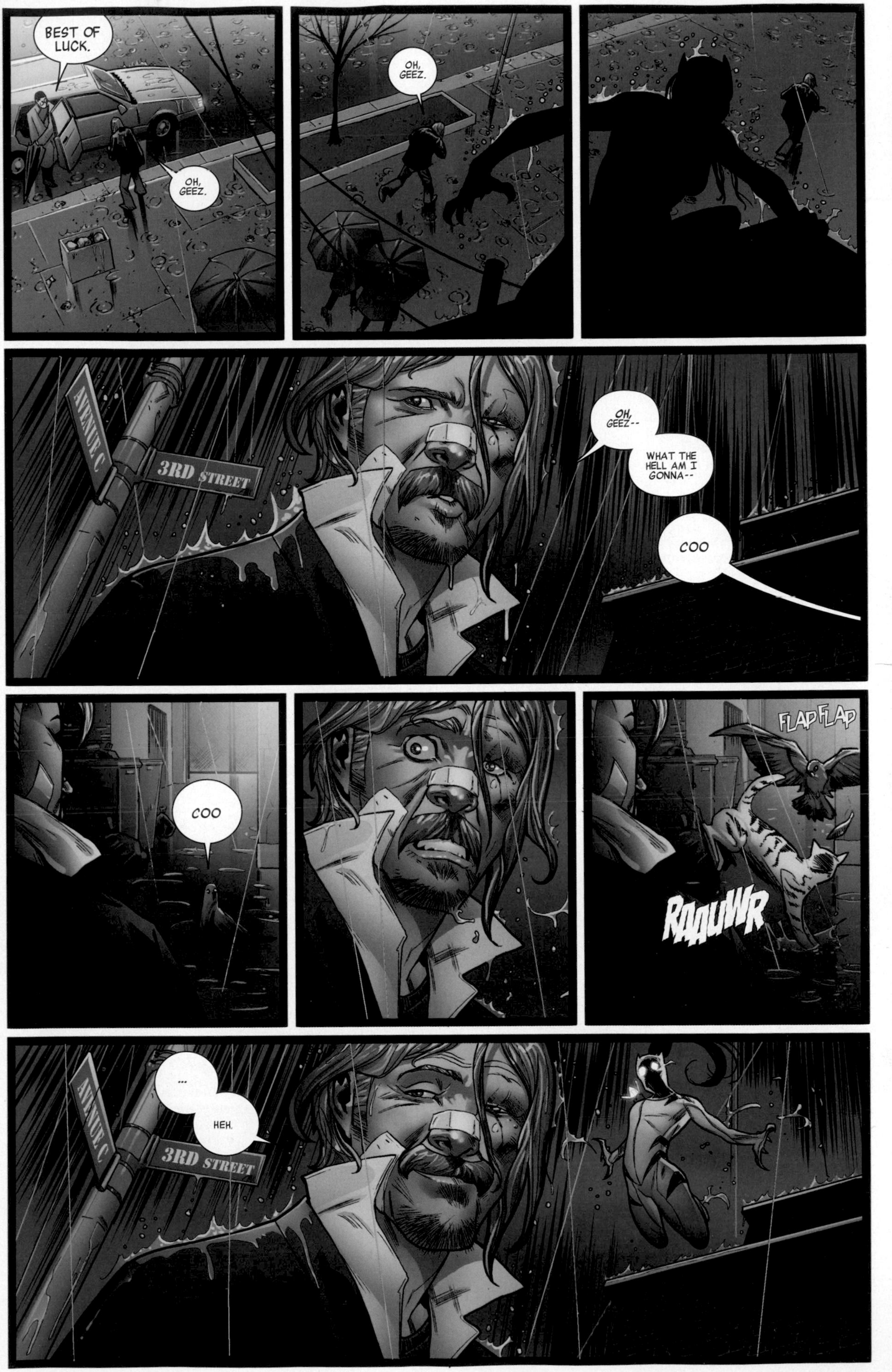
BEST OF LUCK.
OH, GEEZ.
OH, GEEZ.
AVENUE C
3RD STREET
OH, GEEZ--
WHAT THE HELL AM I GONNA--
COO
COO
FLAP FLAP
RAAUWR
AVENUE C
3RD STREET
...
HEH.

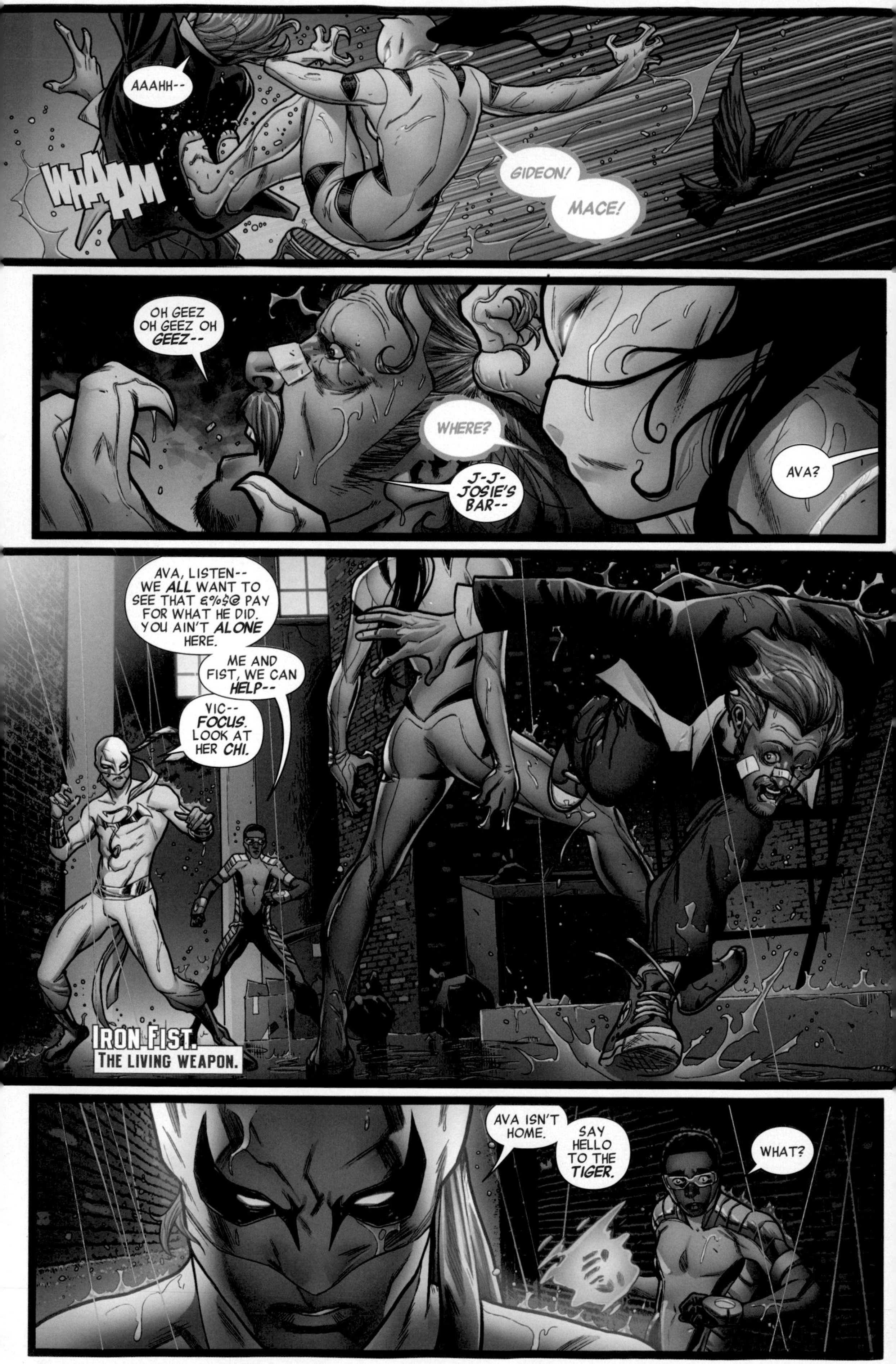
AAAHH--
WHAAAM
GIDEON!
MACE!
OH GEEZ OH GEEZ OH GEEZ--
WHERE?
J-J- JOSIE'S BAR--
AVA?
AVA, LISTEN-- WE ALL WANT TO SEE THAT &%$@ PAY FOR WHAT HE DID. YOU AIN'T ALONE HERE.
ME AND FIST, WE CAN HELP--
VIC-- FOCUS. LOOK AT HER CHI.
IRON FIST. THE LIVING WEAPON.
AVA ISN'T HOME.
SAY HELLO TO THE TIGER.
WHAT?

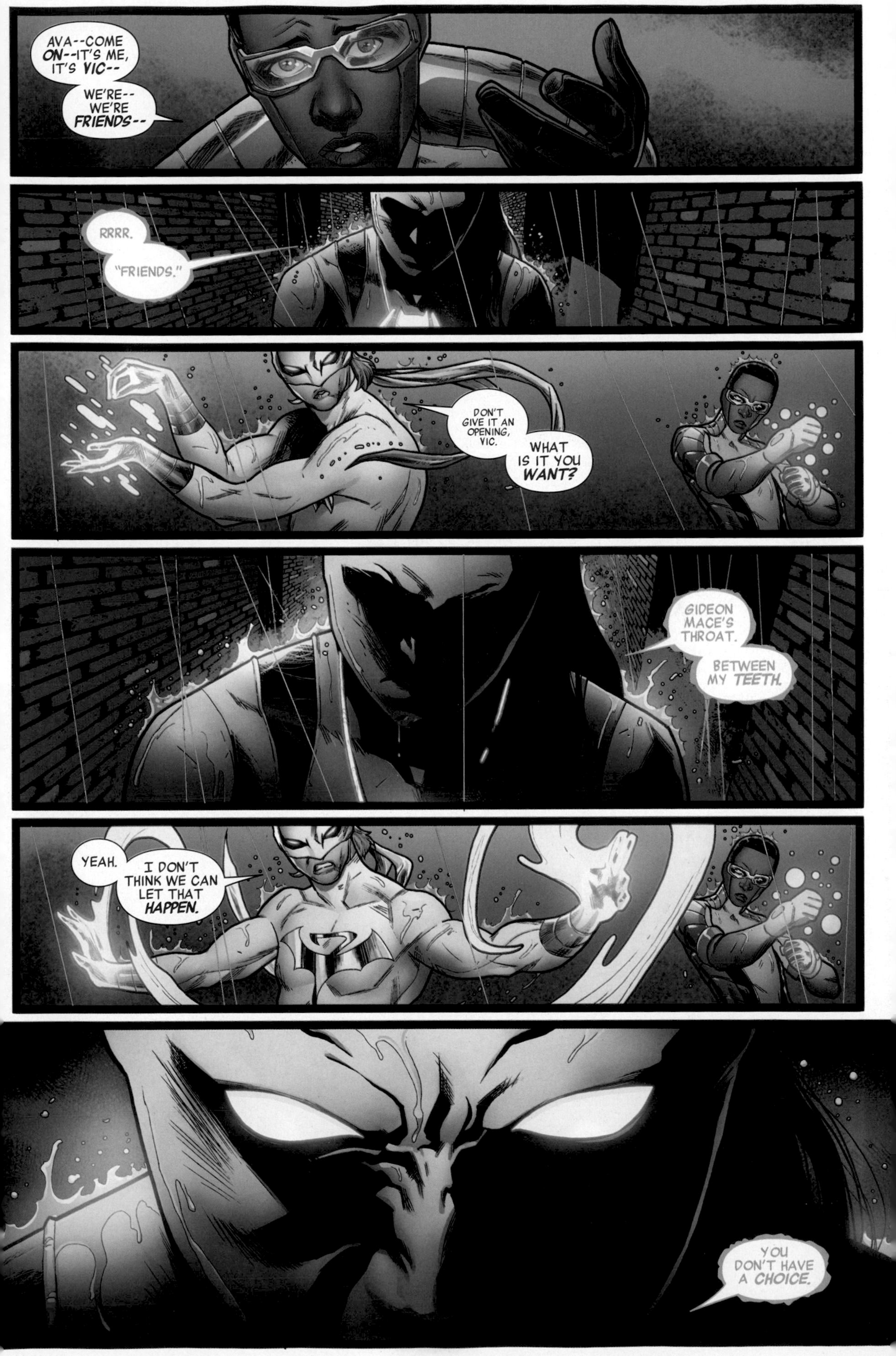

AVA--COME ON--IT'S ME, IT'S VIC--
WE'RE-- WE'RE FRIENDS--
RRRR.
"FRIENDS."
DON'T GIVE IT AN OPENING, VIC.
WHAT IS IT YOU WANT?
GIDEON MACE'S THROAT.
BETWEEN MY TEETH.
YEAH.
I DON'T THINK WE CAN LET THAT HAPPEN.
YOU DON'T HAVE A CHOICE.

SAYS YOU, %£$€#--

VIC, NO-- DON'T JUST--

LET HER GO!

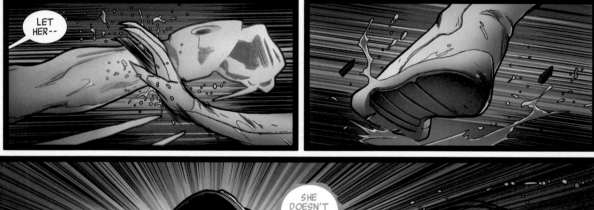

LET HER--

SHE DOESN'T LOVE YOU.

KRAK

NEXT.

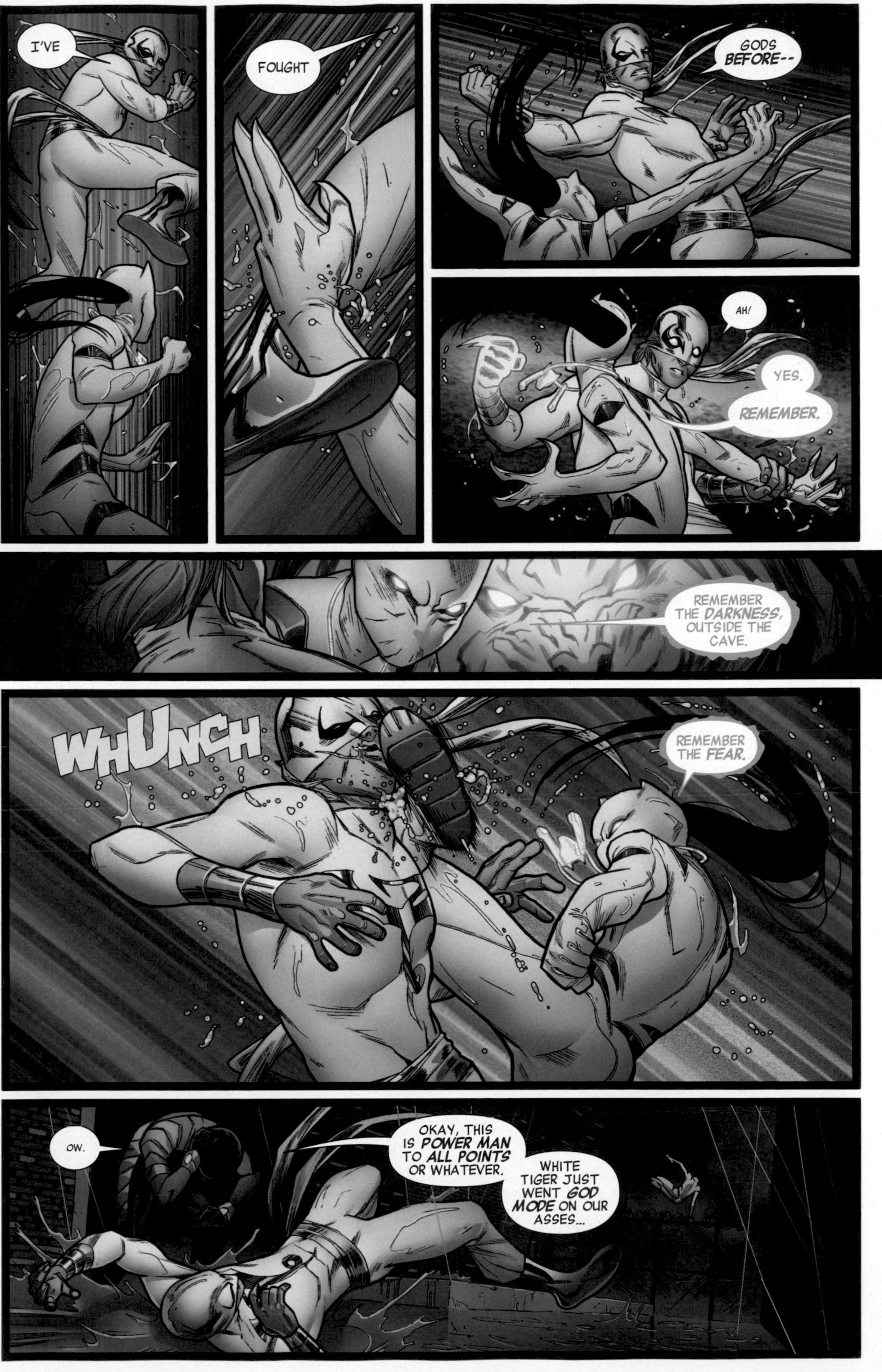
I'VE
FOUGHT
GODS BEFORE--
AH!
YES.
REMEMBER.
REMEMBER THE DARKNESS, OUTSIDE THE CAVE.
WHUNCH
REMEMBER THE FEAR.
OW.
OKAY, THIS IS POWER MAN TO ALL POINTS OR WHATEVER.
WHITE TIGER JUST WENT GOD MODE ON OUR ASSES...

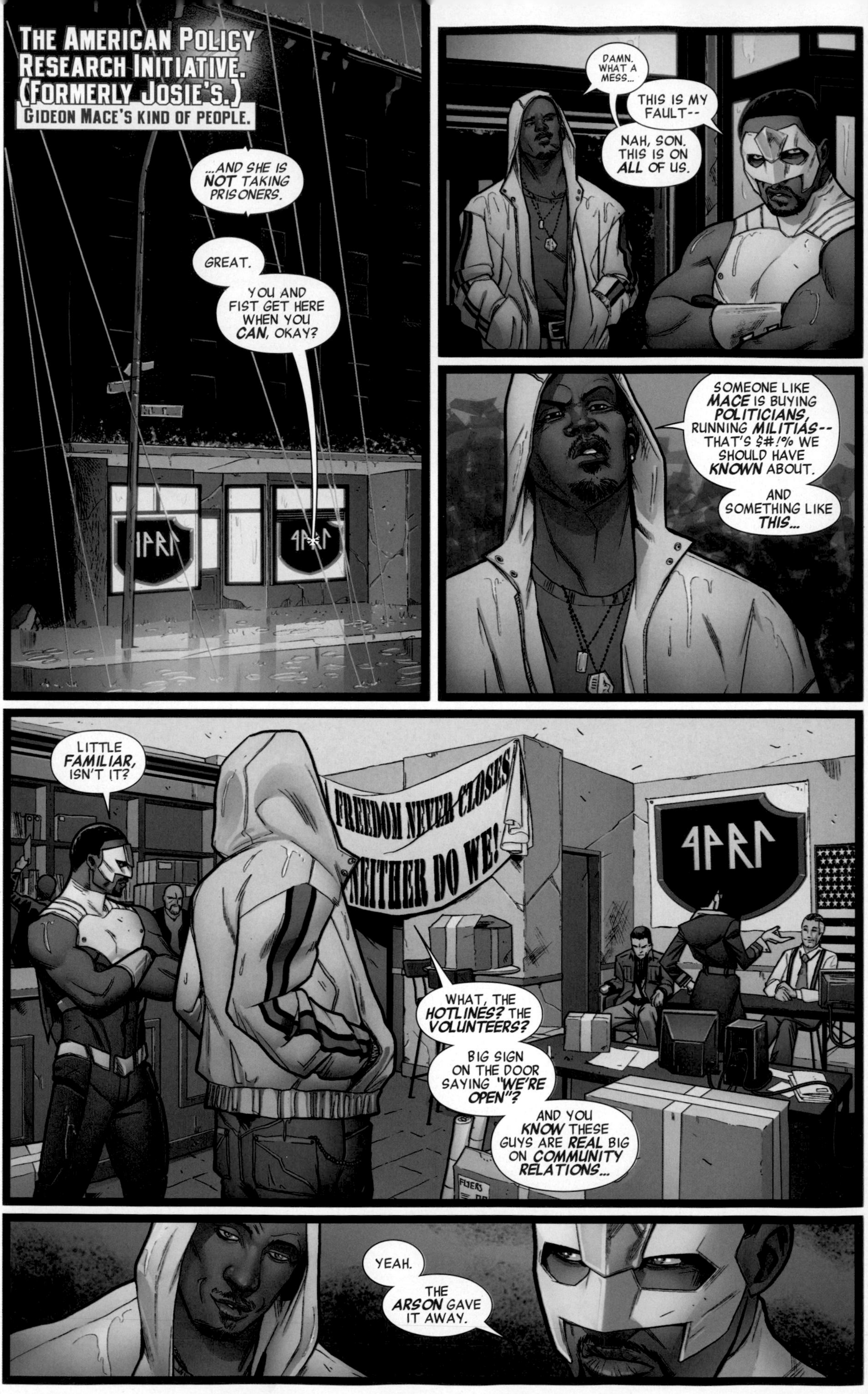
THE AMERICAN POLICY RESEARCH INITIATIVE. (FORMERLY JOSIE'S.)
GIDEON MACE'S KIND OF PEOPLE.
...AND SHE IS NOT TAKING PRISONERS.
GREAT.
YOU AND FIST GET HERE WHEN YOU CAN, OKAY?
APRI
APRI
DAMN. WHAT A MESS...
THIS IS MY FAULT--
NAH, SON. THIS IS ON ALL OF US.
SOMEONE LIKE MACE IS BUYING POLITICIANS, RUNNING MILITIAS--THAT'S $#!% WE SHOULD HAVE KNOWN ABOUT.
AND SOMETHING LIKE THIS...
LITTLE FAMILIAR, ISN'T IT?
FREEDOM NEVER CLOSES NEITHER DO WE!
APRI
WHAT, THE HOTLINES? THE VOLUNTEERS?
BIG SIGN ON THE DOOR SAYING "WE'RE OPEN"?
AND YOU KNOW THESE GUYS ARE REAL BIG ON COMMUNITY RELATIONS...
FLYERS
YEAH.
THE ARSON GAVE IT AWAY.

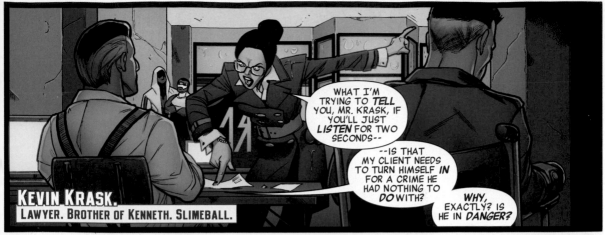

WHAT I'M TRYING TO **TELL** YOU, MR. KRASK, IF YOU'LL JUST **LISTEN** FOR TWO SECONDS--

--IS THAT MY CLIENT NEEDS TO TURN HIMSELF **IN** FOR A CRIME HE HAD NOTHING TO **DO** WITH?

WHY, EXACTLY? IS HE IN **DANGER**?

KEVIN KRASK.
LAWYER. BROTHER OF KENNETH. SLIMEBALL.

WE'RE ALREADY MEETING YOU **HALFWAY**, MS. WALTERS. WE'RE ALLOWING YOUR, AH, **PEOPLE** TO PROVIDE ADDITIONAL **PROTECTION**.

I THINK MR. MACE IS QUITE SAFE **NOW**, DON'T YOU?

DAMN IT.

NEVER GET ANGRY, JEN. ANGRY IS THE **OTHER** HULK--

NOT GOOD NEWS?

NO. WITHOUT **DRISCOLL**, THERE'S NOTHING WE CAN GET **MACE** ON--AND KRASK **KNOWS** THERE'S MORE THAN WE'RE TELLING HIM.

PUT SIMPLY-- IF AVA BUSTS IN HERE **NOW**?

IT'S A **CIVIL SUIT** AND POSSIBLE **CRIMINAL PROCEEDINGS** FOR **HER**--AND A FREE **RECRUITING AD** FOR **THESE** CREEPS.

IF SHE **SUCCEEDS**--IF SHE MANAGES TO **KILL** GIDEON MACE--

--IT'S THE **END** OF THE MIGHTY AVENGERS.

UNHH--

SAM--

OH, HELL--

HULK OUT. WAIT FOR YOUR MOMENT, TRY AND TAKE HER DOWN GENTLY.

WHUDD

I'LL KEEP HER--

--BUSY?

WHOOSHH

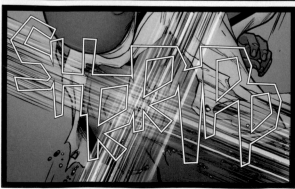

AAAARRRHH!

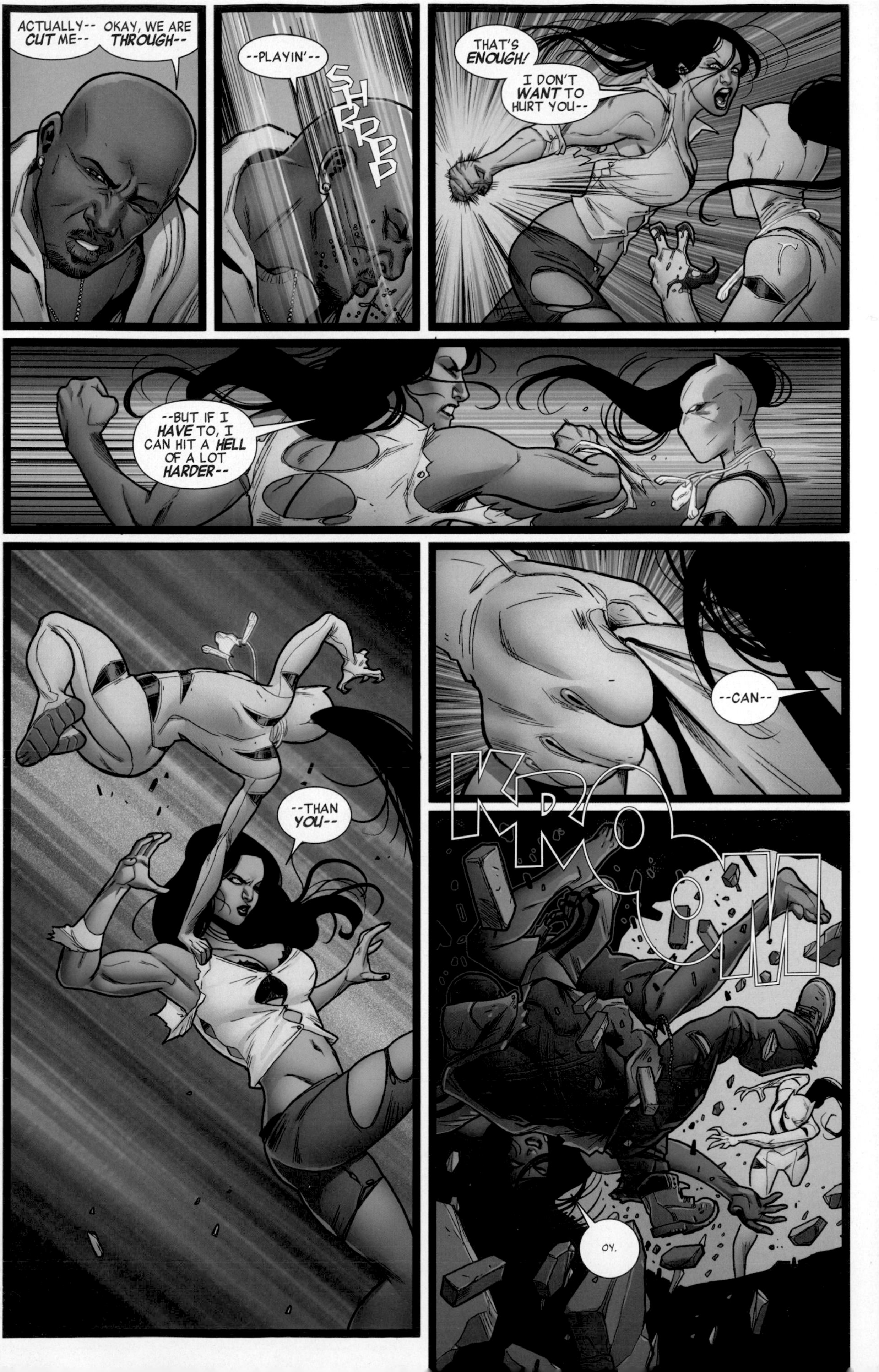
ACTUALLY-- CUT ME--
OKAY, WE ARE THROUGH--
--PLAYIN'--
SHRRPP
THAT'S ENOUGH!
I DON'T WANT TO HURT YOU--
--BUT IF I HAVE TO, I CAN HIT A HELL OF A LOT HARDER--
--THAN YOU--
--CAN--
KROOM
OY.

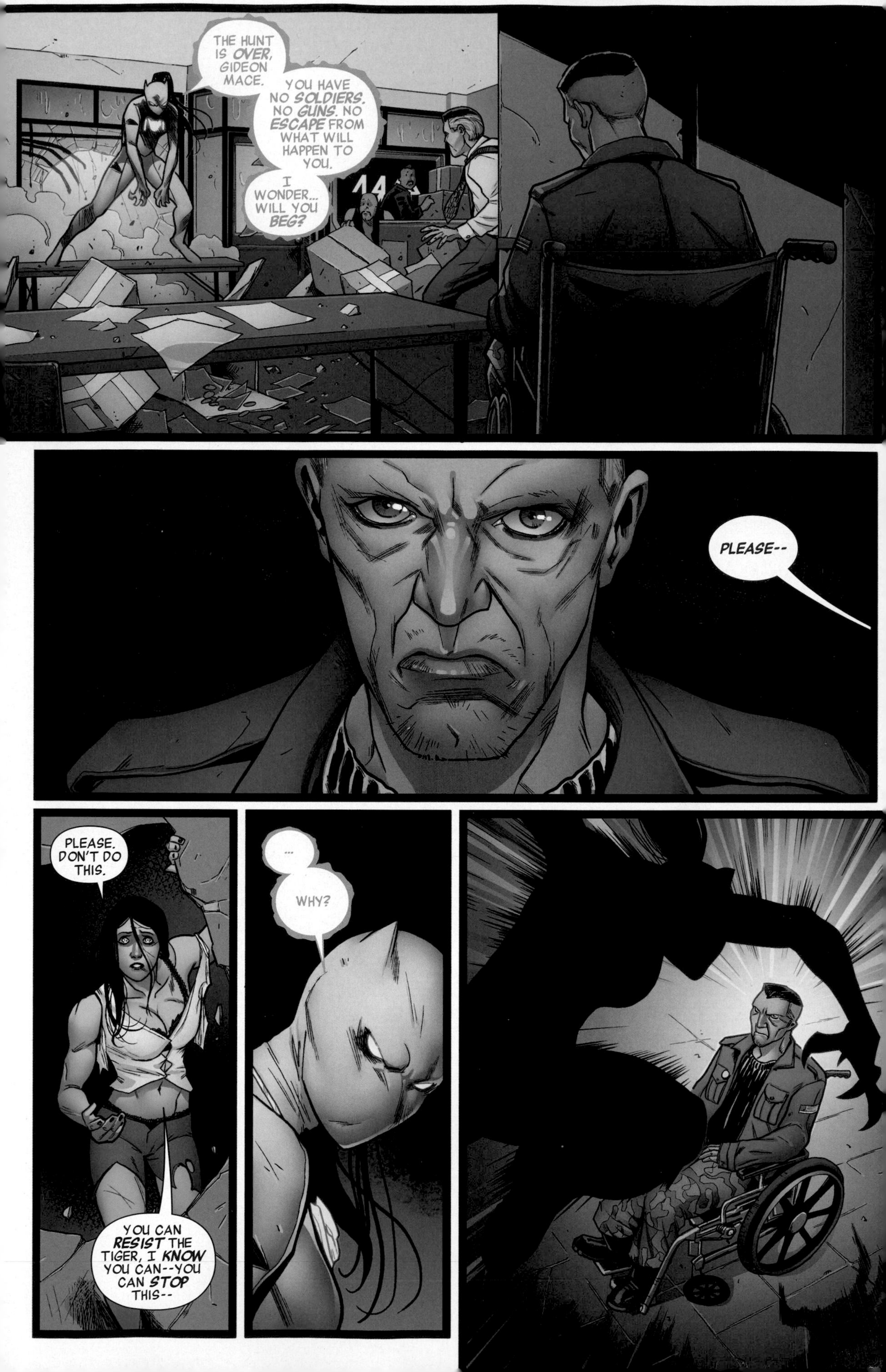
THE HUNT IS OVER, GIDEON MACE.
YOU HAVE NO SOLDIERS. NO GUNS. NO ESCAPE FROM WHAT WILL HAPPEN TO YOU.
I WONDER... WILL YOU BEG?
PLEASE--
PLEASE. DON'T DO THIS.
YOU CAN RESIST THE TIGER, I KNOW YOU CAN--YOU CAN STOP THIS--
...
WHY?

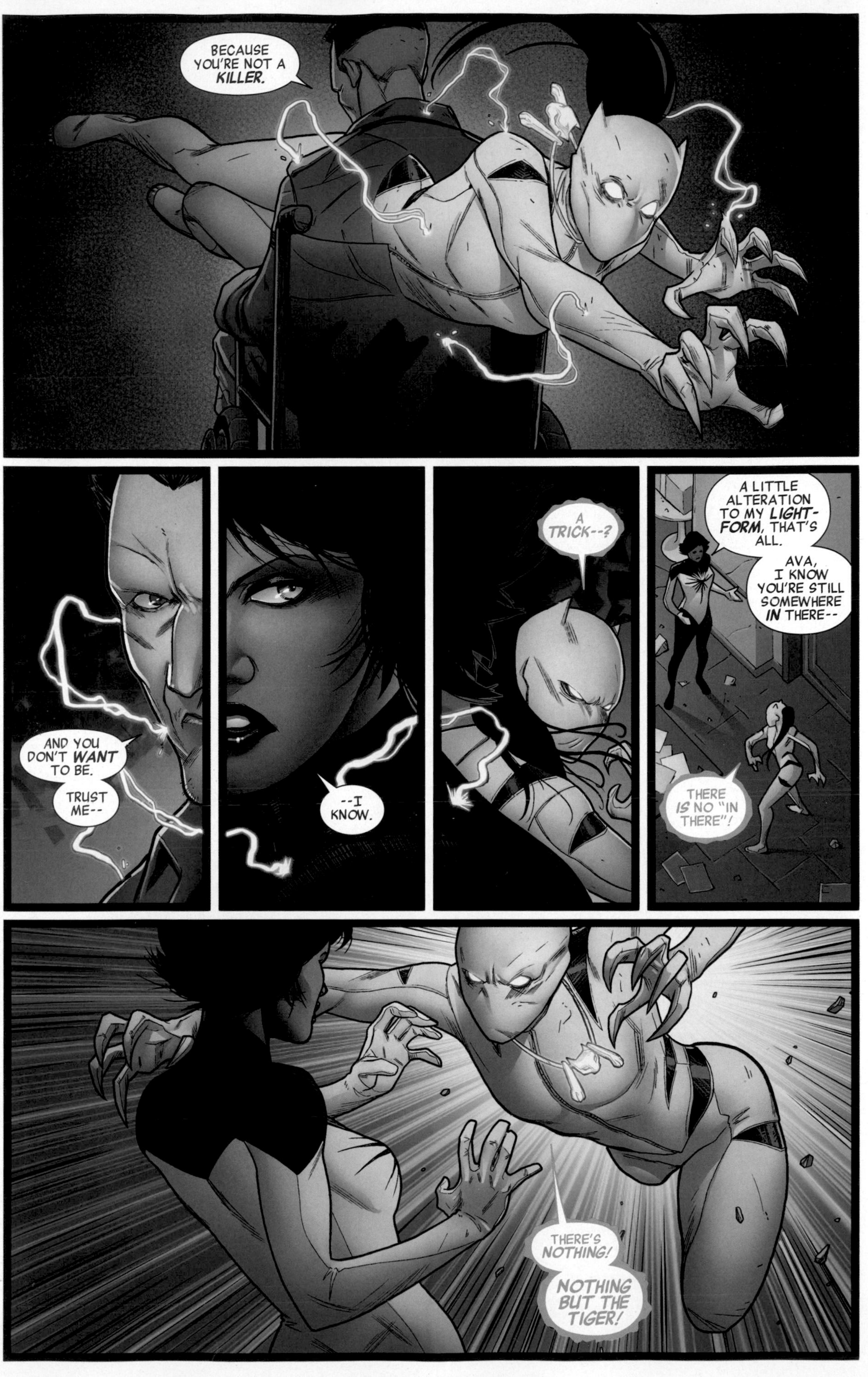
BECAUSE YOU'RE NOT A KILLER.
AND YOU DON'T WANT TO BE.
TRUST ME--
--I KNOW.
A TRICK--?
A LITTLE ALTERATION TO MY LIGHT-FORM, THAT'S ALL.
AVA, I KNOW YOU'RE STILL SOMEWHERE IN THERE--
THERE IS NO "IN THERE"!
THERE'S NOTHING!
NOTHING BUT THE TIGER!

RRAAARRHH!

WELL. THAT'S A SHAME.

BUT I GUESS IT MEANS I DON'T HAVE TO HOLD BACK.

SHZZAKKAOOM!!!

NNAARRRHH--

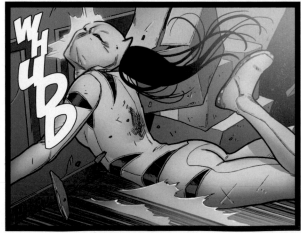

WHUB

SHE'S ALIVE.

THANK GOD.

ACTUALLY, ASIDE FROM THE *POSSESSION* BY AN ANCIENT *TIGER GOD*, SHE SEEMS *FINE*--

SO IT'S JUST THE *REST* OF US NEED THE HOSPITAL, HUH?

MAN, I HOPE THIS DOESN'T *SCAR*...

LUKE? IT'S *JESS*.

WHAT HAPPENED? WE HEARD SOMETHING THAT SOUNDED LIKE A *WRECKING BALL*--

YEAH, THAT WAS ME.

LOOK, WE'RE ON OUR WAY *BACK*, SO--

UH... *LUKE?*

YOU IN THERE! DROP YOUR WEAPONS!

COME OUT WITH YOUR HANDS ABOVE YOUR HEADS!

WE WILL NOT HESITATE TO SHOOT--

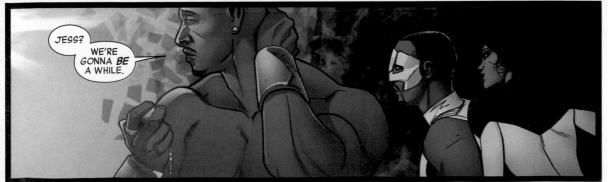

JESS?

WE'RE GONNA *BE* A WHILE.

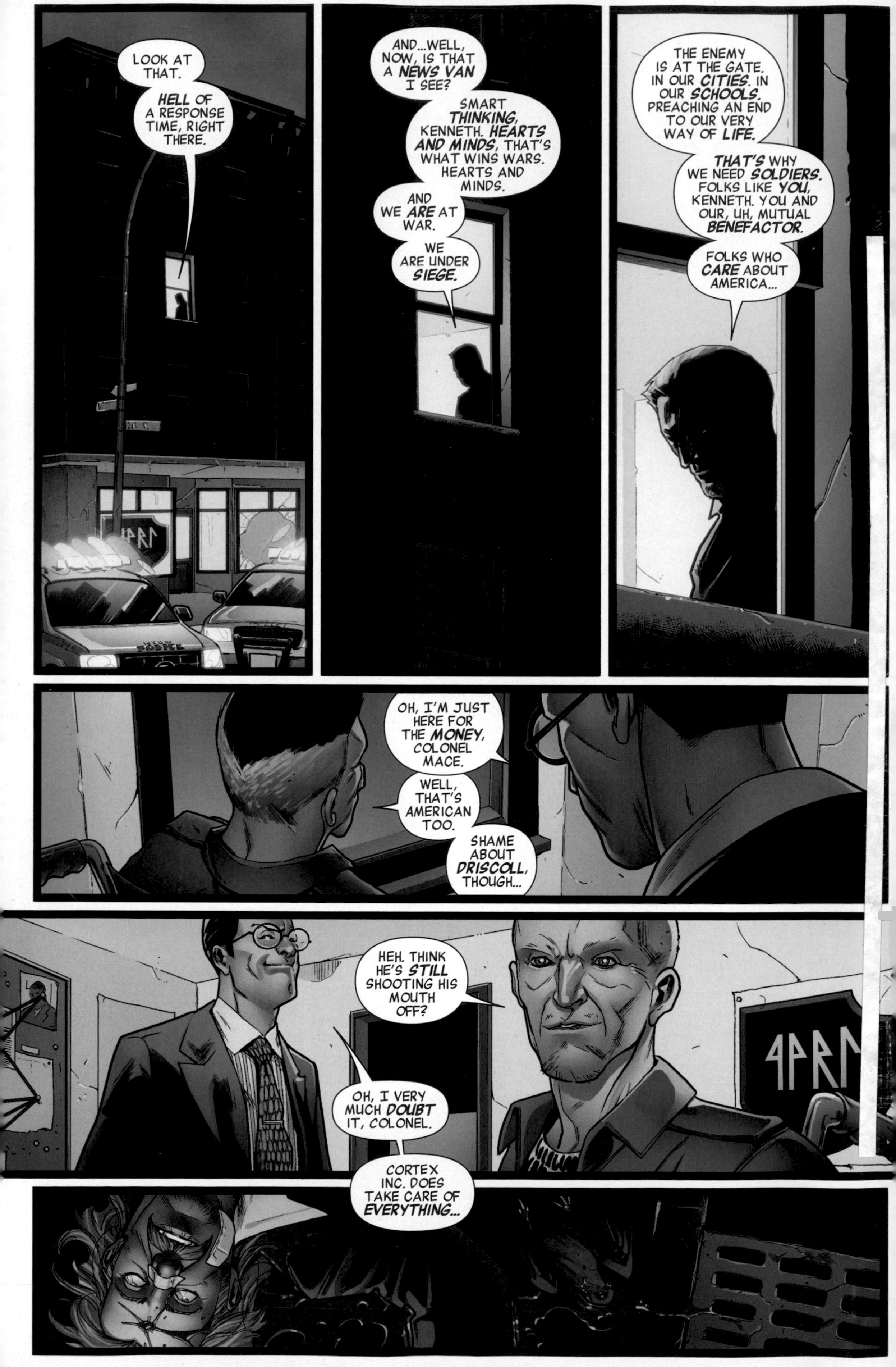
LOOK AT THAT.
HELL OF A RESPONSE TIME, RIGHT THERE.
AND...WELL, NOW, IS THAT A NEWS VAN I SEE?
SMART THINKING, KENNETH. HEARTS AND MINDS, THAT'S WHAT WINS WARS. HEARTS AND MINDS.
AND WE ARE AT WAR.
WE ARE UNDER SIEGE.
THE ENEMY IS AT THE GATE. IN OUR CITIES. IN OUR SCHOOLS. PREACHING AN END TO OUR VERY WAY OF LIFE.
THAT'S WHY WE NEED SOLDIERS. FOLKS LIKE YOU, KENNETH. YOU AND OUR, UH, MUTUAL BENEFACTOR.
FOLKS WHO CARE ABOUT AMERICA...
OH, I'M JUST HERE FOR THE MONEY, COLONEL MACE.
WELL, THAT'S AMERICAN TOO.
SHAME ABOUT DRISCOLL, THOUGH...
HEH. THINK HE'S STILL SHOOTING HIS MOUTH OFF?
OH, I VERY MUCH DOUBT IT, COLONEL.
CORTEX INC. DOES TAKE CARE OF EVERYTHING...

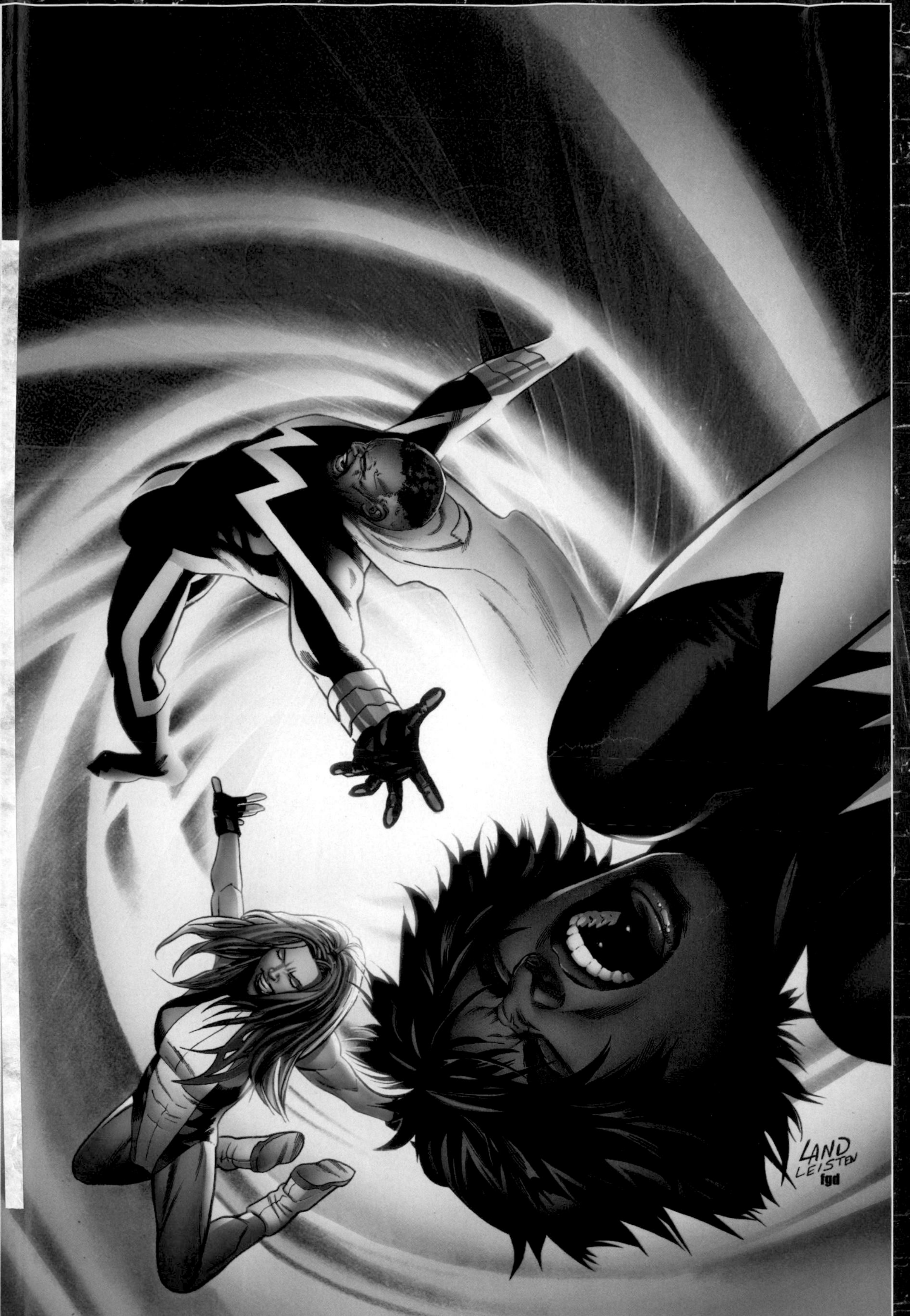
LAND
LEISTEN
fgd

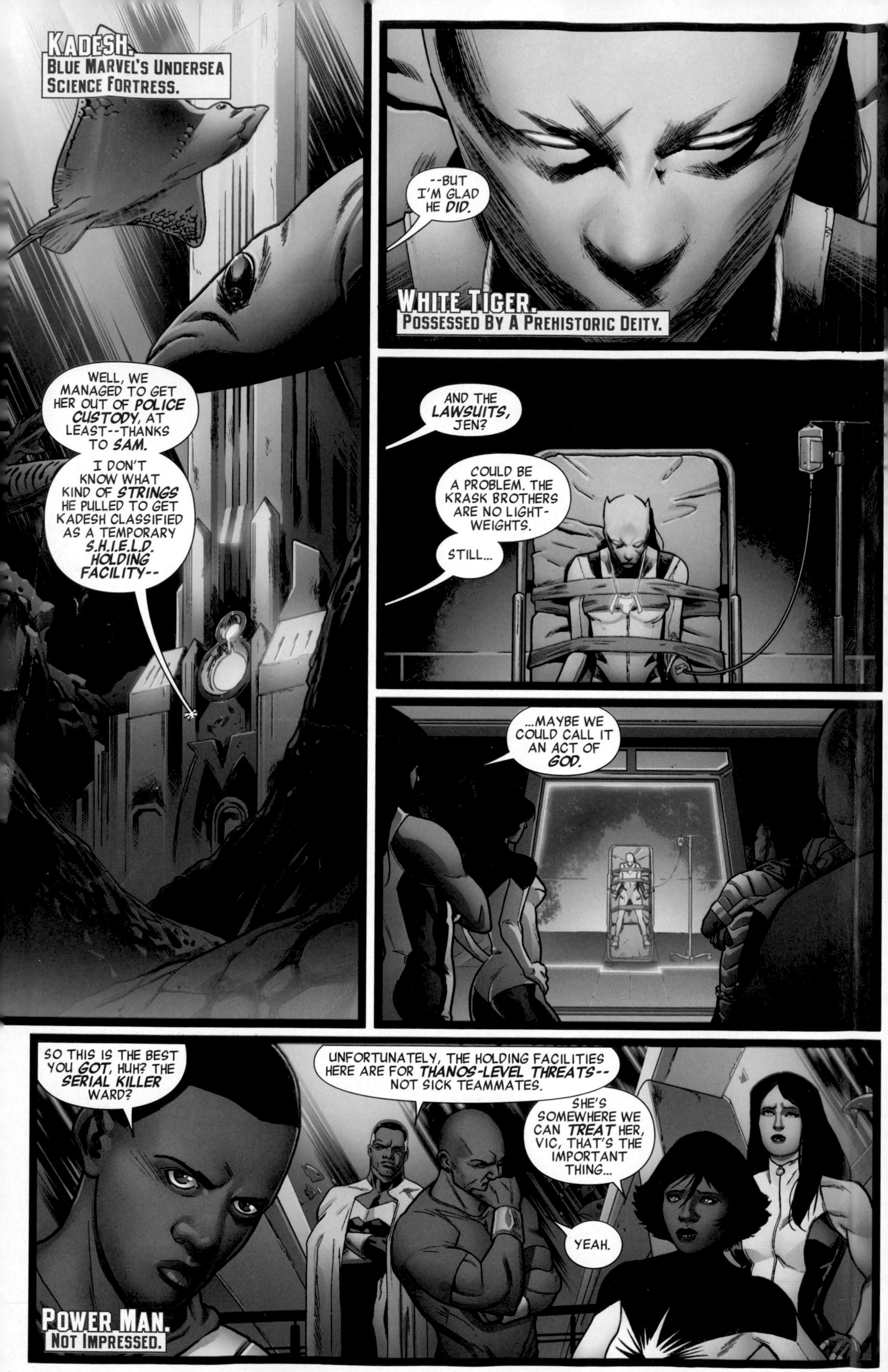
KADESH.
BLUE MARVEL'S UNDERSEA SCIENCE FORTRESS.
WELL, WE MANAGED TO GET HER OUT OF POLICE CUSTODY, AT LEAST--THANKS TO SAM.
I DON'T KNOW WHAT KIND OF STRINGS HE PULLED TO GET KADESH CLASSIFIED AS A TEMPORARY S.H.I.E.L.D. HOLDING FACILITY--
--BUT I'M GLAD HE DID.
WHITE TIGER.
POSSESSED BY A PREHISTORIC DEITY.
AND THE LAWSUITS, JEN?
COULD BE A PROBLEM. THE KRASK BROTHERS ARE NO LIGHT-WEIGHTS.
STILL...
...MAYBE WE COULD CALL IT AN ACT OF GOD.
SO THIS IS THE BEST YOU GOT, HUH? THE SERIAL KILLER WARD?
UNFORTUNATELY, THE HOLDING FACILITIES HERE ARE FOR THANOS-LEVEL THREATS--NOT SICK TEAMMATES.
SHE'S SOMEWHERE WE CAN TREAT HER, VIC, THAT'S THE IMPORTANT THING...
YEAH.
POWER MAN.
NOT IMPRESSED.

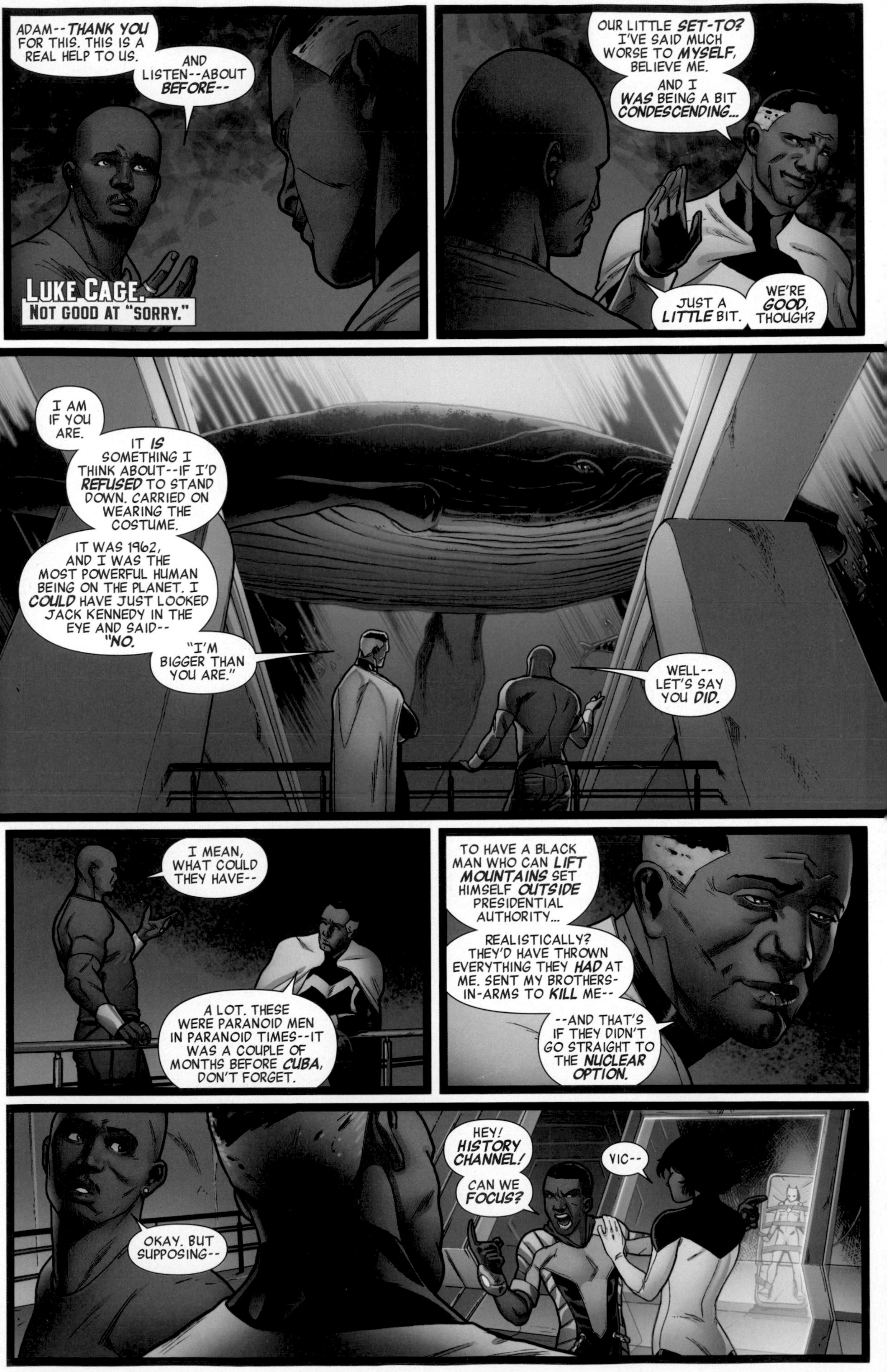

ADAM--THANK YOU FOR THIS. THIS IS A REAL HELP TO US.
AND LISTEN--ABOUT BEFORE--
LUKE CAGE. NOT GOOD AT "SORRY."
OUR LITTLE SET-TO? I'VE SAID MUCH WORSE TO MYSELF, BELIEVE ME.
AND I WAS BEING A BIT CONDESCENDING...
JUST A LITTLE BIT.
WE'RE GOOD, THOUGH?
I AM IF YOU ARE.
IT IS SOMETHING I THINK ABOUT--IF I'D REFUSED TO STAND DOWN. CARRIED ON WEARING THE COSTUME.
IT WAS 1962, AND I WAS THE MOST POWERFUL HUMAN BEING ON THE PLANET. I COULD HAVE JUST LOOKED JACK KENNEDY IN THE EYE AND SAID--"NO.
"I'M BIGGER THAN YOU ARE."
WELL--LET'S SAY YOU DID.
I MEAN, WHAT COULD THEY HAVE--
A LOT. THESE WERE PARANOID MEN IN PARANOID TIMES--IT WAS A COUPLE OF MONTHS BEFORE CUBA, DON'T FORGET.
TO HAVE A BLACK MAN WHO CAN LIFT MOUNTAINS SET HIMSELF OUTSIDE PRESIDENTIAL AUTHORITY...
REALISTICALLY? THEY'D HAVE THROWN EVERYTHING THEY HAD AT ME. SENT MY BROTHERS-IN-ARMS TO KILL ME--
--AND THAT'S IF THEY DIDN'T GO STRAIGHT TO THE NUCLEAR OPTION.
OKAY. BUT SUPPOSING--
HEY! HISTORY CHANNEL! CAN WE FOCUS?
VIC--

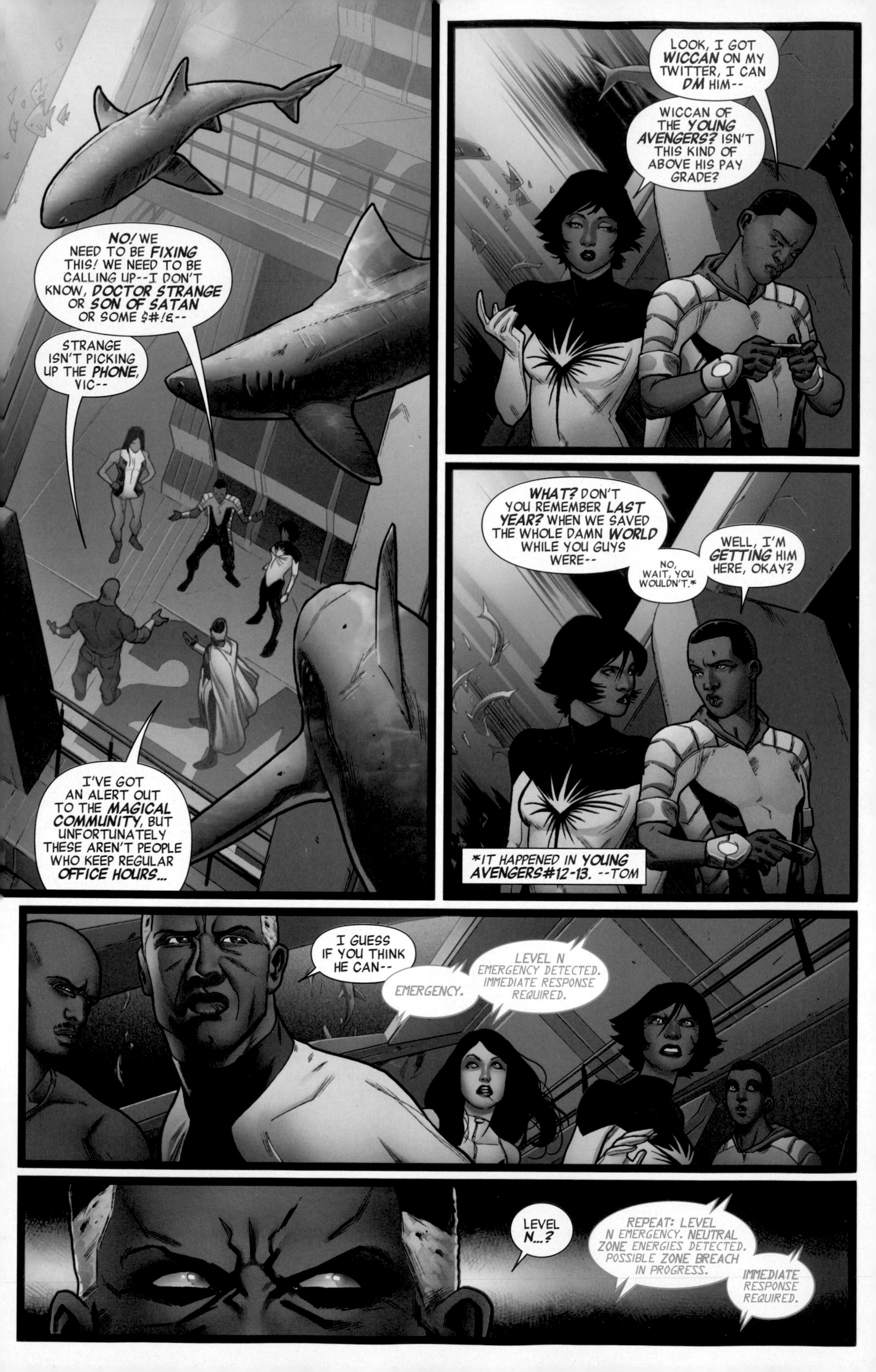
NO! WE NEED TO BE FIXING THIS! WE NEED TO BE CALLING UP--I DON'T KNOW, DOCTOR STRANGE OR SON OF SATAN OR SOME $#!&--
STRANGE ISN'T PICKING UP THE PHONE, VIC--
I'VE GOT AN ALERT OUT TO THE MAGICAL COMMUNITY, BUT UNFORTUNATELY THESE AREN'T PEOPLE WHO KEEP REGULAR OFFICE HOURS...
LOOK, I GOT WICCAN ON MY TWITTER, I CAN DM HIM--
WICCAN OF THE YOUNG AVENGERS? ISN'T THIS KIND OF ABOVE HIS PAY GRADE?
WHAT? DON'T YOU REMEMBER LAST YEAR? WHEN WE SAVED THE WHOLE DAMN WORLD WHILE YOU GUYS WERE--
NO, WAIT, YOU WOULDN'T.*
WELL, I'M GETTING HIM HERE, OKAY?
*IT HAPPENED IN YOUNG AVENGERS #12-13. --TOM
I GUESS IF YOU THINK HE CAN--
EMERGENCY.
LEVEL N EMERGENCY DETECTED. IMMEDIATE RESPONSE REQUIRED.
LEVEL N...?
REPEAT: LEVEL N EMERGENCY. NEUTRAL ZONE ENERGIES DETECTED. POSSIBLE ZONE BREACH IN PROGRESS.
IMMEDIATE RESPONSE REQUIRED.

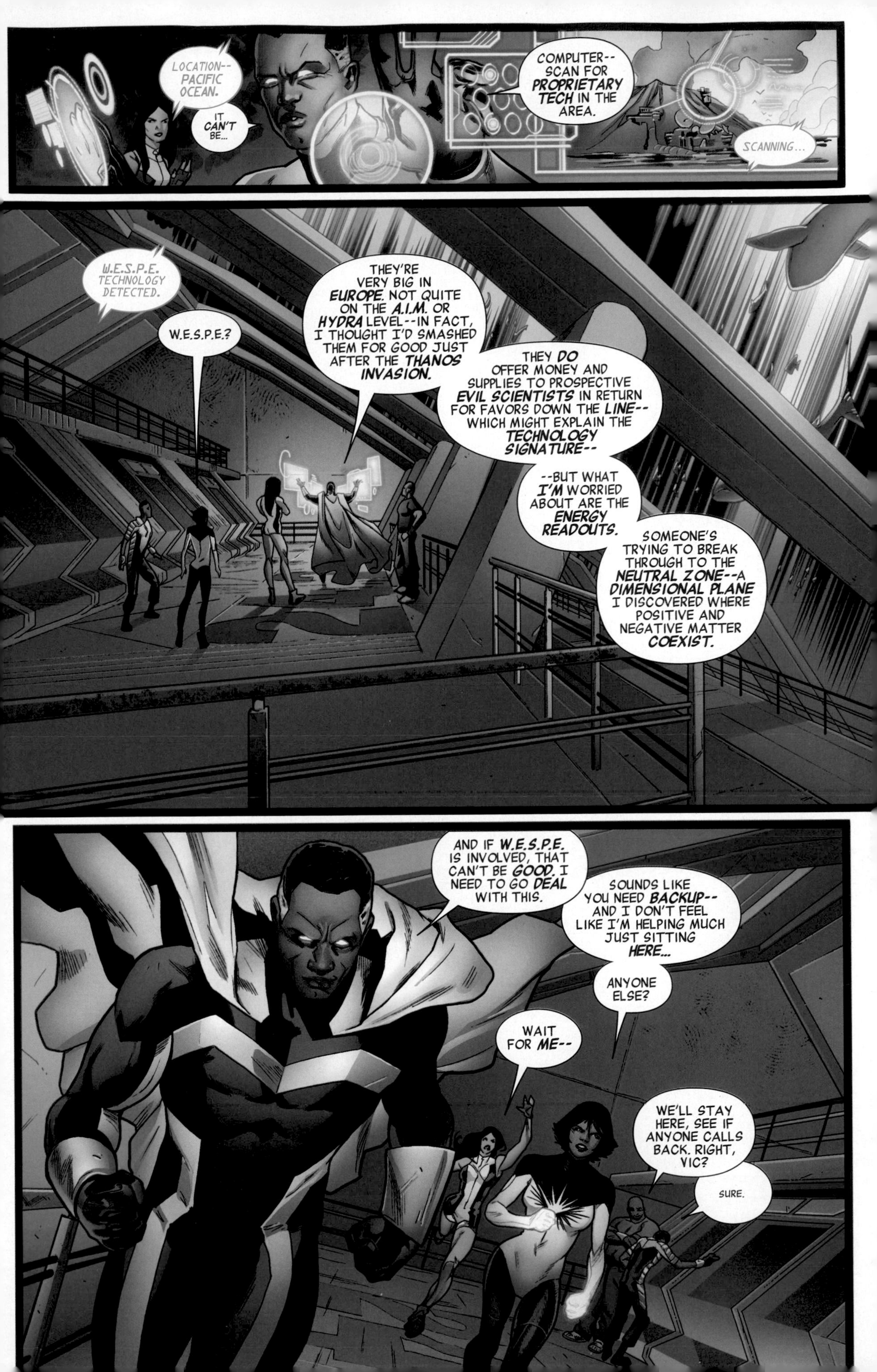
LOCATION--PACIFIC OCEAN.
IT CAN'T BE...
COMPUTER--SCAN FOR PROPRIETARY TECH IN THE AREA.
SCANNING...
W.E.S.P.E. TECHNOLOGY DETECTED.
W.E.S.P.E.?
THEY'RE VERY BIG IN EUROPE. NOT QUITE ON THE A.I.M. OR HYDRA LEVEL--IN FACT, I THOUGHT I'D SMASHED THEM FOR GOOD JUST AFTER THE THANOS INVASION.
THEY DO OFFER MONEY AND SUPPLIES TO PROSPECTIVE EVIL SCIENTISTS IN RETURN FOR FAVORS DOWN THE LINE--WHICH MIGHT EXPLAIN THE TECHNOLOGY SIGNATURE--
--BUT WHAT I'M WORRIED ABOUT ARE THE ENERGY READOUTS.
SOMEONE'S TRYING TO BREAK THROUGH TO THE NEUTRAL ZONE--A DIMENSIONAL PLANE I DISCOVERED WHERE POSITIVE AND NEGATIVE MATTER COEXIST.
AND IF W.E.S.P.E. IS INVOLVED, THAT CAN'T BE GOOD. I NEED TO GO DEAL WITH THIS.
SOUNDS LIKE YOU NEED BACKUP--AND I DON'T FEEL LIKE I'M HELPING MUCH JUST SITTING HERE...
ANYONE ELSE?
WAIT FOR ME--
WE'LL STAY HERE, SEE IF ANYONE CALLS BACK. RIGHT, VIC?
SURE.

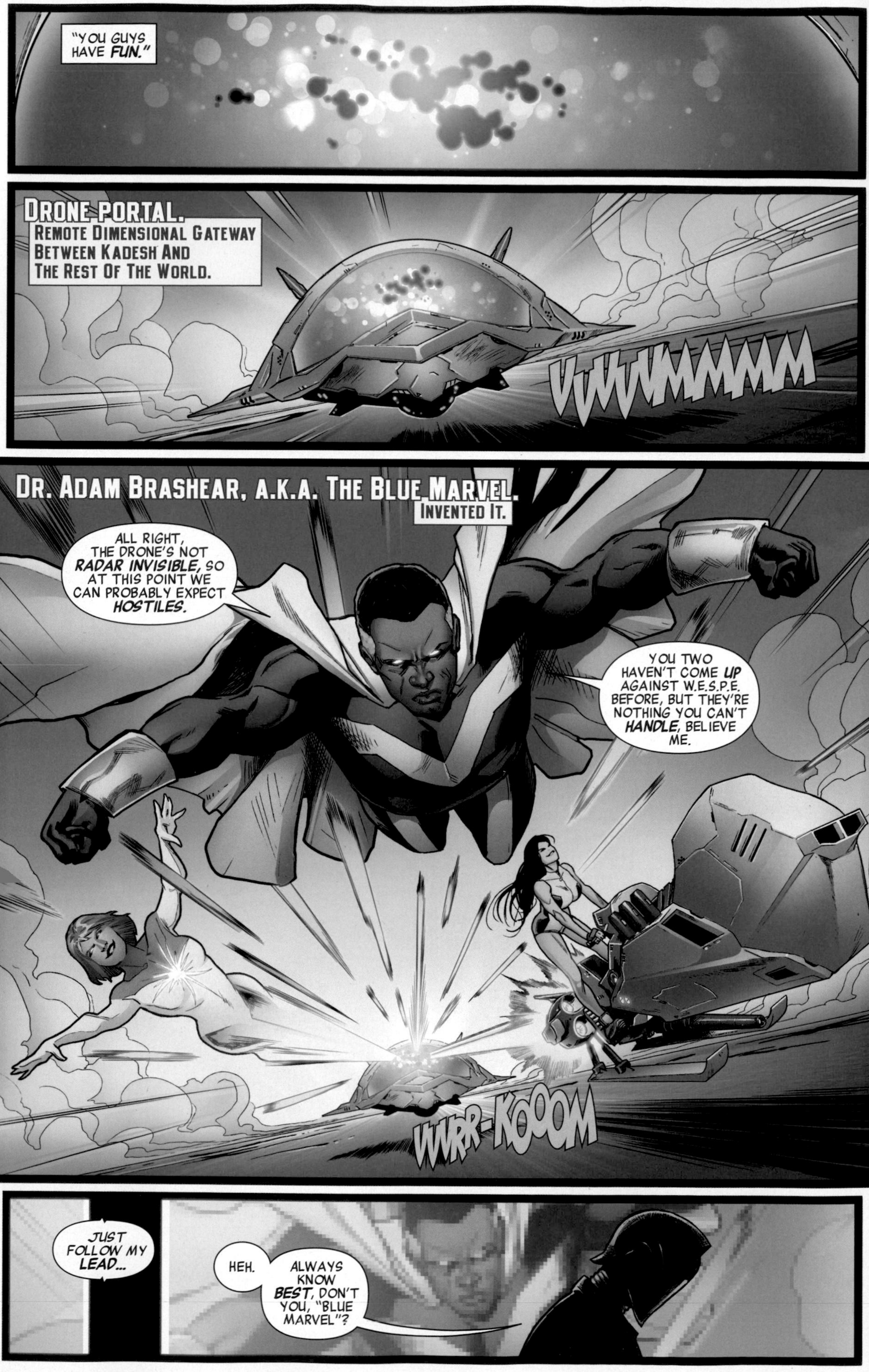

"YOU GUYS HAVE FUN."
DRONE PORTAL.
REMOTE DIMENSIONAL GATEWAY BETWEEN KADESH AND THE REST OF THE WORLD.
VVVUMMMMM
DR. ADAM BRASHEAR, A.K.A. THE BLUE MARVEL.
INVENTED IT.
ALL RIGHT, THE DRONE'S NOT RADAR INVISIBLE, SO AT THIS POINT WE CAN PROBABLY EXPECT HOSTILES.
YOU TWO HAVEN'T COME UP AGAINST W.E.S.P.E. BEFORE, BUT THEY'RE NOTHING YOU CAN'T HANDLE, BELIEVE ME.
VVRR-KOOOM
JUST FOLLOW MY LEAD...
HEH.
ALWAYS KNOW BEST, DON'T YOU, "BLUE MARVEL"?

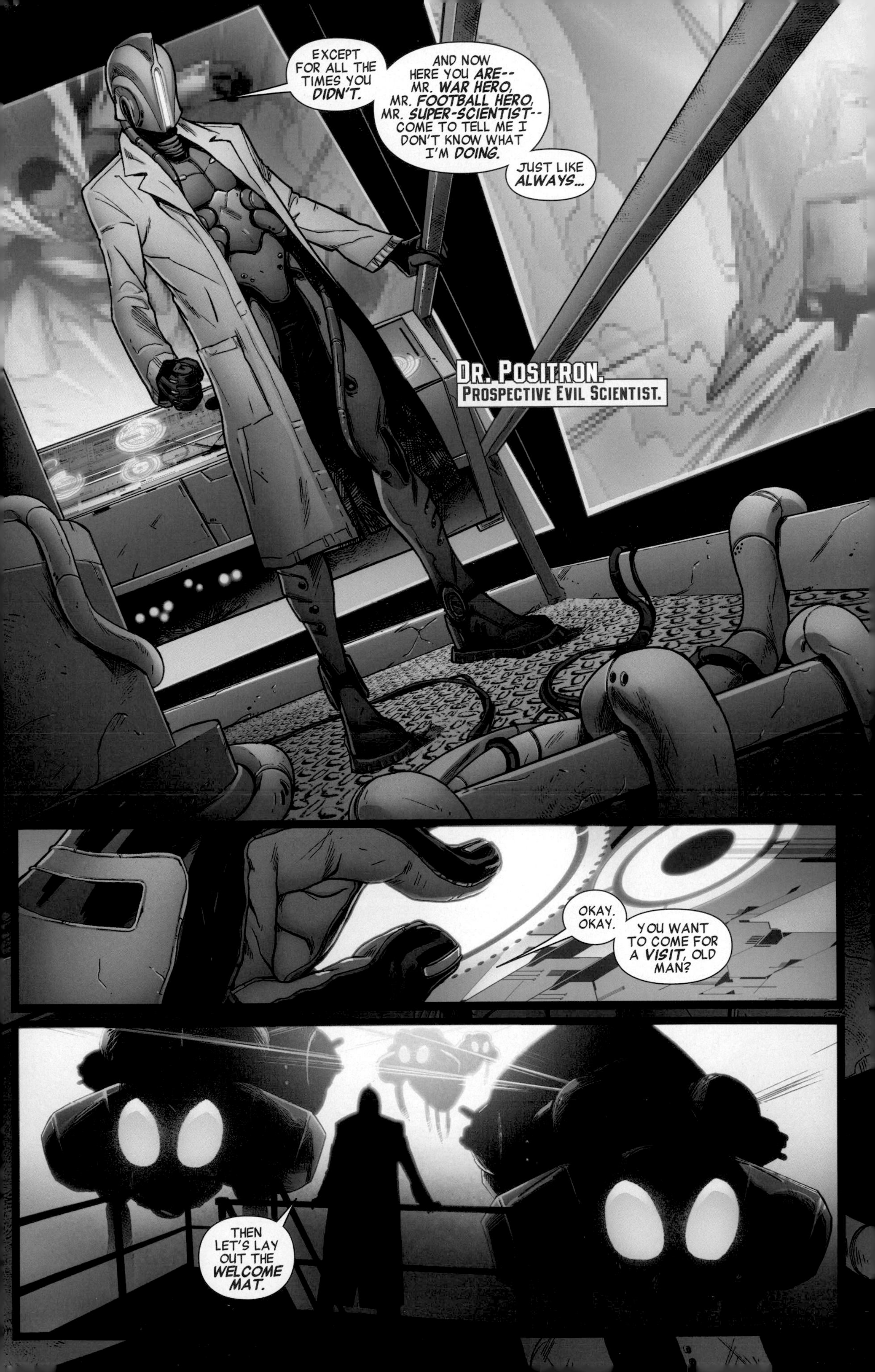
EXCEPT FOR ALL THE TIMES YOU DIDN'T.
AND NOW HERE YOU ARE-- MR. WAR HERO, MR. FOOTBALL HERO, MR. SUPER-SCIENTIST-- COME TO TELL ME I DON'T KNOW WHAT I'M DOING.
JUST LIKE ALWAYS...
DR. POSITRON.
PROSPECTIVE EVIL SCIENTIST.
OKAY. OKAY.
YOU WANT TO COME FOR A VISIT, OLD MAN?
THEN LET'S LAY OUT THE WELCOME MAT.

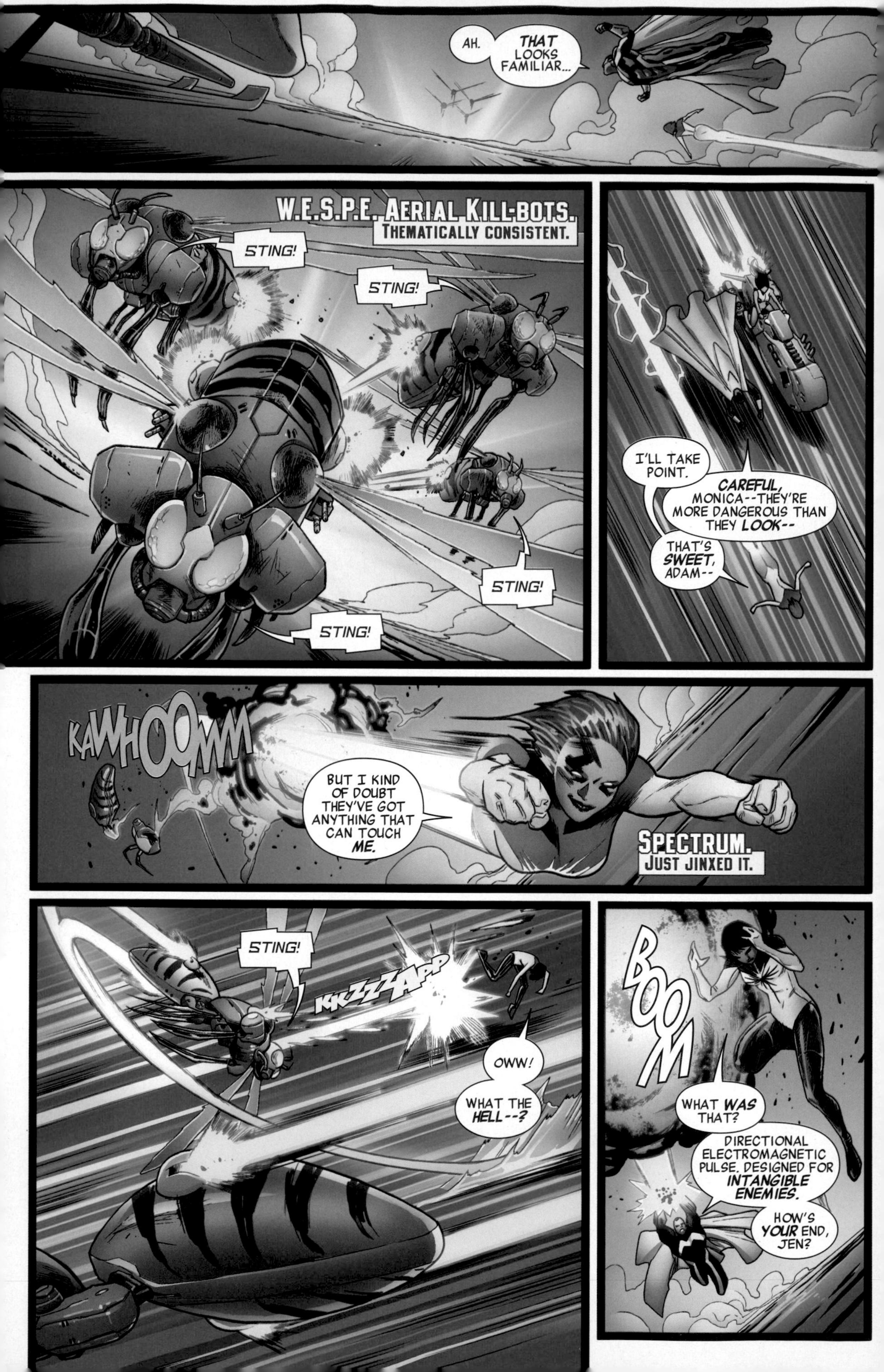
AH.
THAT LOOKS FAMILIAR...
W.E.S.P.E. AERIAL KILL-BOTS.
THEMATICALLY CONSISTENT.
STING!
STING!
STING!
STING!
I'LL TAKE POINT.
CAREFUL, MONICA--THEY'RE MORE DANGEROUS THAN THEY LOOK--
THAT'S SWEET, ADAM--
KAWHOOMM
BUT I KIND OF DOUBT THEY'VE GOT ANYTHING THAT CAN TOUCH ME.
SPECTRUM.
JUST JINXED IT.
STING!
KKZZZAPP
OWW!
WHAT THE HELL--?
BOOM
WHAT WAS THAT?
DIRECTIONAL ELECTROMAGNETIC PULSE, DESIGNED FOR INTANGIBLE ENEMIES.
HOW'S YOUR END, JEN?

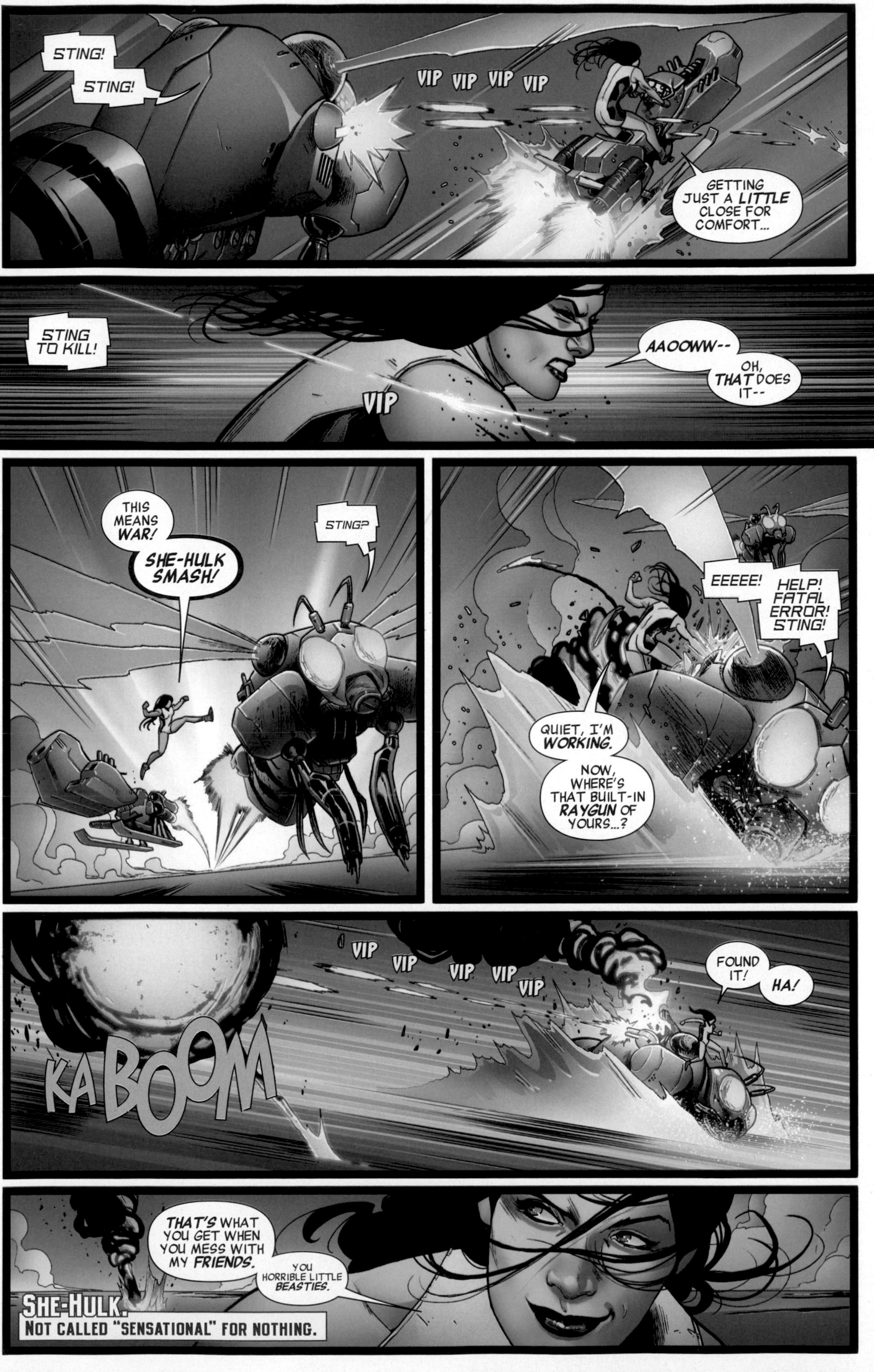
STING!
STING!
VIP VIP VIP VIP
GETTING JUST A LITTLE CLOSE FOR COMFORT...
STING TO KILL!
VIP
AAOOWW--
OH, THAT DOES IT--
THIS MEANS WAR!
SHE-HULK SMASH!
STING?
EEEEE!
HELP! FATAL ERROR! STING!
QUIET, I'M WORKING.
NOW, WHERE'S THAT BUILT-IN RAYGUN OF YOURS...?
KABOOM
VIP VIP VIP VIP VIP
FOUND IT!
HA!
THAT'S WHAT YOU GET WHEN YOU MESS WITH MY FRIENDS.
YOU HORRIBLE LITTLE BEASTIES.
SHE-HULK:
NOT CALLED "SENSATIONAL" FOR NOTHING.

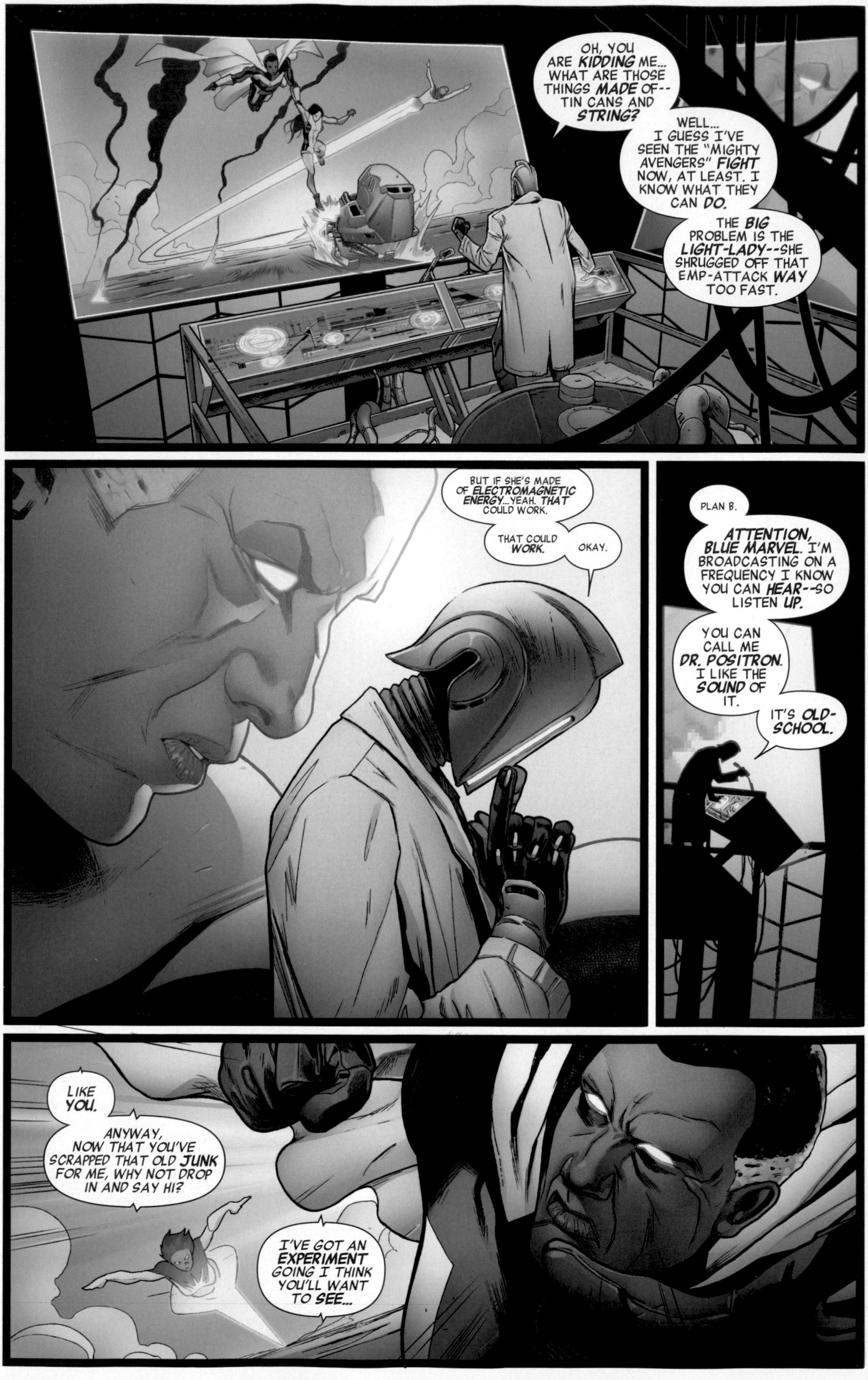
OH, YOU ARE KIDDING ME... WHAT ARE THOSE THINGS MADE OF-- TIN CANS AND STRING?
WELL... I GUESS I'VE SEEN THE "MIGHTY AVENGERS" FIGHT NOW, AT LEAST. I KNOW WHAT THEY CAN DO.
THE BIG PROBLEM IS THE LIGHT-LADY--SHE SHRUGGED OFF THAT EMP-ATTACK WAY TOO FAST.
BUT IF SHE'S MADE OF ELECTROMAGNETIC ENERGY...YEAH. THAT COULD WORK.
THAT COULD WORK.
OKAY.
PLAN B.
ATTENTION, BLUE MARVEL. I'M BROADCASTING ON A FREQUENCY I KNOW YOU CAN HEAR--SO LISTEN UP.
YOU CAN CALL ME DR. POSITRON. I LIKE THE SOUND OF IT.
IT'S OLD-SCHOOL.
LIKE YOU.
ANYWAY, NOW THAT YOU'VE SCRAPPED THAT OLD JUNK FOR ME, WHY NOT DROP IN AND SAY HI?
I'VE GOT AN EXPERIMENT GOING I THINK YOU'LL WANT TO SEE...

...SO WHEN YOU **DO** GET A HOLD OF **CLEA**, CAN YOU TELL HER TO CALL THIS NUMBER?

THANKS, MISTY. I OWE YOU.

MAN, HELL OF A **SIGNAL** DOWN HERE...

BIP!

OH, HEY-- SOME **TEXTS** MADE IT THROUGH--

Hi Vic! Sorry, got hands full :-(

OF 1000000000 EUROS!!!! 8-O ha ha!

Anyway am holding up casino right now but hope Ava better soon. HUGS. --L

DAMN.

FALSE ALARM.

*FOR THE FULL STORY SEE **LOKI: AGENT OF ASGARD #2**, ON SALE NOW! --WIL

THOUGH I GUESS THAT ONE WAS KIND OF A **LAST RESORT**...

OKAY. I'M GONNA GET A **COFFEE** BEFORE WE START THIS **OVER** AGAIN.

YOU COMING?

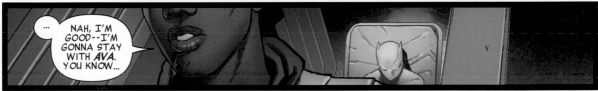

... NAH, I'M GOOD--I'M GONNA STAY WITH **AVA**. YOU KNOW...

...JUST IN CASE.

NNNH!

AVATAR.

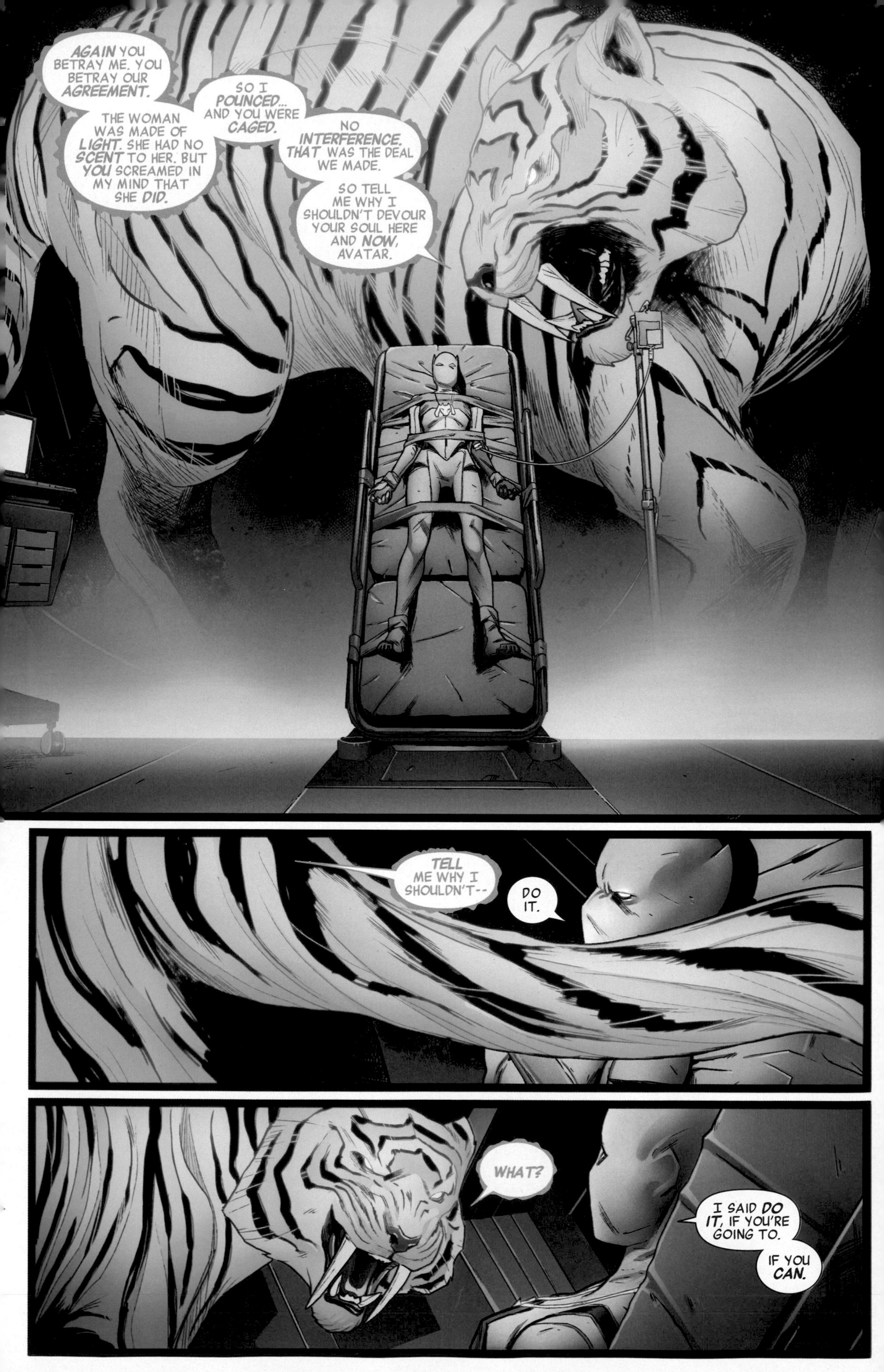
AGAIN YOU BETRAY ME. YOU BETRAY OUR AGREEMENT.
THE WOMAN WAS MADE OF LIGHT. SHE HAD NO SCENT TO HER. BUT YOU SCREAMED IN MY MIND THAT SHE DID.
SO I POUNCED... AND YOU WERE CAGED.
NO INTERFERENCE. THAT WAS THE DEAL WE MADE.
SO TELL ME WHY I SHOULDN'T DEVOUR YOUR SOUL HERE AND NOW, AVATAR.
TELL ME WHY I SHOULDN'T--
DO IT.
WHAT?
I SAID DO IT, IF YOU'RE GOING TO.
IF YOU CAN.

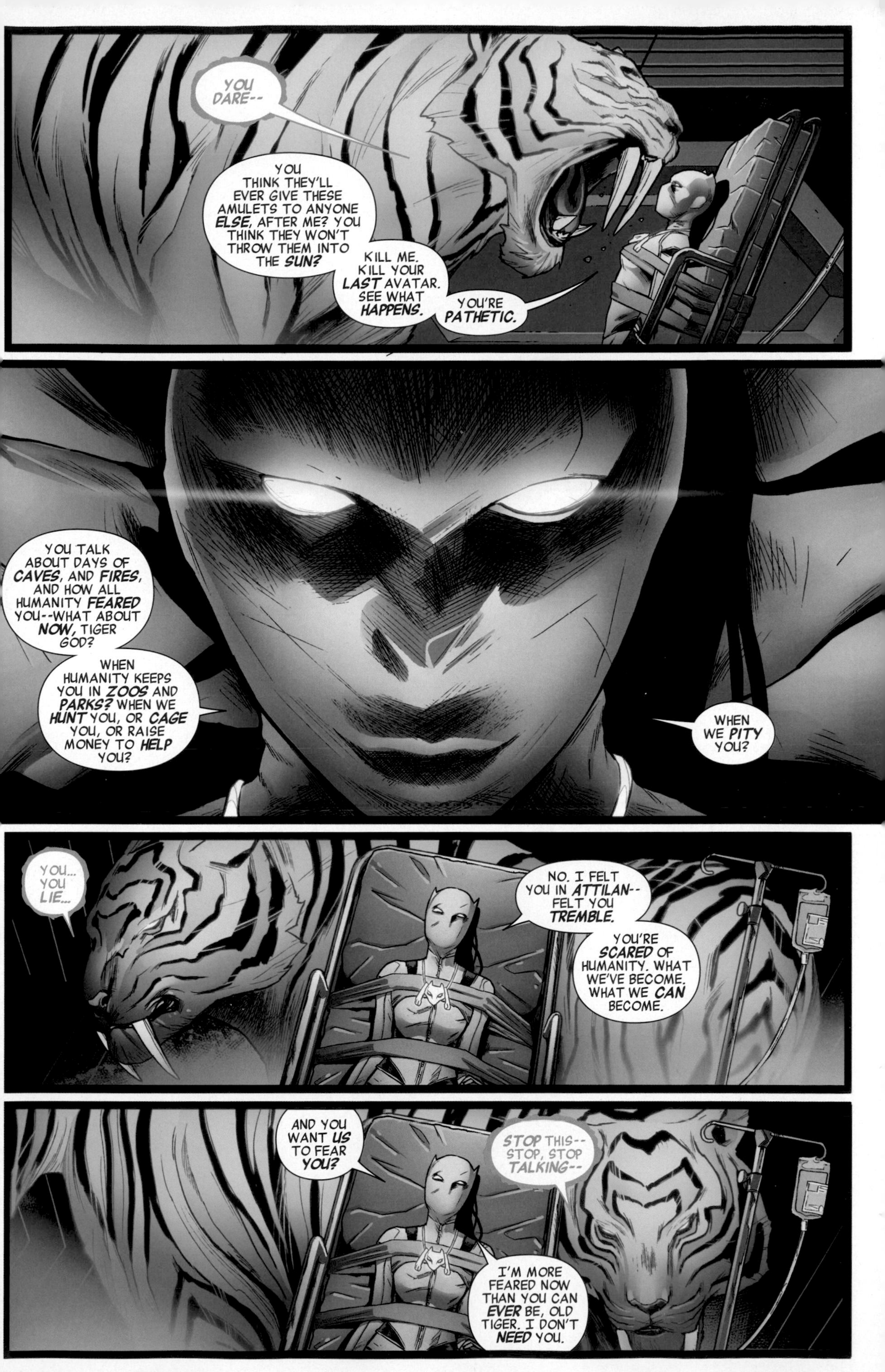
YOU DARE--
YOU THINK THEY'LL EVER GIVE THESE AMULETS TO ANYONE ELSE, AFTER ME? YOU THINK THEY WON'T THROW THEM INTO THE SUN?
KILL ME. KILL YOUR LAST AVATAR. SEE WHAT HAPPENS.
YOU'RE PATHETIC.
YOU TALK ABOUT DAYS OF CAVES, AND FIRES, AND HOW ALL HUMANITY FEARED YOU--WHAT ABOUT NOW, TIGER GOD?
WHEN HUMANITY KEEPS YOU IN ZOOS AND PARKS? WHEN WE HUNT YOU, OR CAGE YOU, OR RAISE MONEY TO HELP YOU?
WHEN WE PITY YOU?
YOU... YOU LIE...
NO. I FELT YOU IN ATTILAN-- FELT YOU TREMBLE.
YOU'RE SCARED OF HUMANITY. WHAT WE'VE BECOME. WHAT WE CAN BECOME.
AND YOU WANT US TO FEAR YOU?
STOP THIS-- STOP, STOP TALKING--
I'M MORE FEARED NOW THAN YOU CAN EVER BE, OLD TIGER. I DON'T NEED YOU.

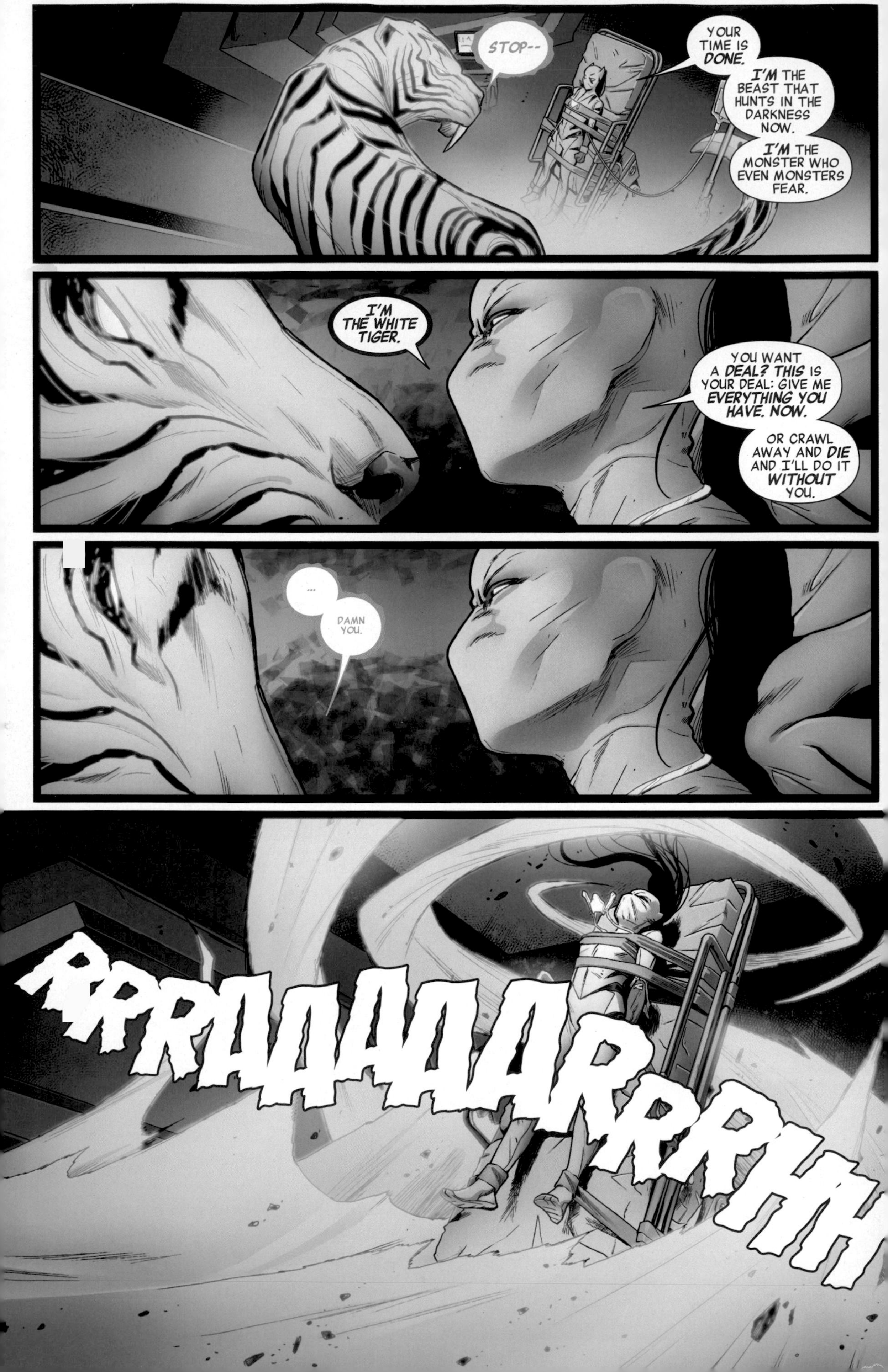
STOP--
YOUR TIME IS DONE.
I'M THE BEAST THAT HUNTS IN THE DARKNESS NOW.
I'M THE MONSTER WHO EVEN MONSTERS FEAR.
I'M THE WHITE TIGER.
YOU WANT A DEAL? THIS IS YOUR DEAL: GIVE ME EVERYTHING YOU HAVE. NOW.
OR CRAWL AWAY AND DIE AND I'LL DO IT WITHOUT YOU.
...
DAMN YOU.
RRRAAAAARRRHH

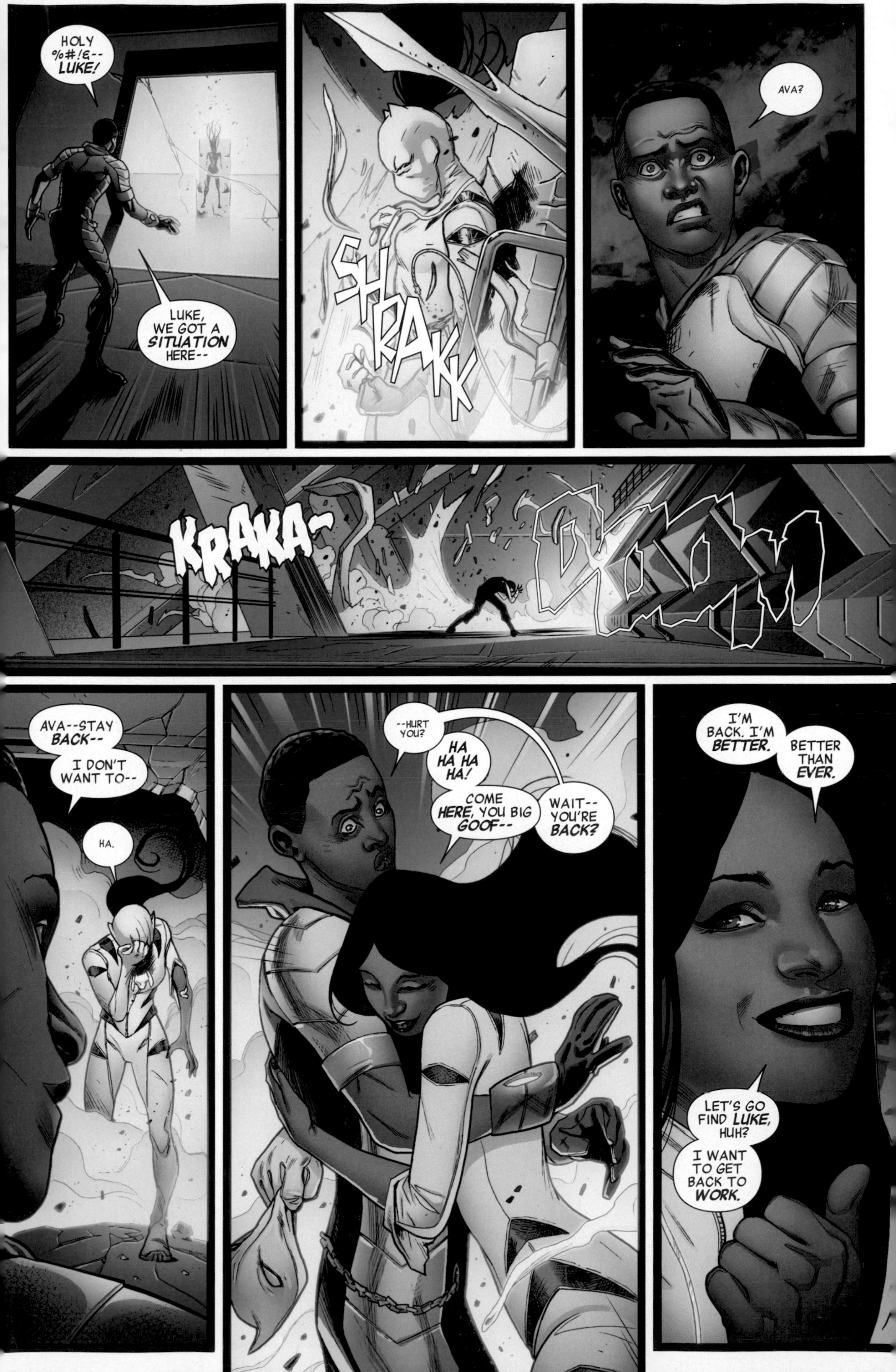
HOLY %#!&-- LUKE!
LUKE, WE GOT A SITUATION HERE--
SHRAKK
AVA?
KRAKA-
DOOOM
AVA--STAY BACK--
I DON'T WANT TO--
HA.
--HURT YOU?
HA HA HA HA!
COME HERE, YOU BIG GOOF--
WAIT-- YOU'RE BACK?
I'M BACK. I'M BETTER.
BETTER THAN EVER.
LET'S GO FIND LUKE, HUH?
I WANT TO GET BACK TO WORK.

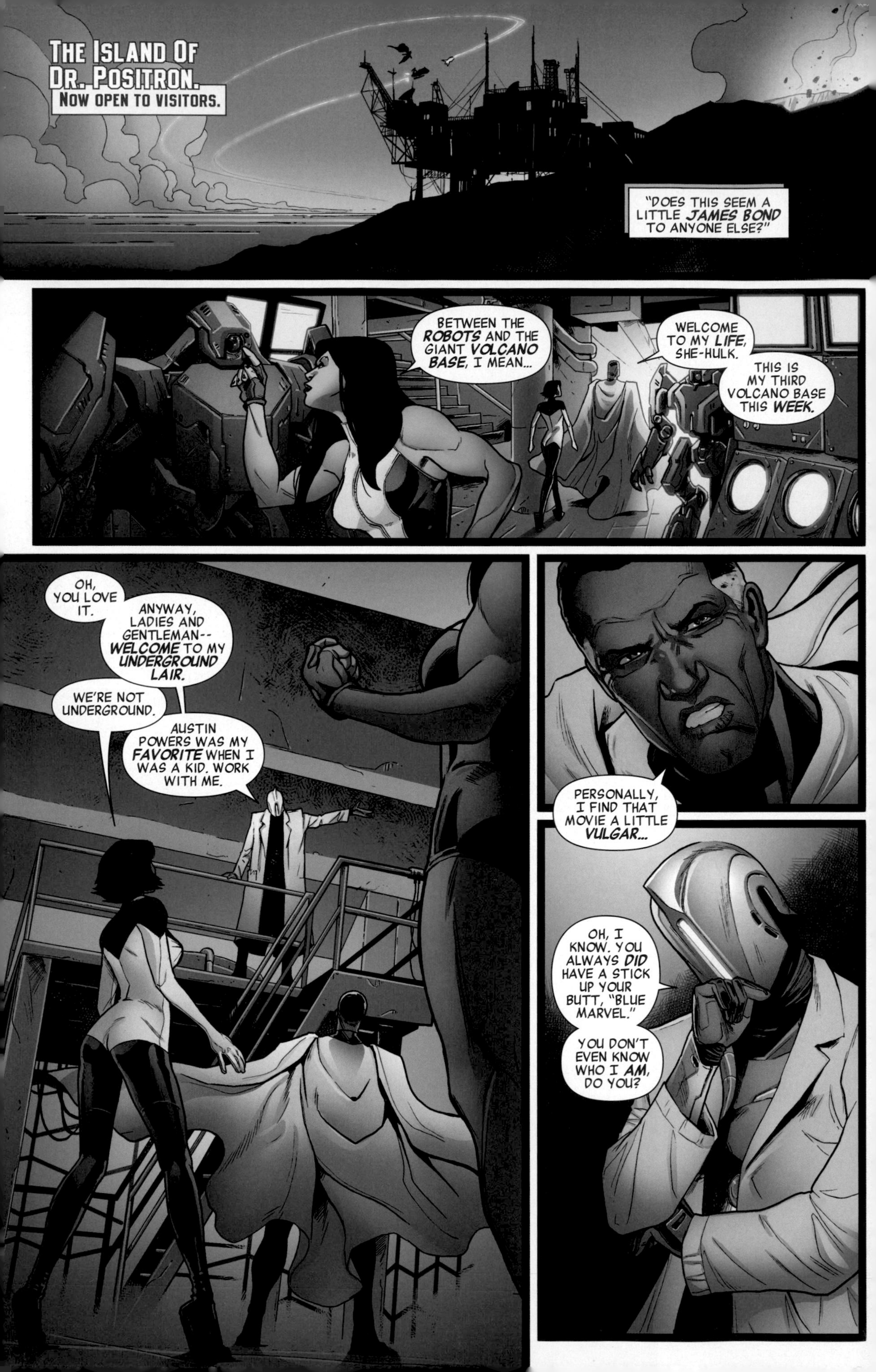
THE ISLAND OF DR. POSITRON.
NOW OPEN TO VISITORS.
"DOES THIS SEEM A LITTLE JAMES BOND TO ANYONE ELSE?"
BETWEEN THE ROBOTS AND THE GIANT VOLCANO BASE, I MEAN...
WELCOME TO MY LIFE, SHE-HULK.
THIS IS MY THIRD VOLCANO BASE THIS WEEK.
OH, YOU LOVE IT.
ANYWAY, LADIES AND GENTLEMAN-- WELCOME TO MY UNDERGROUND LAIR.
WE'RE NOT UNDERGROUND.
AUSTIN POWERS WAS MY FAVORITE WHEN I WAS A KID. WORK WITH ME.
PERSONALLY, I FIND THAT MOVIE A LITTLE VULGAR...
OH, I KNOW. YOU ALWAYS DID HAVE A STICK UP YOUR BUTT, "BLUE MARVEL."
YOU DON'T EVEN KNOW WHO I AM, DO YOU?

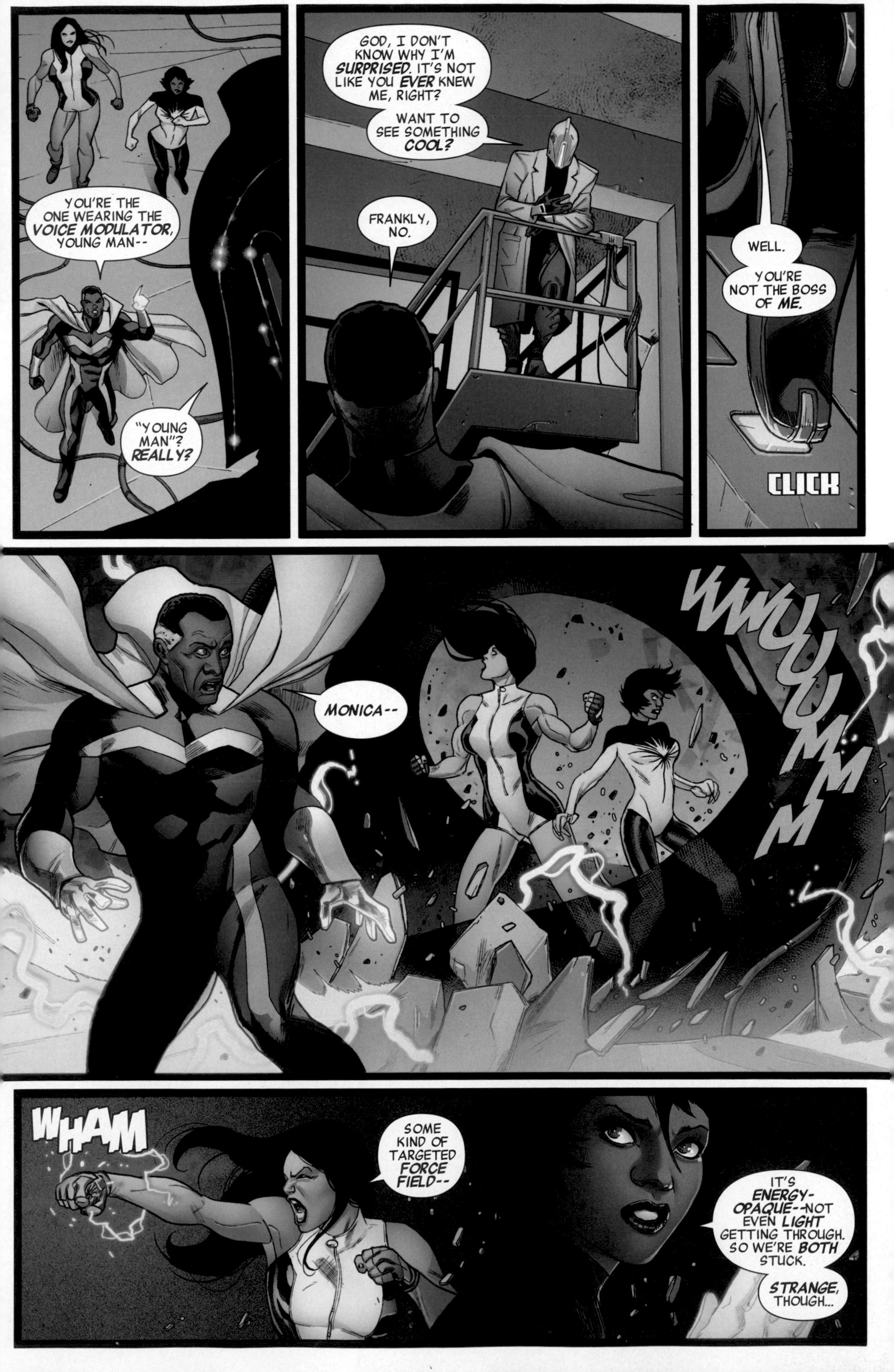
YOU'RE THE ONE WEARING THE VOICE MODULATOR, YOUNG MAN--
"YOUNG MAN"? REALLY?
GOD, I DON'T KNOW WHY I'M SURPRISED. IT'S NOT LIKE YOU EVER KNEW ME, RIGHT?
WANT TO SEE SOMETHING COOL?
FRANKLY, NO.
WELL.
YOU'RE NOT THE BOSS OF ME.
CLICK
VWUUUMMM
MONICA--
WHAM
SOME KIND OF TARGETED FORCE FIELD--
IT'S ENERGY-OPAQUE--NOT EVEN LIGHT GETTING THROUGH. SO WE'RE BOTH STUCK.
STRANGE, THOUGH...

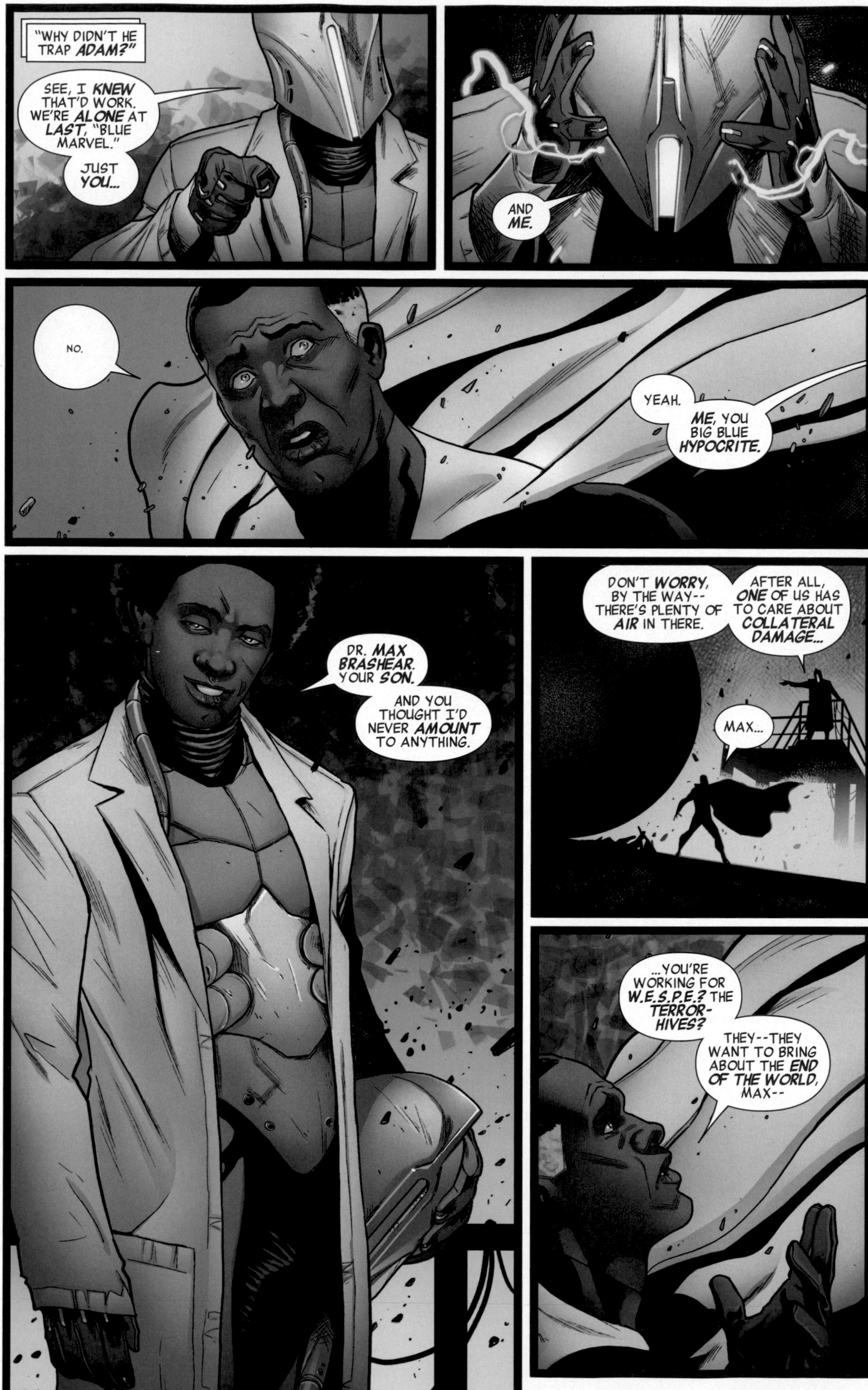
"WHY DIDN'T HE TRAP ADAM?"
SEE, I KNEW THAT'D WORK. WE'RE ALONE AT LAST, "BLUE MARVEL."
JUST YOU...
AND ME.
NO.
YEAH.
ME, YOU BIG BLUE HYPOCRITE.
DR. MAX BRASHEAR. YOUR SON.
AND YOU THOUGHT I'D NEVER AMOUNT TO ANYTHING.
DON'T WORRY, BY THE WAY-- THERE'S PLENTY OF AIR IN THERE.
AFTER ALL, ONE OF US HAS TO CARE ABOUT COLLATERAL DAMAGE...
MAX...
...YOU'RE WORKING FOR W.E.S.P.E.? THE TERROR-HIVES?
THEY--THEY WANT TO BRING ABOUT THE END OF THE WORLD, MAX--

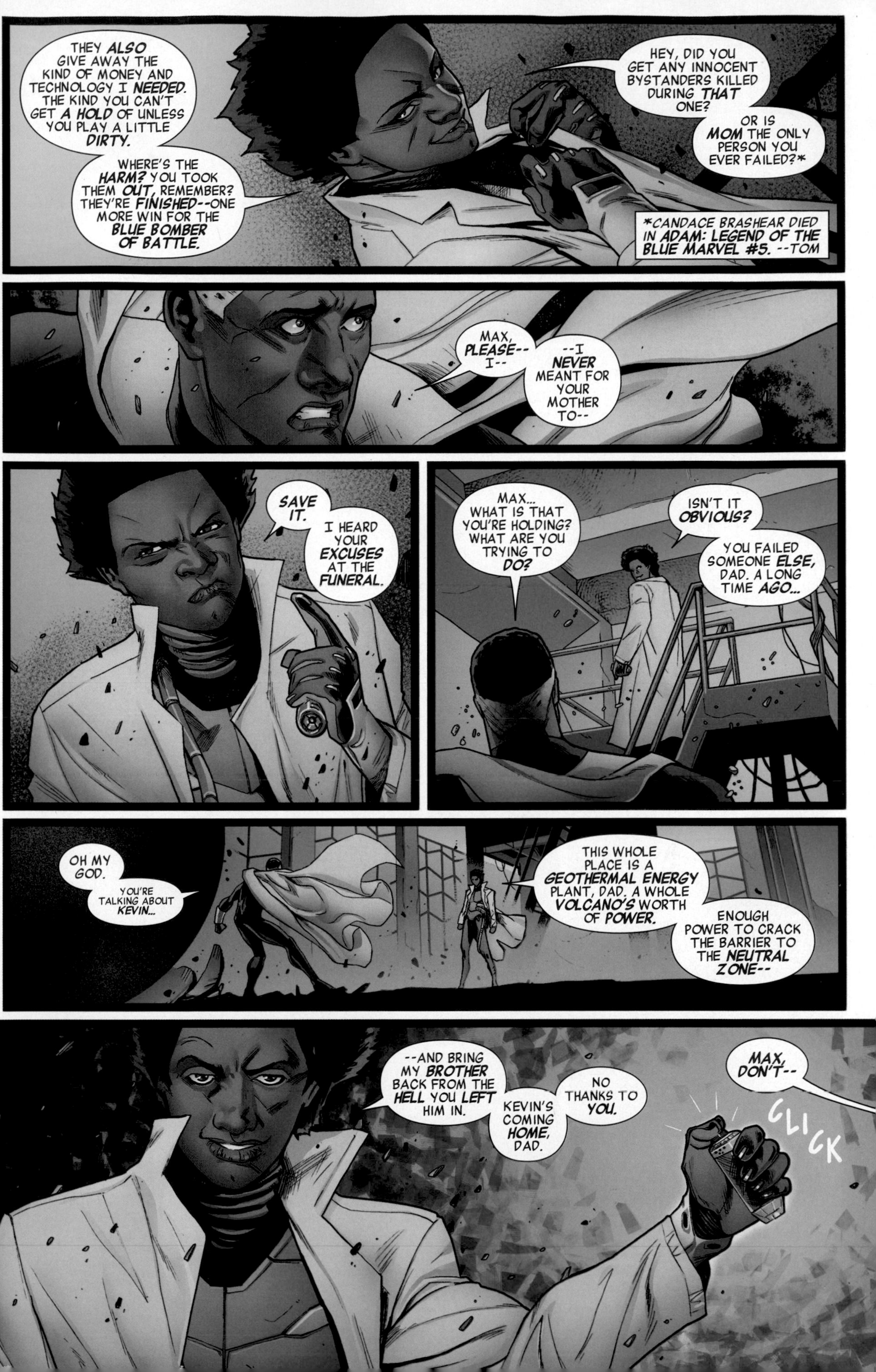

THEY ALSO GIVE AWAY THE KIND OF MONEY AND TECHNOLOGY I NEEDED. THE KIND YOU CAN'T GET A HOLD OF UNLESS YOU PLAY A LITTLE DIRTY.
WHERE'S THE HARM? YOU TOOK THEM OUT, REMEMBER? THEY'RE FINISHED--ONE MORE WIN FOR THE BLUE BOMBER OF BATTLE.
HEY, DID YOU GET ANY INNOCENT BYSTANDERS KILLED DURING THAT ONE?
OR IS MOM THE ONLY PERSON YOU EVER FAILED?*
*CANDACE BRASHEAR DIED IN ADAM: LEGEND OF THE BLUE MARVEL #5. --TOM
MAX, PLEASE-- I--
--I NEVER MEANT FOR YOUR MOTHER TO--
SAVE IT.
I HEARD YOUR EXCUSES AT THE FUNERAL.
MAX... WHAT IS THAT YOU'RE HOLDING? WHAT ARE YOU TRYING TO DO?
ISN'T IT OBVIOUS?
YOU FAILED SOMEONE ELSE, DAD. A LONG TIME AGO...
OH MY GOD.
YOU'RE TALKING ABOUT KEVIN...
THIS WHOLE PLACE IS A GEOTHERMAL ENERGY PLANT, DAD. A WHOLE VOLCANO'S WORTH OF POWER.
ENOUGH POWER TO CRACK THE BARRIER TO THE NEUTRAL ZONE--
--AND BRING MY BROTHER BACK FROM THE HELL YOU LEFT HIM IN.
KEVIN'S COMING HOME, DAD.
NO THANKS TO YOU.
MAX, DON'T--
CLICK

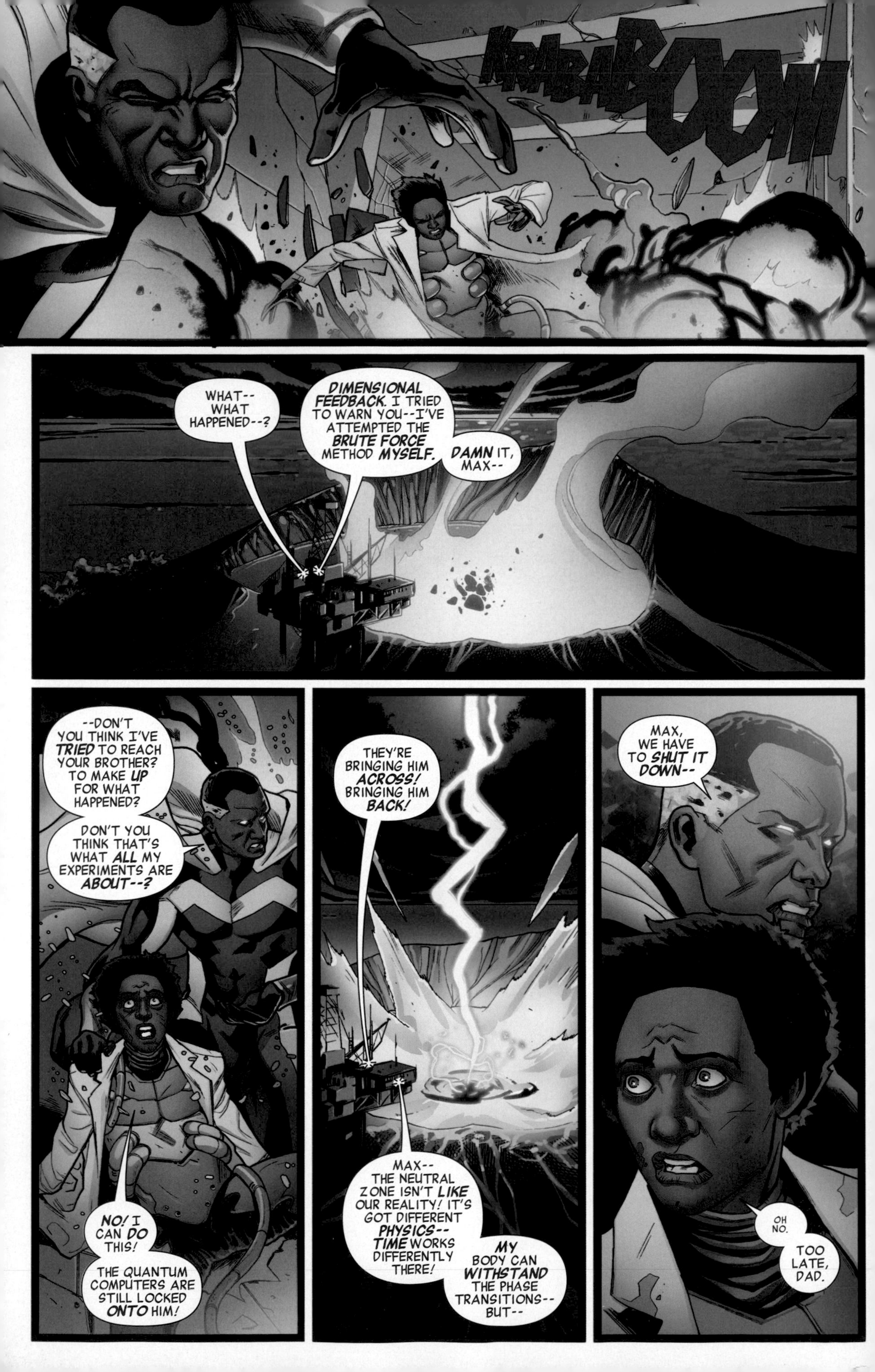
KRABABOOM
WHAT-- WHAT HAPPENED--?
DIMENSIONAL FEEDBACK. I TRIED TO WARN YOU--I'VE ATTEMPTED THE BRUTE FORCE METHOD MYSELF.
DAMN IT, MAX--
--DON'T YOU THINK I'VE TRIED TO REACH YOUR BROTHER? TO MAKE UP FOR WHAT HAPPENED?
DON'T YOU THINK THAT'S WHAT ALL MY EXPERIMENTS ARE ABOUT--?
NO! I CAN DO THIS!
THE QUANTUM COMPUTERS ARE STILL LOCKED ONTO HIM!
THEY'RE BRINGING HIM ACROSS! BRINGING HIM BACK!
MAX-- THE NEUTRAL ZONE ISN'T LIKE OUR REALITY! IT'S GOT DIFFERENT PHYSICS-- TIME WORKS DIFFERENTLY THERE!
MY BODY CAN WITHSTAND THE PHASE TRANSITIONS-- BUT--
MAX, WE HAVE TO SHUT IT DOWN--
OH NO.
TOO LATE, DAD.

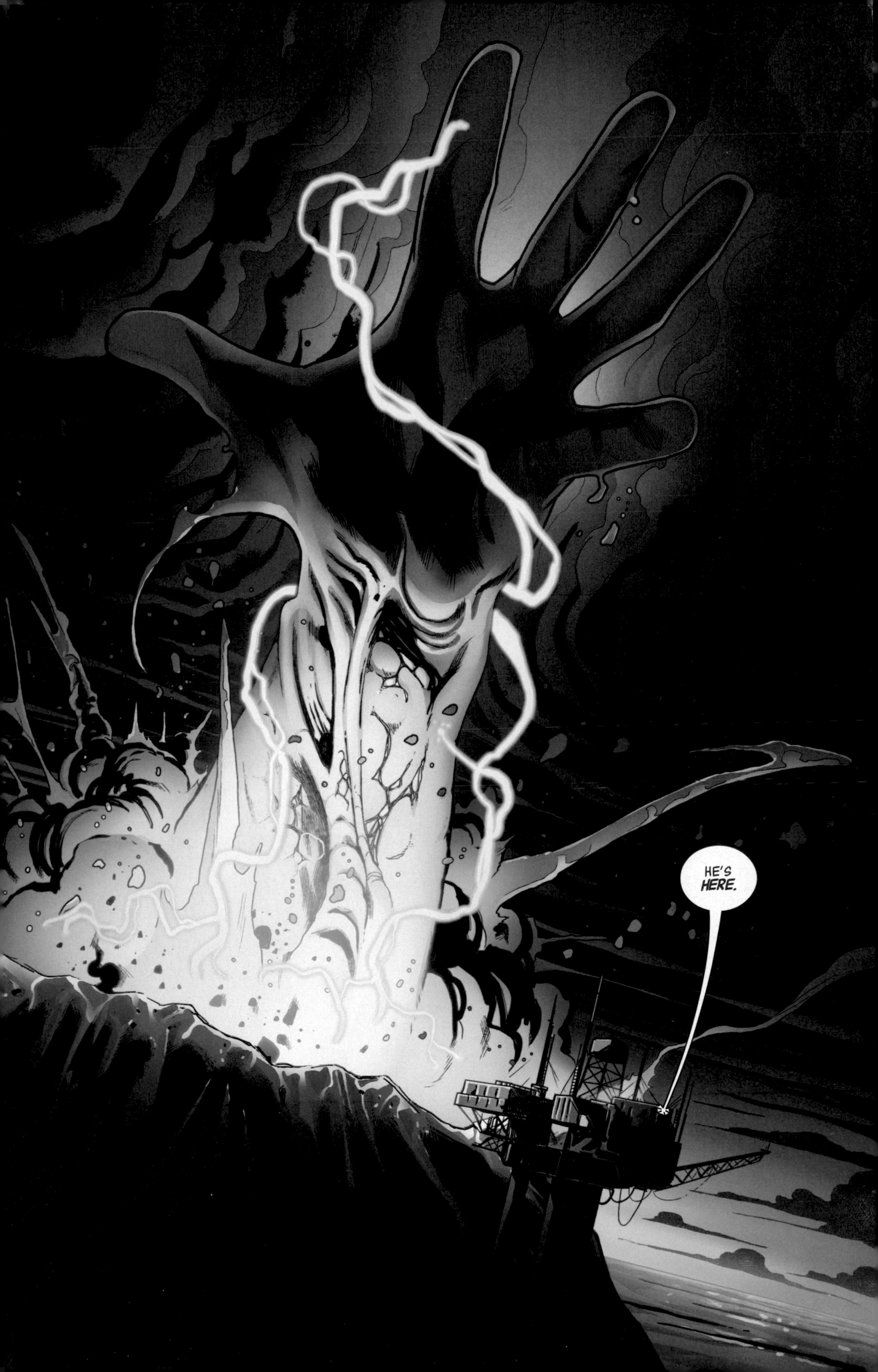
HE'S HERE.

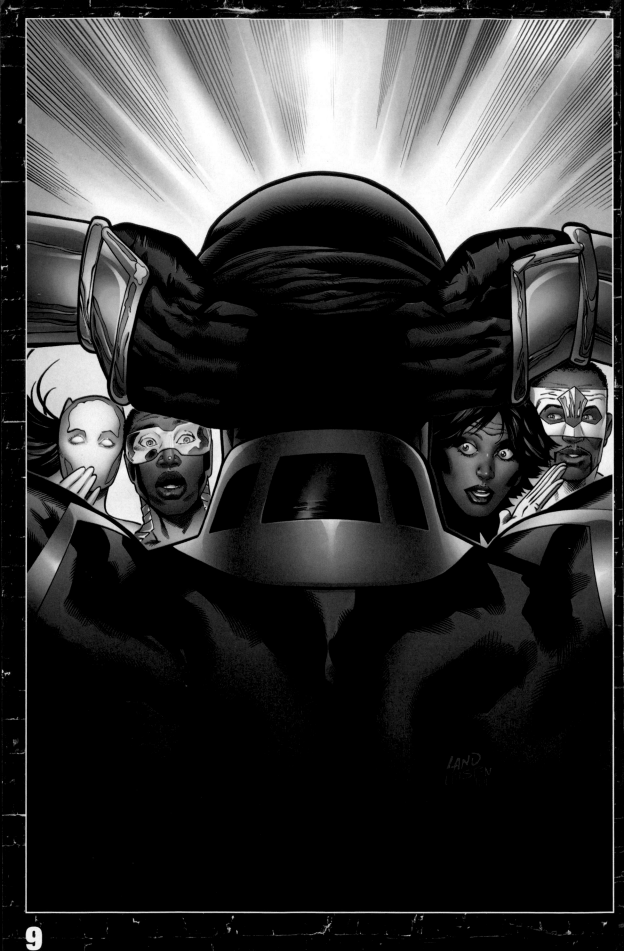

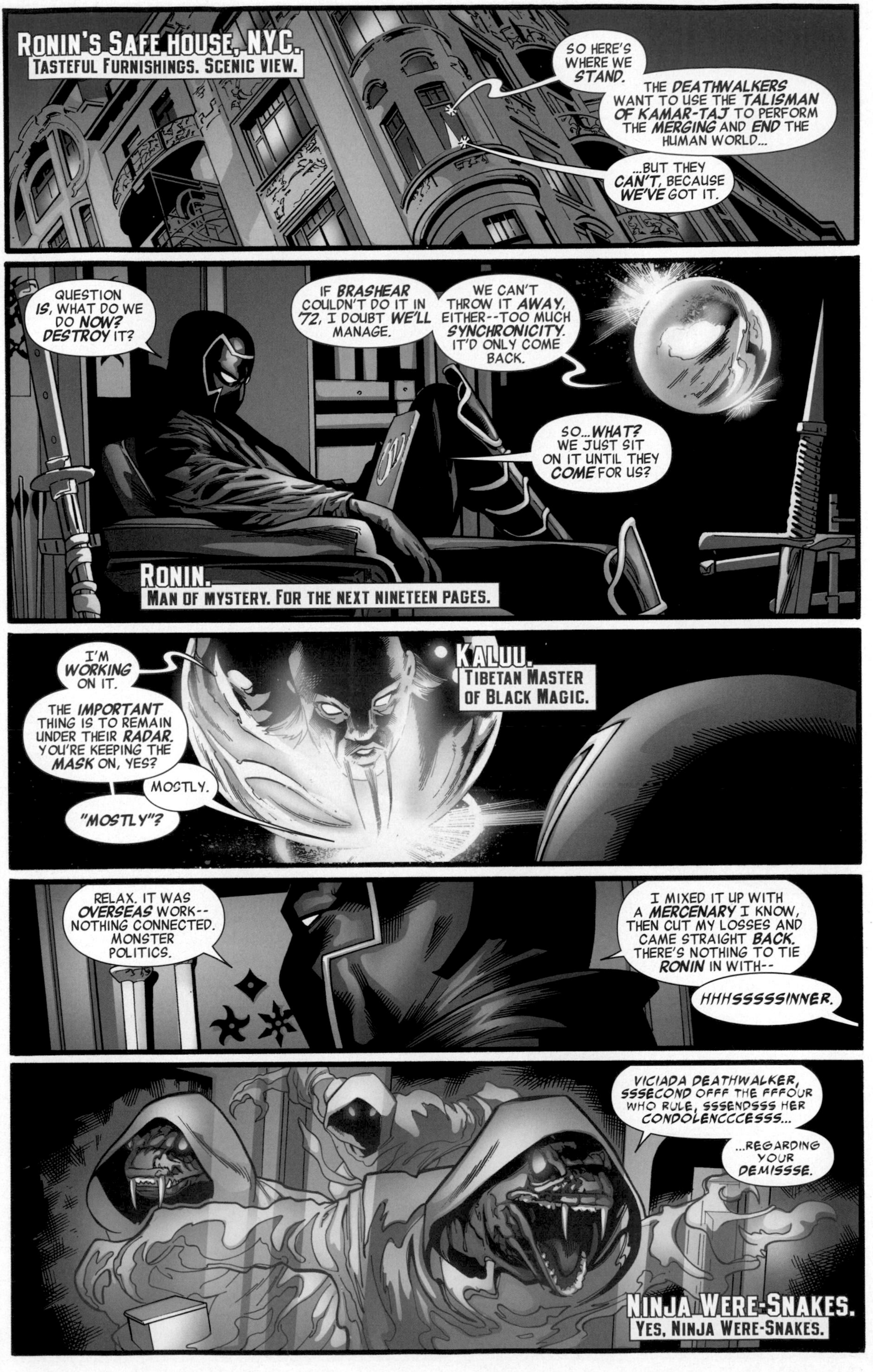
RONIN'S SAFE HOUSE, NYC.
TASTEFUL FURNISHINGS. SCENIC VIEW.
SO HERE'S WHERE WE STAND.
THE DEATHWALKERS WANT TO USE THE TALISMAN OF KAMAR-TAJ TO PERFORM THE MERGING AND END THE HUMAN WORLD...
...BUT THEY CAN'T, BECAUSE WE'VE GOT IT.
QUESTION IS, WHAT DO WE DO NOW? DESTROY IT?
IF BRASHEAR COULDN'T DO IT IN '72, I DOUBT WE'LL MANAGE.
WE CAN'T THROW IT AWAY, EITHER--TOO MUCH SYNCHRONICITY. IT'D ONLY COME BACK.
SO...WHAT? WE JUST SIT ON IT UNTIL THEY COME FOR US?
RONIN.
MAN OF MYSTERY. FOR THE NEXT NINETEEN PAGES.
I'M WORKING ON IT.
KALUU.
TIBETAN MASTER OF BLACK MAGIC.
THE IMPORTANT THING IS TO REMAIN UNDER THEIR RADAR. YOU'RE KEEPING THE MASK ON, YES?
MOSTLY.
"MOSTLY"?
RELAX. IT WAS OVERSEAS WORK--NOTHING CONNECTED. MONSTER POLITICS.
I MIXED IT UP WITH A MERCENARY I KNOW, THEN CUT MY LOSSES AND CAME STRAIGHT BACK. THERE'S NOTHING TO TIE RONIN IN WITH--
HHHSSSSSINNER.
VICIADA DEATHWALKER, SSSECOND OFFF THE FFFOUR WHO RULE, SSSENDSSS HER CONDOLENCCCESSS...
...REGARDING YOUR DEMISSSE.
NINJA WERE-SNAKES.
YES, NINJA WERE-SNAKES.

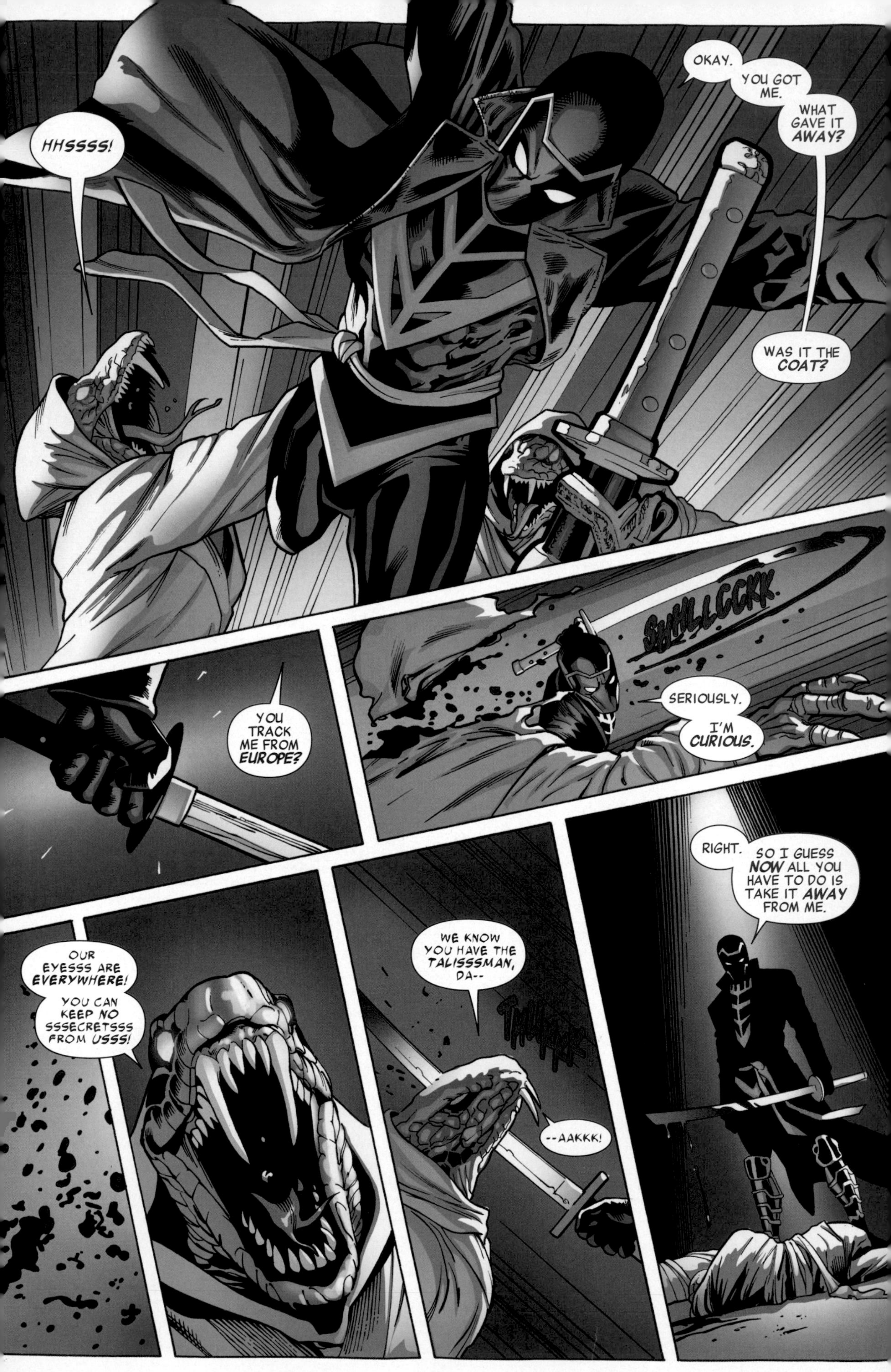
HHSSSS!
OKAY.
YOU GOT ME.
WHAT GAVE IT AWAY?
WAS IT THE COAT?
SHHLLCCKK
SERIOUSLY.
I'M CURIOUS.
YOU TRACK ME FROM EUROPE?
OUR EYESSS ARE EVERYWHERE!
YOU CAN KEEP NO SSSECRETSSS FROM USSS!
WE KNOW YOU HAVE THE TALISSSMAN, DA--
--AAKKK!
RIGHT.
SO I GUESS NOW ALL YOU HAVE TO DO IS TAKE IT AWAY FROM ME.

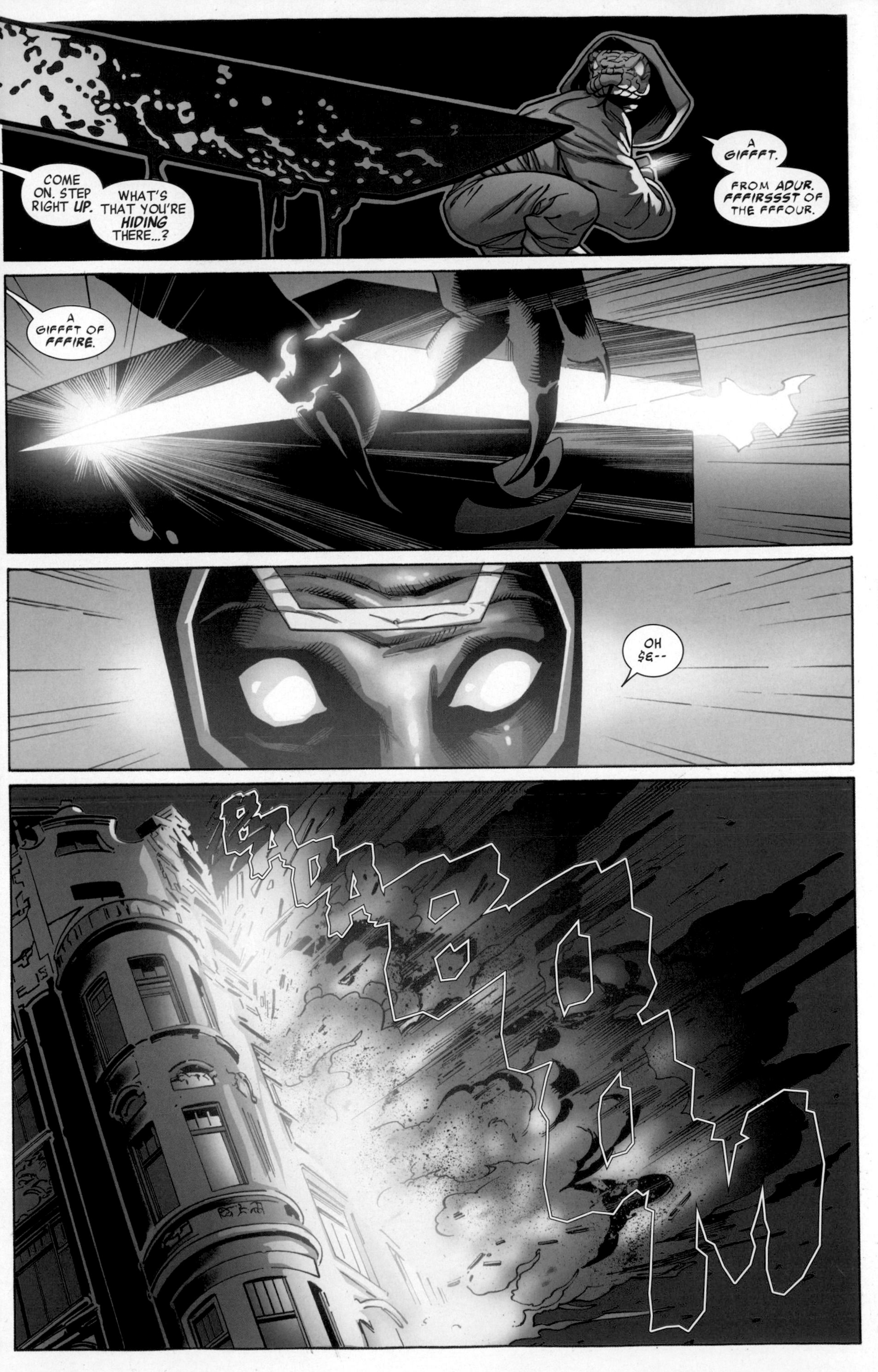
COME ON. STEP RIGHT UP.
WHAT'S THAT YOU'RE HIDING THERE...?
A GIFFFT.
FROM ADUR. FFFIRSSST OF THE FFFOUR.
A GIFFFT OF FFFIRE.
OH $&--
BADABOOOM

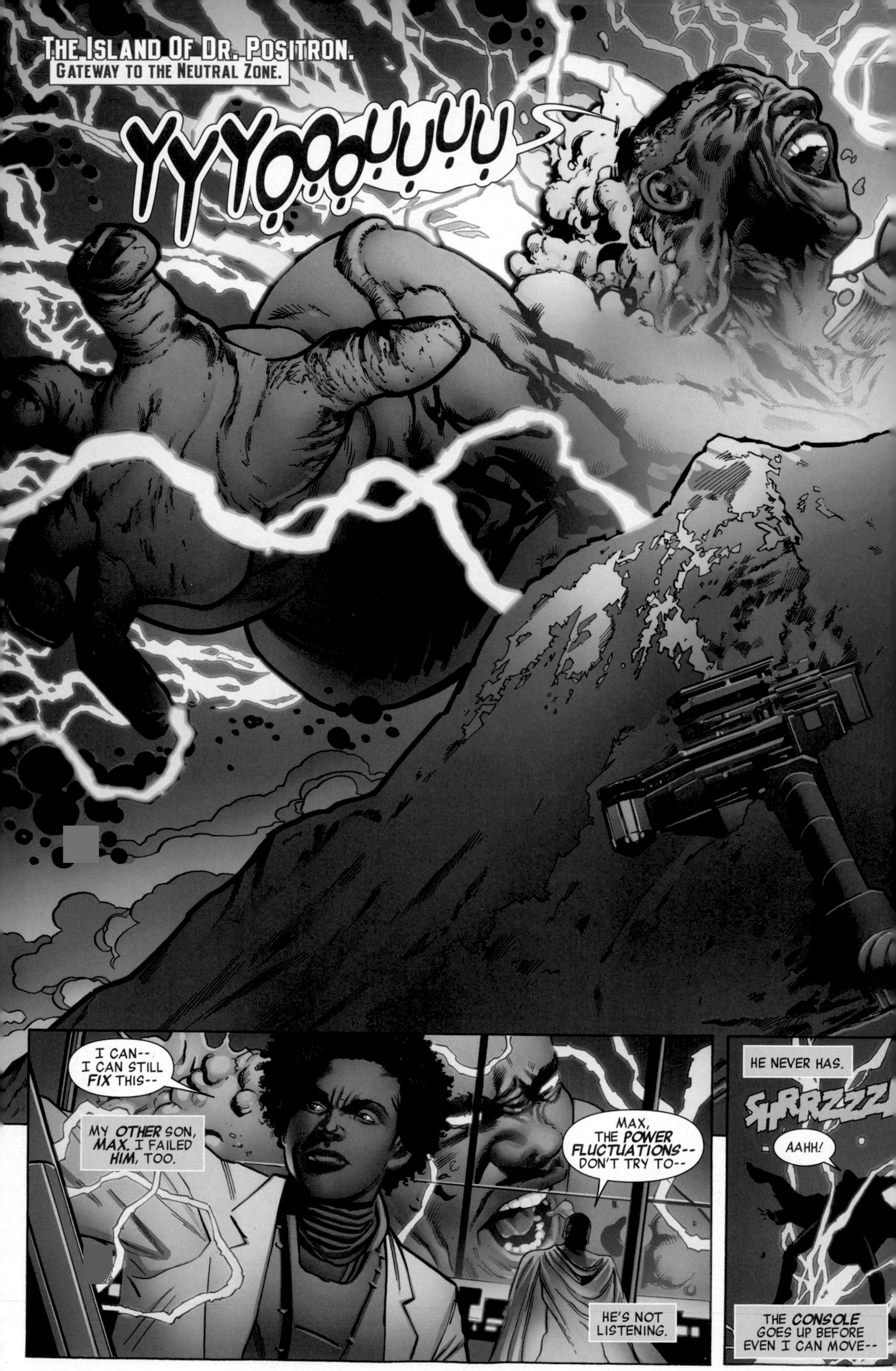
THE ISLAND OF DR. POSITRON.
GATEWAY TO THE NEUTRAL ZONE.
YYYOOOUUUU
I CAN-- I CAN STILL FIX THIS--
MY OTHER SON, MAX. I FAILED HIM, TOO.
MAX, THE POWER FLUCTUATIONS-- DON'T TRY TO--
HE'S NOT LISTENING.
HE NEVER HAS.
SHRRZZZ
AAHH!
THE CONSOLE GOES UP BEFORE EVEN I CAN MOVE--

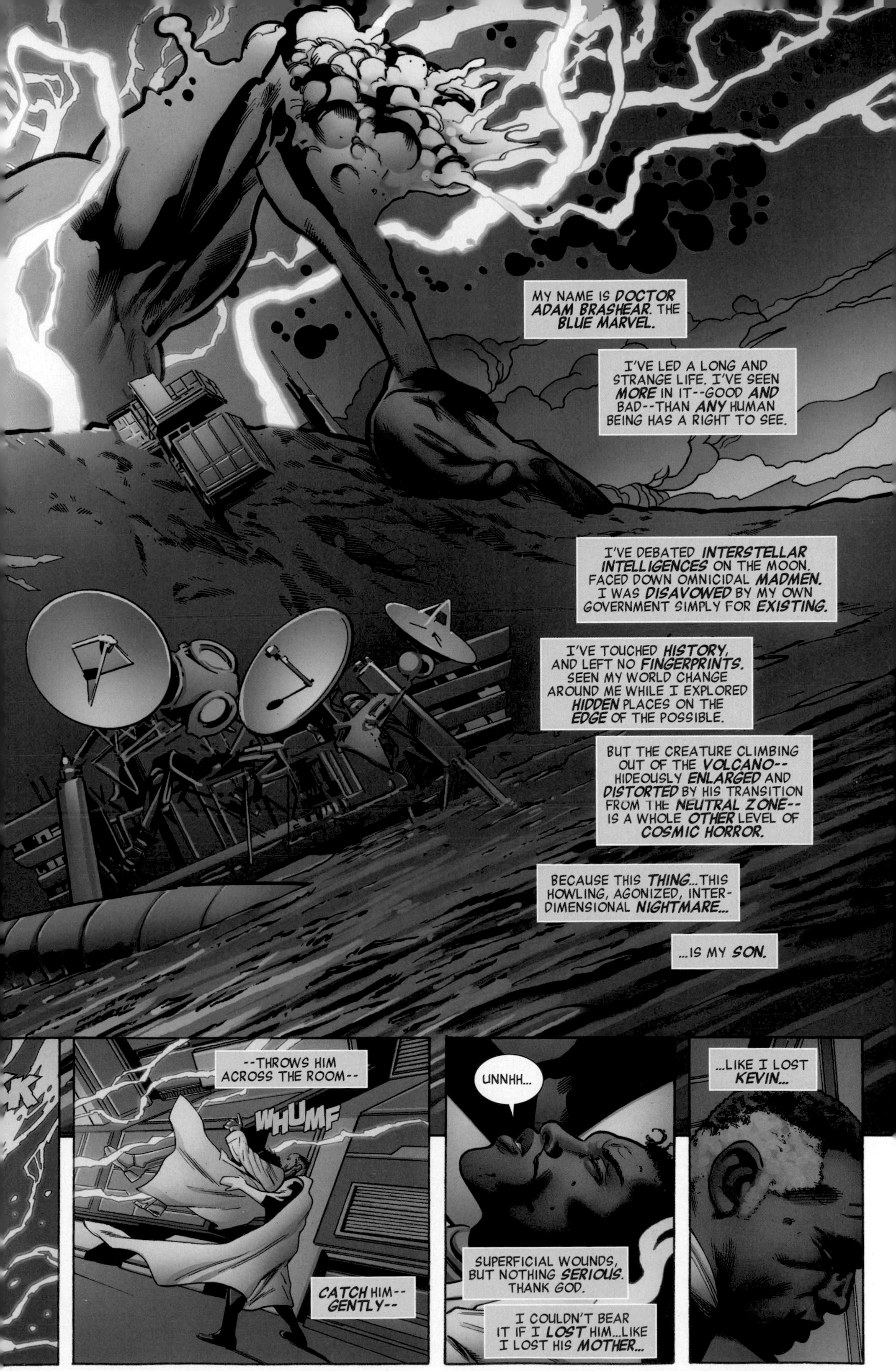

MY NAME IS DOCTOR ADAM BRASHEAR. THE BLUE MARVEL.
I'VE LED A LONG AND STRANGE LIFE. I'VE SEEN MORE IN IT--GOOD AND BAD--THAN ANY HUMAN BEING HAS A RIGHT TO SEE.
I'VE DEBATED INTERSTELLAR INTELLIGENCES ON THE MOON. FACED DOWN OMNICIDAL MADMEN. I WAS DISAVOWED BY MY OWN GOVERNMENT SIMPLY FOR EXISTING.
I'VE TOUCHED HISTORY, AND LEFT NO FINGERPRINTS. SEEN MY WORLD CHANGE AROUND ME WHILE I EXPLORED HIDDEN PLACES ON THE EDGE OF THE POSSIBLE.
BUT THE CREATURE CLIMBING OUT OF THE VOLCANO-- HIDEOUSLY ENLARGED AND DISTORTED BY HIS TRANSITION FROM THE NEUTRAL ZONE-- IS A WHOLE OTHER LEVEL OF COSMIC HORROR.
BECAUSE THIS THING...THIS HOWLING, AGONIZED, INTER-DIMENSIONAL NIGHTMARE...
...IS MY SON.
--THROWS HIM ACROSS THE ROOM--
WHUMF
CATCH HIM-- GENTLY--
UNNHH...
SUPERFICIAL WOUNDS, BUT NOTHING SERIOUS. THANK GOD.
I COULDN'T BEAR IT IF I LOST HIM...LIKE I LOST HIS MOTHER...
...LIKE I LOST KEVIN...

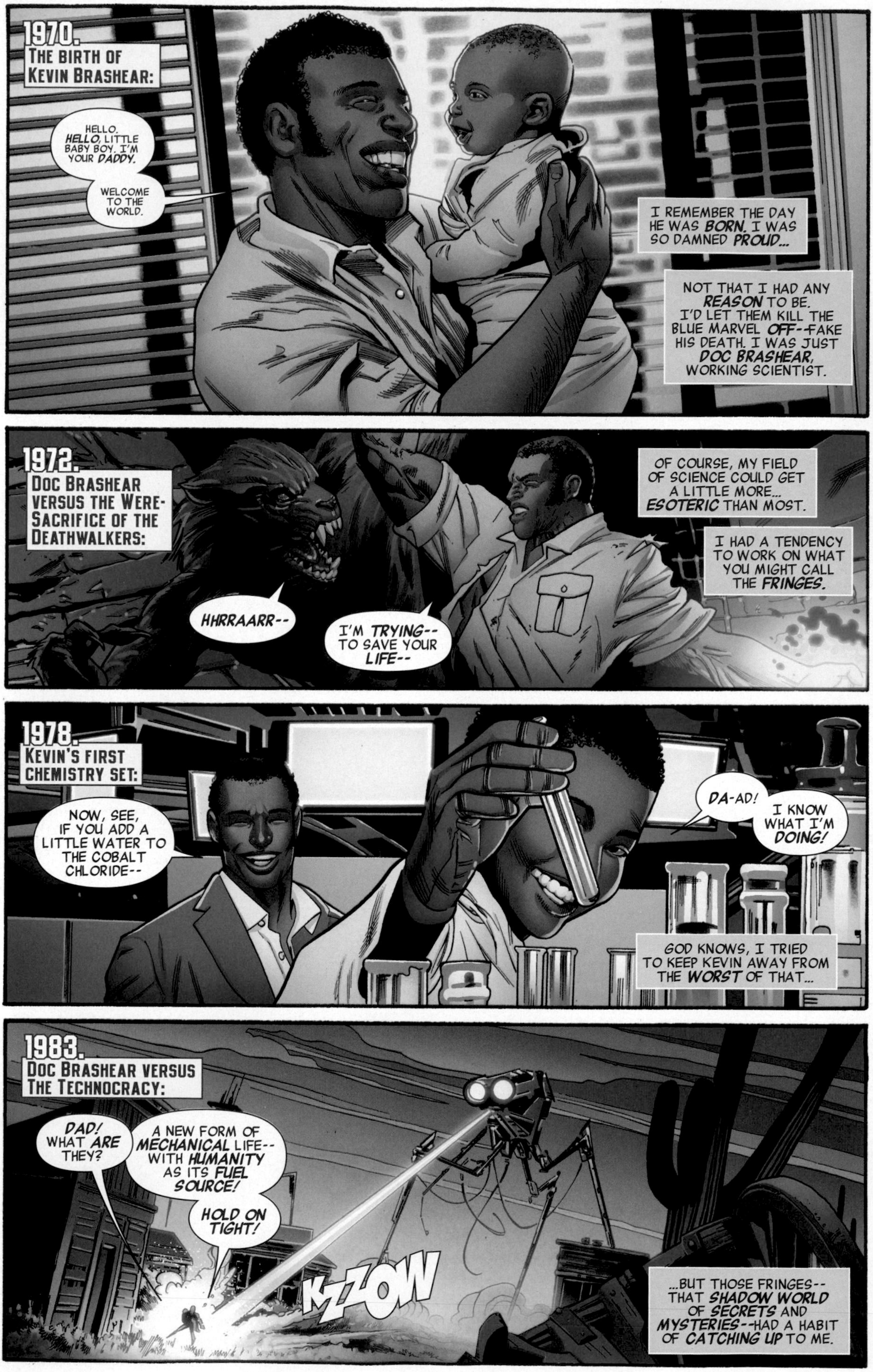
1970.
THE BIRTH OF KEVIN BRASHEAR:
HELLO. HELLO, LITTLE BABY BOY. I'M YOUR DADDY.
WELCOME TO THE WORLD.
I REMEMBER THE DAY HE WAS BORN. I WAS SO DAMNED PROUD...
NOT THAT I HAD ANY REASON TO BE. I'D LET THEM KILL THE BLUE MARVEL OFF--FAKE HIS DEATH. I WAS JUST DOC BRASHEAR, WORKING SCIENTIST.
1972.
DOC BRASHEAR VERSUS THE WERE-SACRIFICE OF THE DEATHWALKERS:
OF COURSE, MY FIELD OF SCIENCE COULD GET A LITTLE MORE... ESOTERIC THAN MOST.
I HAD A TENDENCY TO WORK ON WHAT YOU MIGHT CALL THE FRINGES.
HHRRAARR--
I'M TRYING--TO SAVE YOUR LIFE--
1978.
KEVIN'S FIRST CHEMISTRY SET:
NOW, SEE, IF YOU ADD A LITTLE WATER TO THE COBALT CHLORIDE--
DA-AD!
I KNOW WHAT I'M DOING!
GOD KNOWS, I TRIED TO KEEP KEVIN AWAY FROM THE WORST OF THAT...
1983.
DOC BRASHEAR VERSUS THE TECHNOCRACY:
DAD! WHAT ARE THEY?
A NEW FORM OF MECHANICAL LIFE--WITH HUMANITY AS ITS FUEL SOURCE!
HOLD ON TIGHT!
KZZOW
...BUT THOSE FRINGES--THAT SHADOW WORLD OF SECRETS AND MYSTERIES--HAD A HABIT OF CATCHING UP TO ME.

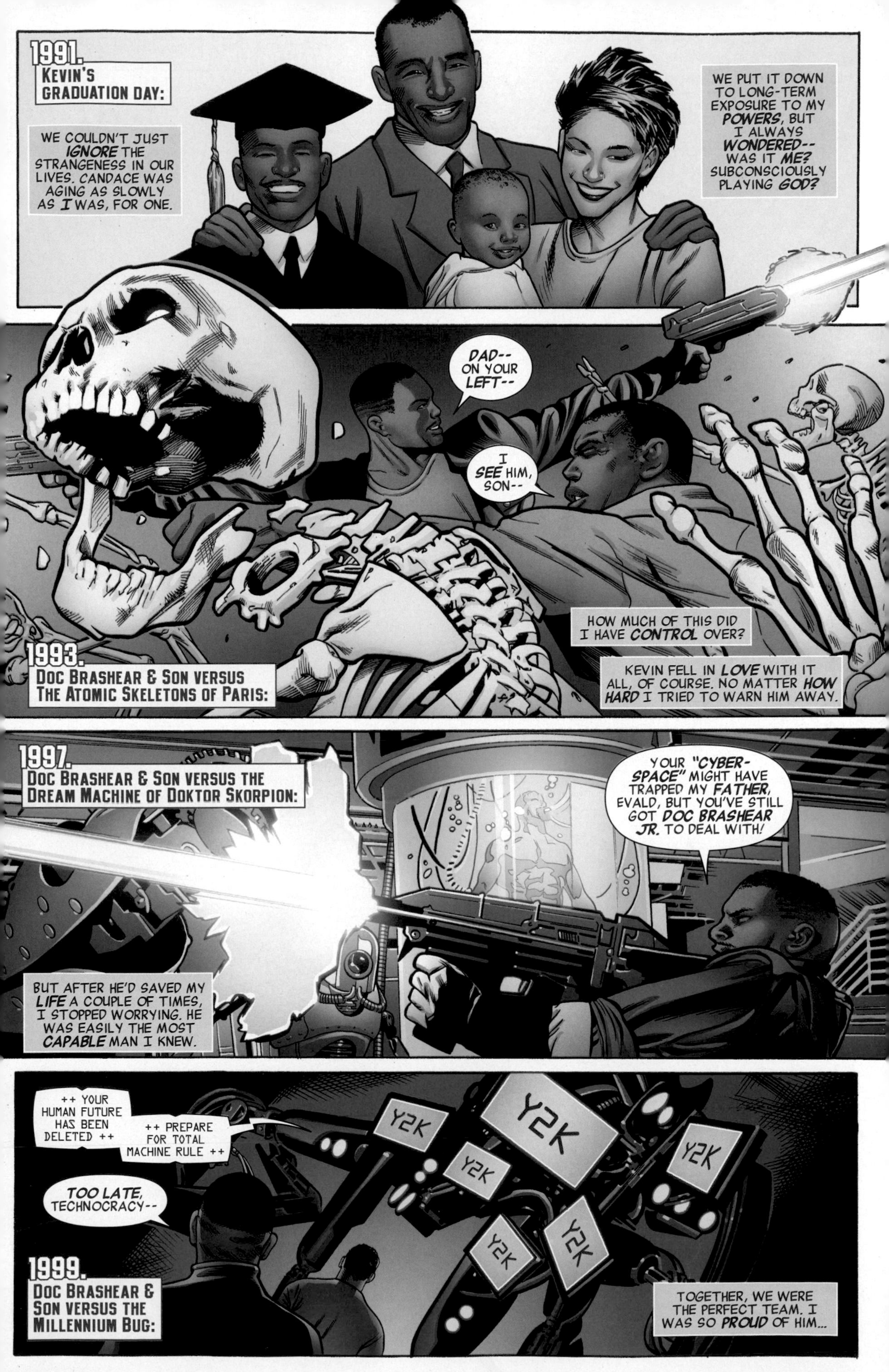
1991.
KEVIN'S GRADUATION DAY:
WE COULDN'T JUST IGNORE THE STRANGENESS IN OUR LIVES. CANDACE WAS AGING AS SLOWLY AS I WAS, FOR ONE.
WE PUT IT DOWN TO LONG-TERM EXPOSURE TO MY POWERS, BUT I ALWAYS WONDERED-- WAS IT ME? SUBCONSCIOUSLY PLAYING GOD?
DAD-- ON YOUR LEFT--
I SEE HIM, SON--
1993.
DOC BRASHEAR & SON VERSUS THE ATOMIC SKELETONS OF PARIS:
HOW MUCH OF THIS DID I HAVE CONTROL OVER?
KEVIN FELL IN LOVE WITH IT ALL, OF COURSE. NO MATTER HOW HARD I TRIED TO WARN HIM AWAY.
1997.
DOC BRASHEAR & SON VERSUS THE DREAM MACHINE OF DOKTOR SKORPION:
YOUR "CYBER-SPACE" MIGHT HAVE TRAPPED MY FATHER, EVALD, BUT YOU'VE STILL GOT DOC BRASHEAR JR. TO DEAL WITH!
BUT AFTER HE'D SAVED MY LIFE A COUPLE OF TIMES, I STOPPED WORRYING. HE WAS EASILY THE MOST CAPABLE MAN I KNEW.
++ YOUR HUMAN FUTURE HAS BEEN DELETED ++
++ PREPARE FOR TOTAL MACHINE RULE ++
Y2K
TOO LATE, TECHNOCRACY--
1999.
DOC BRASHEAR & SON VERSUS THE MILLENNIUM BUG:
TOGETHER, WE WERE THE PERFECT TEAM. I WAS SO PROUD OF HIM...

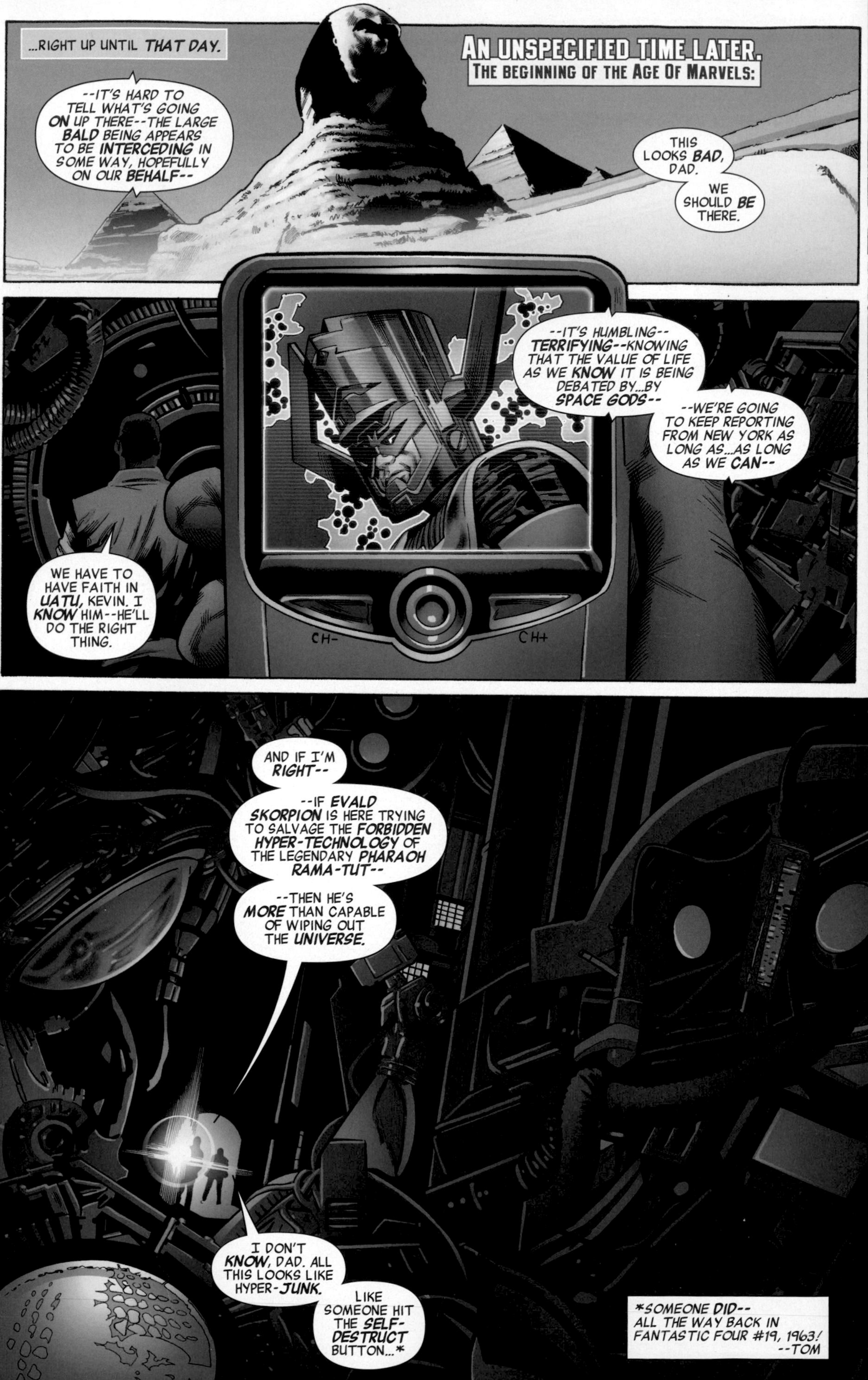

...RIGHT UP UNTIL THAT DAY.
AN UNSPECIFIED TIME LATER.
THE BEGINNING OF THE AGE OF MARVELS:
--IT'S HARD TO TELL WHAT'S GOING ON UP THERE--THE LARGE BALD BEING APPEARS TO BE INTERCEDING IN SOME WAY, HOPEFULLY ON OUR BEHALF--
THIS LOOKS BAD, DAD.
WE SHOULD BE THERE.
--IT'S HUMBLING--TERRIFYING--KNOWING THAT THE VALUE OF LIFE AS WE KNOW IT IS BEING DEBATED BY...BY SPACE GODS--
--WE'RE GOING TO KEEP REPORTING FROM NEW YORK AS LONG AS...AS LONG AS WE CAN--
WE HAVE TO HAVE FAITH IN UATU, KEVIN. I KNOW HIM--HE'LL DO THE RIGHT THING.
CH-
CH+
AND IF I'M RIGHT--
--IF EVALD SKORPION IS HERE TRYING TO SALVAGE THE FORBIDDEN HYPER-TECHNOLOGY OF THE LEGENDARY PHARAOH RAMA-TUT--
--THEN HE'S MORE THAN CAPABLE OF WIPING OUT THE UNIVERSE.
I DON'T KNOW, DAD. ALL THIS LOOKS LIKE HYPER-JUNK.
LIKE SOMEONE HIT THE SELF-DESTRUCT BUTTON...*
*SOMEONE DID--ALL THE WAY BACK IN FANTASTIC FOUR #19, 1963! --TOM

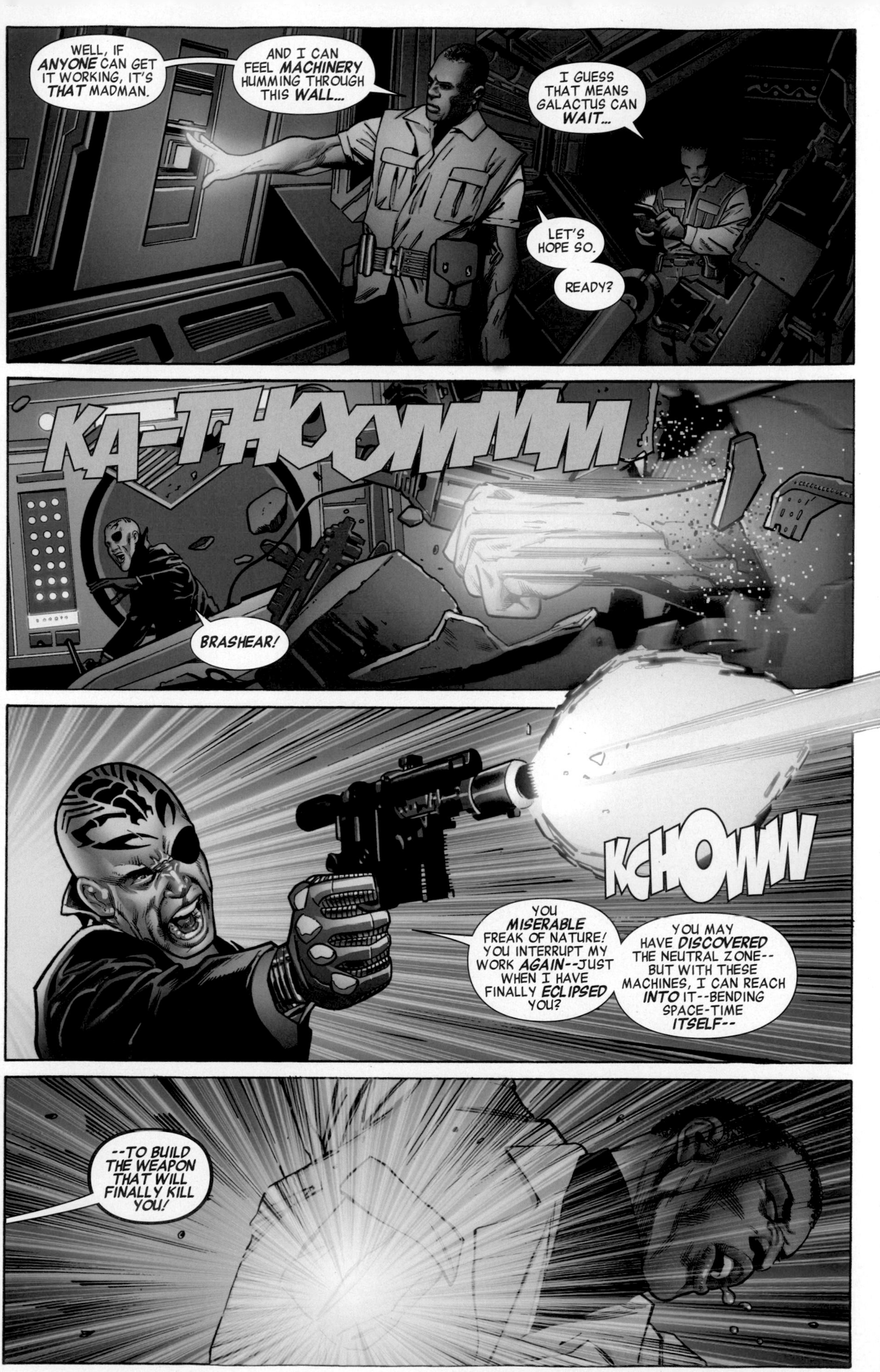
WELL, IF ANYONE CAN GET IT WORKING, IT'S THAT MADMAN.
AND I CAN FEEL MACHINERY HUMMING THROUGH THIS WALL...
I GUESS THAT MEANS GALACTUS CAN WAIT...
LET'S HOPE SO.
READY?
KA-THOOMMM
BRASHEAR!
KCHOWW
YOU MISERABLE FREAK OF NATURE! YOU INTERRUPT MY WORK AGAIN--JUST WHEN I HAVE FINALLY ECLIPSED YOU?
YOU MAY HAVE DISCOVERED THE NEUTRAL ZONE--BUT WITH THESE MACHINES, I CAN REACH INTO IT--BENDING SPACE-TIME ITSELF--
--TO BUILD THE WEAPON THAT WILL FINALLY KILL YOU!

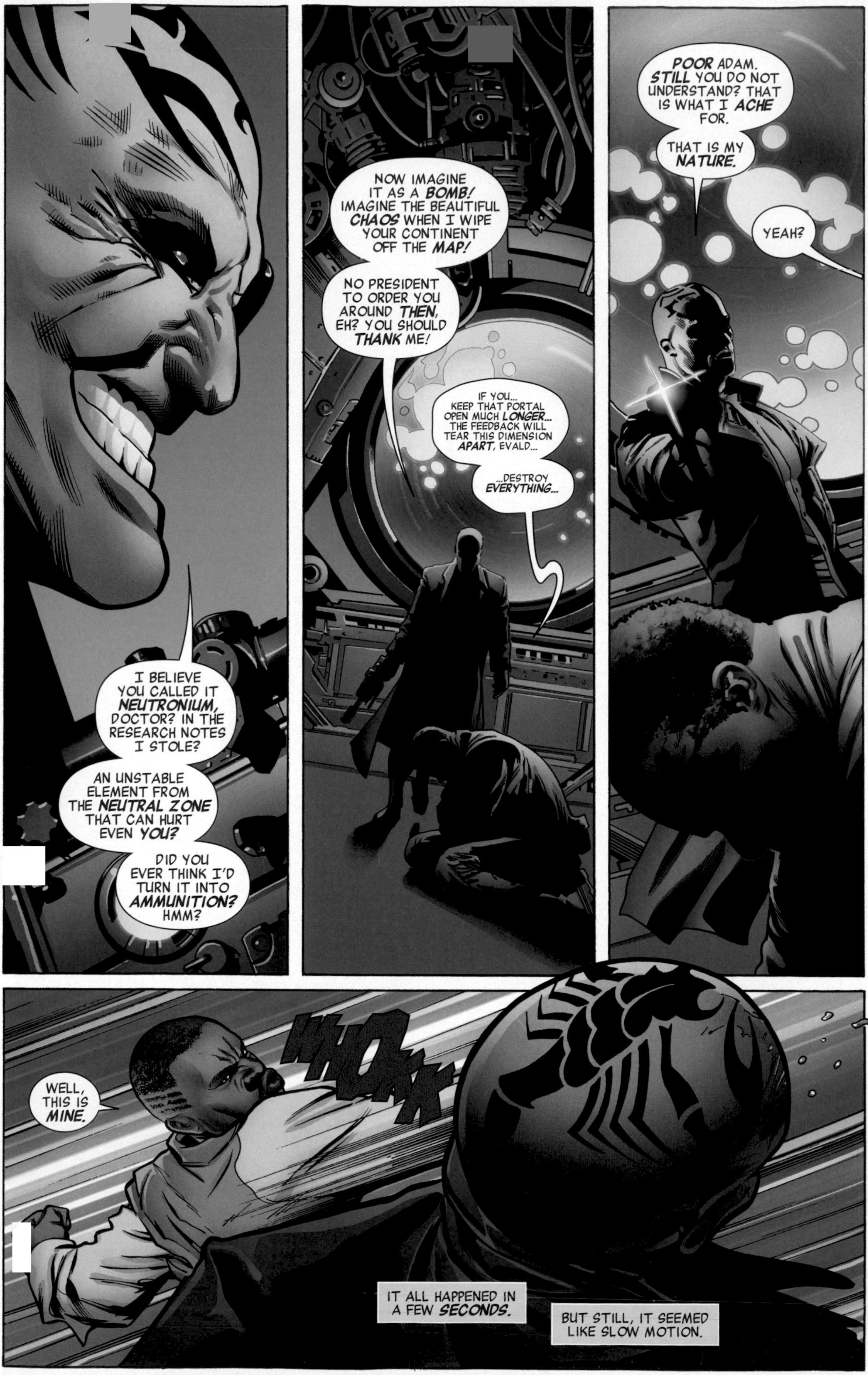
I BELIEVE YOU CALLED IT NEUTRONIUM, DOCTOR? IN THE RESEARCH NOTES I STOLE?
AN UNSTABLE ELEMENT FROM THE NEUTRAL ZONE THAT CAN HURT EVEN YOU?
DID YOU EVER THINK I'D TURN IT INTO AMMUNITION? HMM?
NOW IMAGINE IT AS A BOMB! IMAGINE THE BEAUTIFUL CHAOS WHEN I WIPE YOUR CONTINENT OFF THE MAP!
NO PRESIDENT TO ORDER YOU AROUND THEN, EH? YOU SHOULD THANK ME!
IF YOU... KEEP THAT PORTAL OPEN MUCH LONGER... THE FEEDBACK WILL TEAR THIS DIMENSION APART, EVALD...
...DESTROY EVERYTHING...
POOR ADAM. STILL YOU DO NOT UNDERSTAND? THAT IS WHAT I ACHE FOR.
THAT IS MY NATURE.
YEAH?
WELL, THIS IS MINE.
WHOKK
IT ALL HAPPENED IN A FEW SECONDS.
BUT STILL, IT SEEMED LIKE SLOW MOTION.

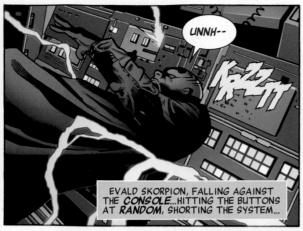

UNNH--

KRZZZTT

EVALD SKORPION, FALLING AGAINST THE **CONSOLE**...HITTING THE BUTTONS AT **RANDOM**, SHORTING THE SYSTEM...

...THE PORTAL **EXPANDING**...THE SHIMMERING SURFACE OF IT **BULGING**, SEEMING ALMOST HUNGRY...

DAD--

...MY **SON** VANISHING INTO ITS MAW.

KEVIN!

NO!

NO!!

INSTINCTIVELY, I LAUNCHED **FORWARD**, INTO THE PORTAL'S MAELSTROM--TRYING TO **GRAB** HIM, TO SNATCH HIM **BACK** SOMEHOW--

KRAAKOOM

BUT I COULDN'T GET WITHIN SIX FEET OF IT.

OUT OF THE CORNER OF MY EYE, I SAW POOR, MAD EVALD BEING **PULLED APART**, MOLECULE BY MOLECULE. I THINK...

I THINK HE WAS **LAUGHING**.

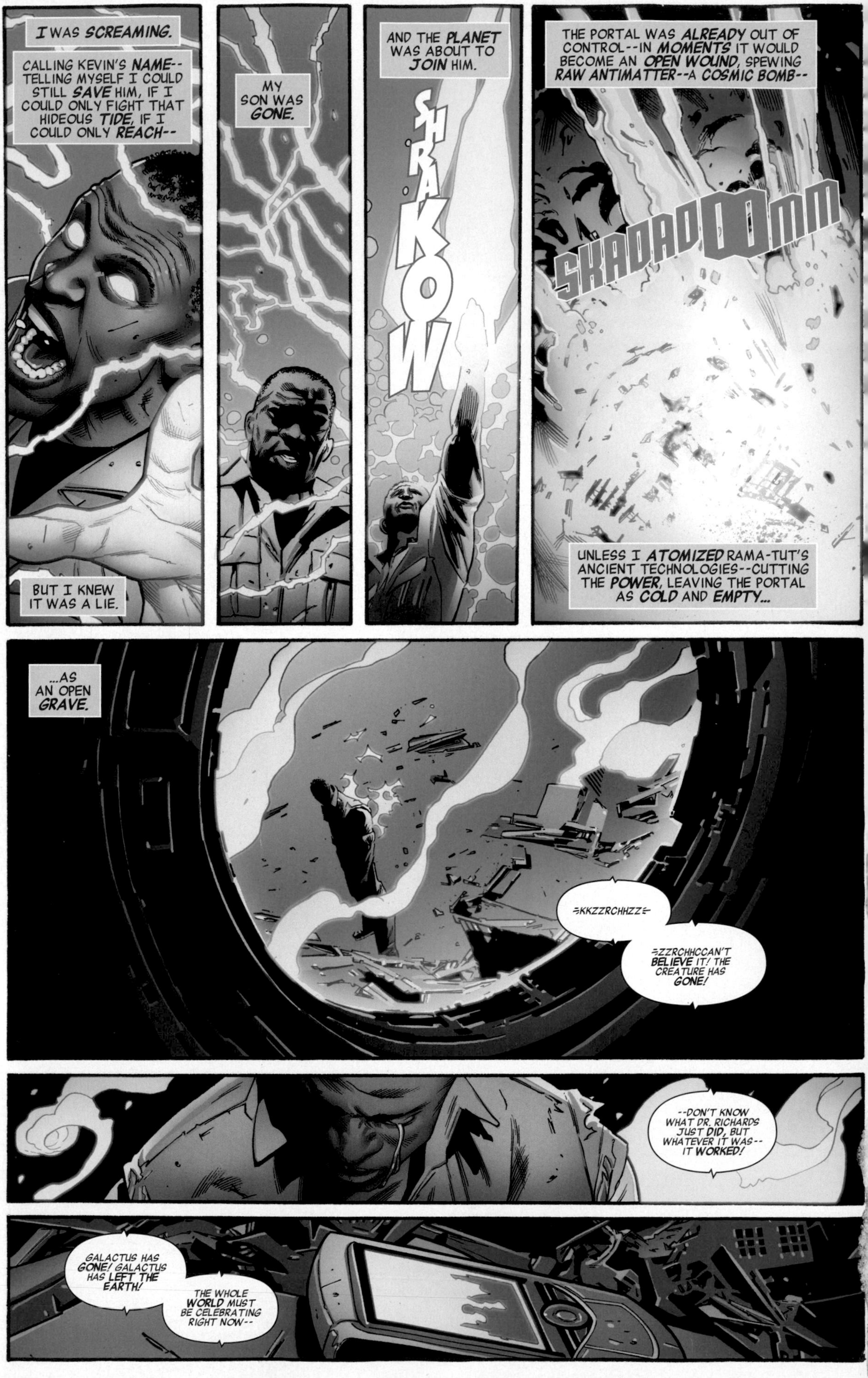
I WAS SCREAMING.
CALLING KEVIN'S NAME--TELLING MYSELF I COULD STILL SAVE HIM, IF I COULD ONLY FIGHT THAT HIDEOUS TIDE, IF I COULD ONLY REACH--
BUT I KNEW IT WAS A LIE.
MY SON WAS GONE.
AND THE PLANET WAS ABOUT TO JOIN HIM.
SHRAKOW
THE PORTAL WAS ALREADY OUT OF CONTROL--IN MOMENTS IT WOULD BECOME AN OPEN WOUND, SPEWING RAW ANTIMATTER--A COSMIC BOMB--
SKADADOOMM
UNLESS I ATOMIZED RAMA-TUT'S ANCIENT TECHNOLOGIES--CUTTING THE POWER, LEAVING THE PORTAL AS COLD AND EMPTY...
...AS AN OPEN GRAVE.
=KKZZRCHHZZ=
=ZZRCHHCCAN'T BELIEVE IT! THE CREATURE HAS GONE!
--DON'T KNOW WHAT DR. RICHARDS JUST DID, BUT WHATEVER IT WAS--IT WORKED!
GALACTUS HAS GONE! GALACTUS HAS LEFT THE EARTH!
THE WHOLE WORLD MUST BE CELEBRATING RIGHT NOW--

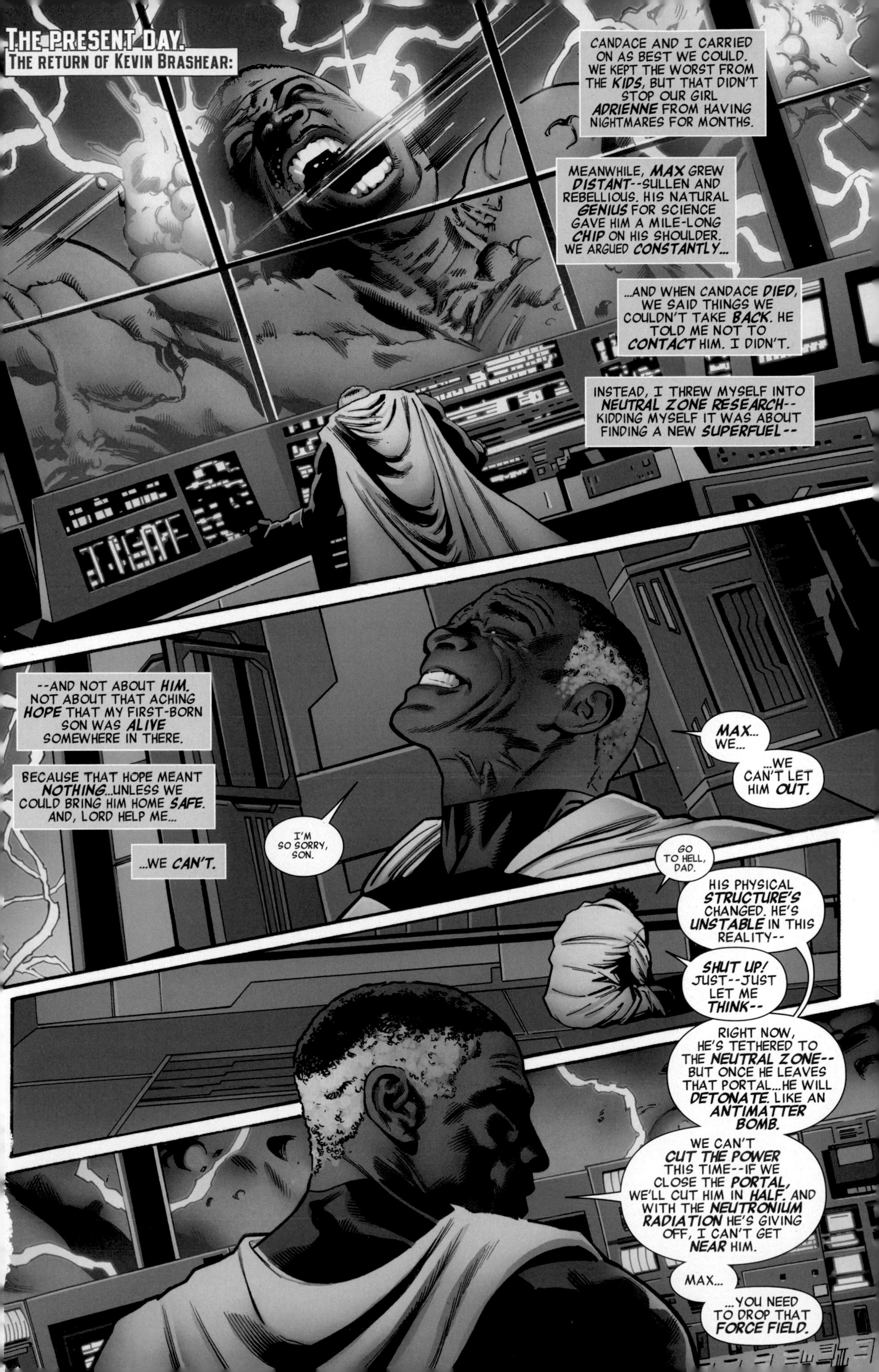
THE PRESENT DAY.
THE RETURN OF KEVIN BRASHEAR:
CANDACE AND I CARRIED ON AS BEST WE COULD. WE KEPT THE WORST FROM THE KIDS, BUT THAT DIDN'T STOP OUR GIRL ADRIENNE FROM HAVING NIGHTMARES FOR MONTHS.
MEANWHILE, MAX GREW DISTANT--SULLEN AND REBELLIOUS. HIS NATURAL GENIUS FOR SCIENCE GAVE HIM A MILE-LONG CHIP ON HIS SHOULDER. WE ARGUED CONSTANTLY...
...AND WHEN CANDACE DIED, WE SAID THINGS WE COULDN'T TAKE BACK. HE TOLD ME NOT TO CONTACT HIM. I DIDN'T.
INSTEAD, I THREW MYSELF INTO NEUTRAL ZONE RESEARCH--KIDDING MYSELF IT WAS ABOUT FINDING A NEW SUPERFUEL--
--AND NOT ABOUT HIM. NOT ABOUT THAT ACHING HOPE THAT MY FIRST-BORN SON WAS ALIVE SOMEWHERE IN THERE.
BECAUSE THAT HOPE MEANT NOTHING...UNLESS WE COULD BRING HIM HOME SAFE. AND, LORD HELP ME...
...WE CAN'T.
MAX... WE...
...WE CAN'T LET HIM OUT.
I'M SO SORRY, SON.
GO TO HELL, DAD.
HIS PHYSICAL STRUCTURE'S CHANGED. HE'S UNSTABLE IN THIS REALITY--
SHUT UP! JUST--JUST LET ME THINK--
RIGHT NOW, HE'S TETHERED TO THE NEUTRAL ZONE--BUT ONCE HE LEAVES THAT PORTAL...HE WILL DETONATE. LIKE AN ANTIMATTER BOMB.
WE CAN'T CUT THE POWER THIS TIME--IF WE CLOSE THE PORTAL, WE'LL CUT HIM IN HALF. AND WITH THE NEUTRONIUM RADIATION HE'S GIVING OFF, I CAN'T GET NEAR HIM.
MAX...
...YOU NEED TO DROP THAT FORCE FIELD.

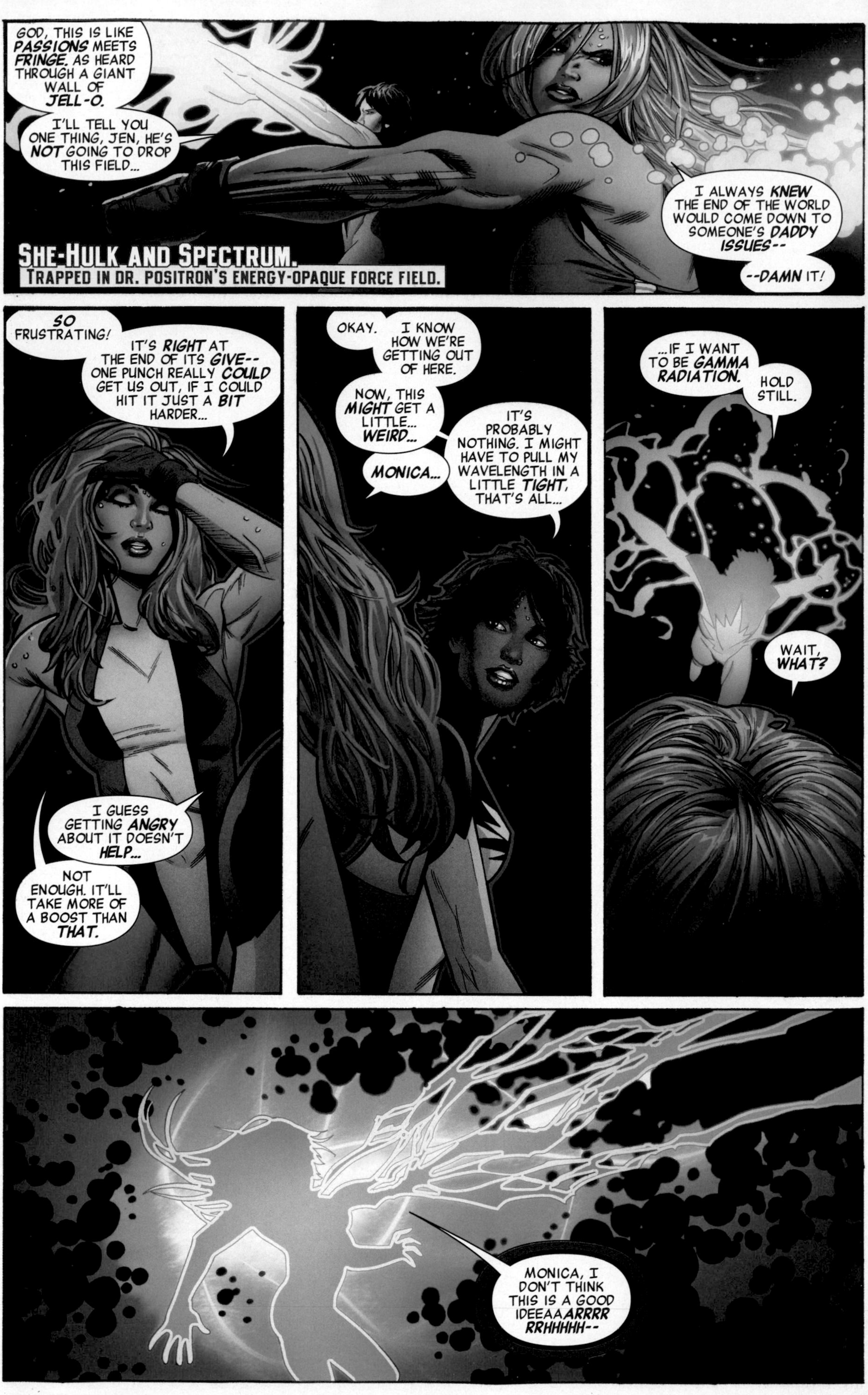
GOD, THIS IS LIKE PASSIONS MEETS FRINGE, AS HEARD THROUGH A GIANT WALL OF JELL-O.
I'LL TELL YOU ONE THING, JEN, HE'S NOT GOING TO DROP THIS FIELD...
I ALWAYS KNEW THE END OF THE WORLD WOULD COME DOWN TO SOMEONE'S DADDY ISSUES--
--DAMN IT!
SHE-HULK AND SPECTRUM.
TRAPPED IN DR. POSITRON'S ENERGY-OPAQUE FORCE FIELD.
SO FRUSTRATING!
IT'S RIGHT AT THE END OF ITS GIVE-- ONE PUNCH REALLY COULD GET US OUT, IF I COULD HIT IT JUST A BIT HARDER...
I GUESS GETTING ANGRY ABOUT IT DOESN'T HELP...
NOT ENOUGH. IT'LL TAKE MORE OF A BOOST THAN THAT.
OKAY.
I KNOW HOW WE'RE GETTING OUT OF HERE.
NOW, THIS MIGHT GET A LITTLE... WEIRD...
MONICA...
IT'S PROBABLY NOTHING. I MIGHT HAVE TO PULL MY WAVELENGTH IN A LITTLE TIGHT, THAT'S ALL...
...IF I WANT TO BE GAMMA RADIATION.
HOLD STILL.
WAIT, WHAT?
MONICA, I DON'T THINK THIS IS A GOOD IDEEAAARRRR RRHHHHH--

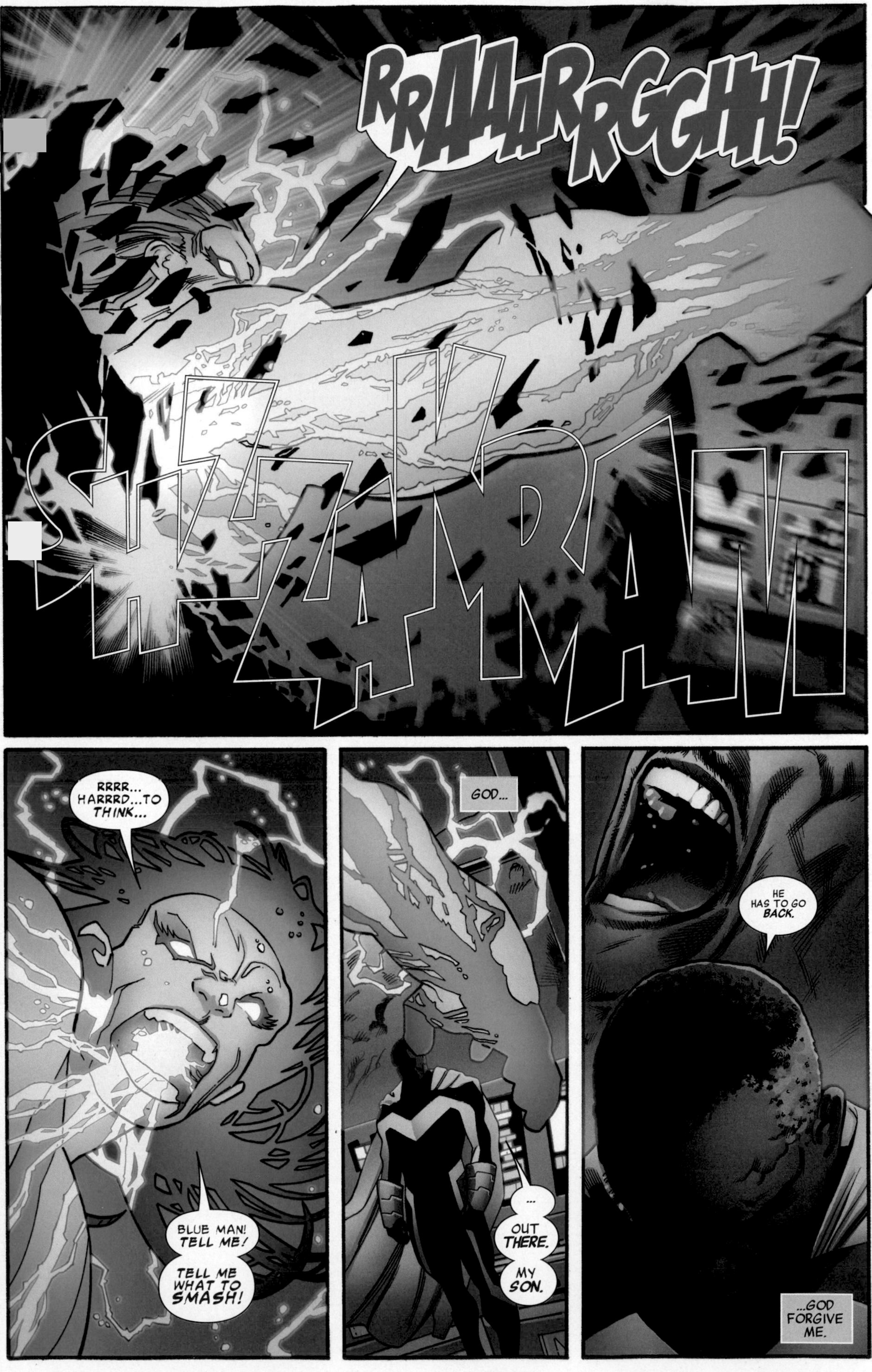
RRAAARRGGHH!
SHZZAKRAM
RRRR... HARRRD...TO THINK...
BLUE MAN! TELL ME!
TELL ME WHAT TO SMASH!
GOD...
... OUT THERE.
MY SON.
HE HAS TO GO BACK.
...GOD FORGIVE ME.

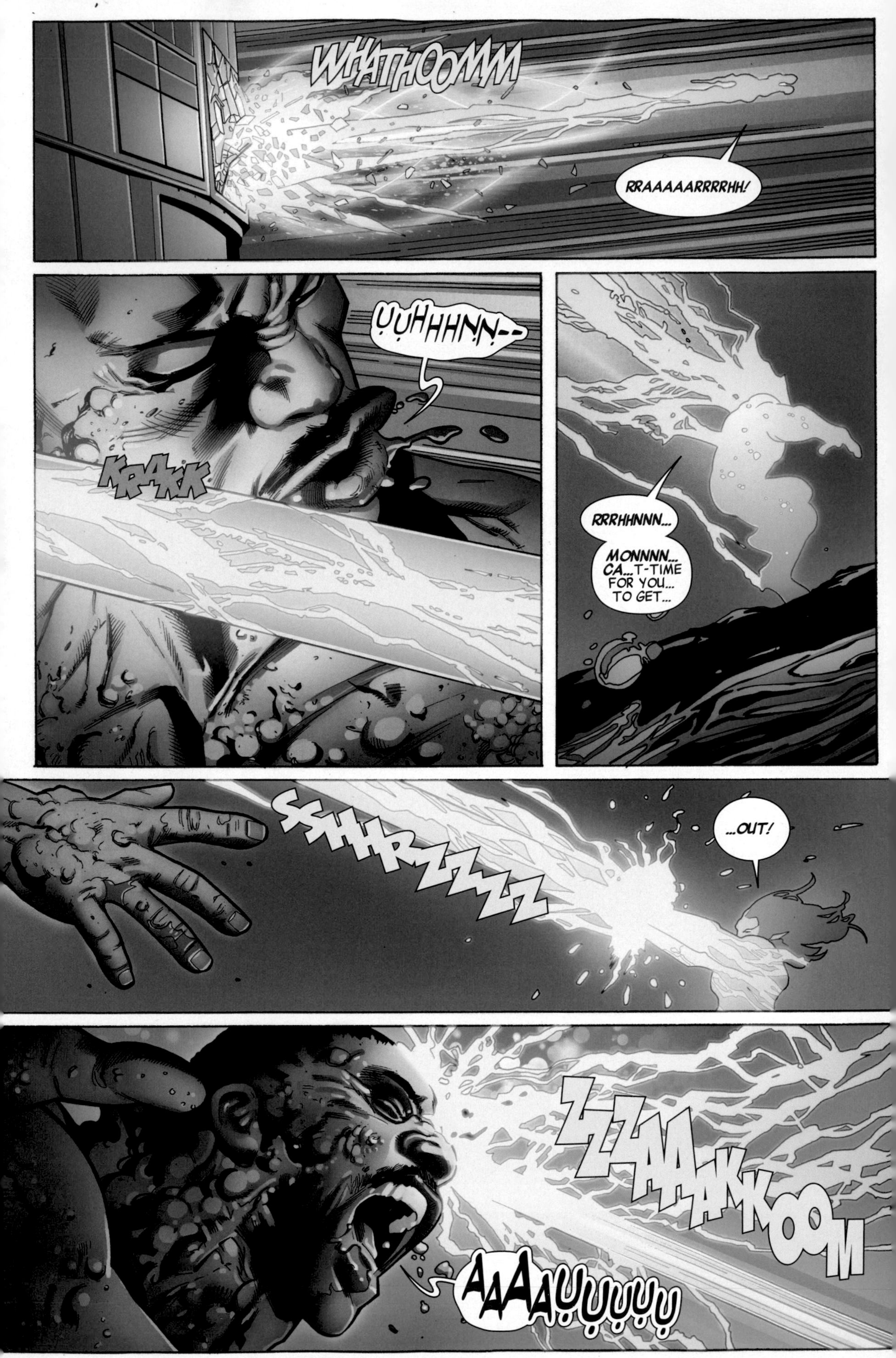
WHATHOOMM
RRAAAAARRRRH!
UUHHHNN--
KRAKK
RRRHHNNN...
MONNNN... CA... T-TIME FOR YOU... TO GET...
SSHHRZZZZZ
...OUT!
ZZZAAAKKOOM
AAAAUUUUU

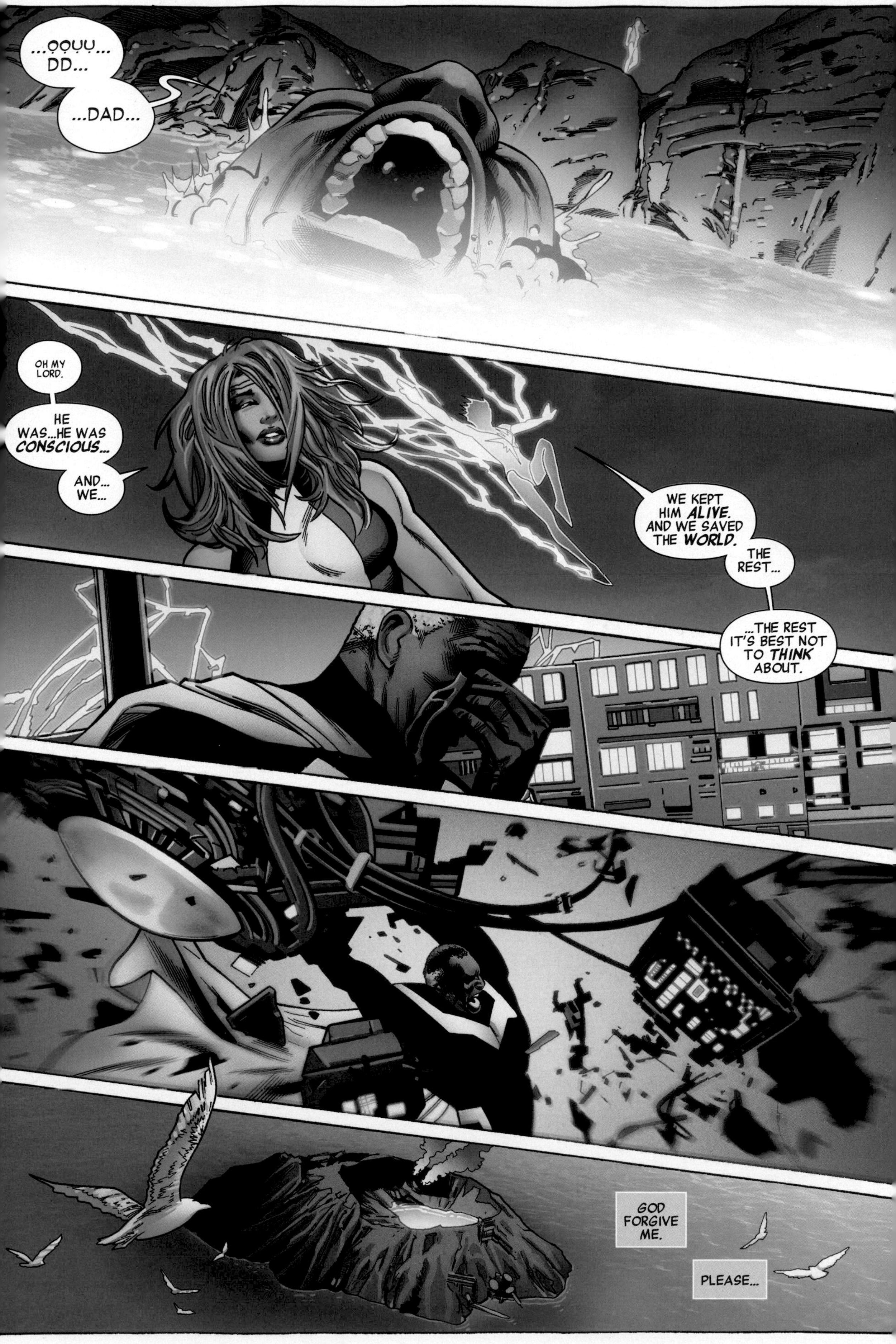

...OOUU...
DD...
...DAD...
OH MY LORD.
HE WAS...HE WAS CONSCIOUS...
AND... WE...
WE KEPT HIM ALIVE. AND WE SAVED THE WORLD.
THE REST...
...THE REST IT'S BEST NOT TO THINK ABOUT.
GOD FORGIVE ME.
PLEASE...

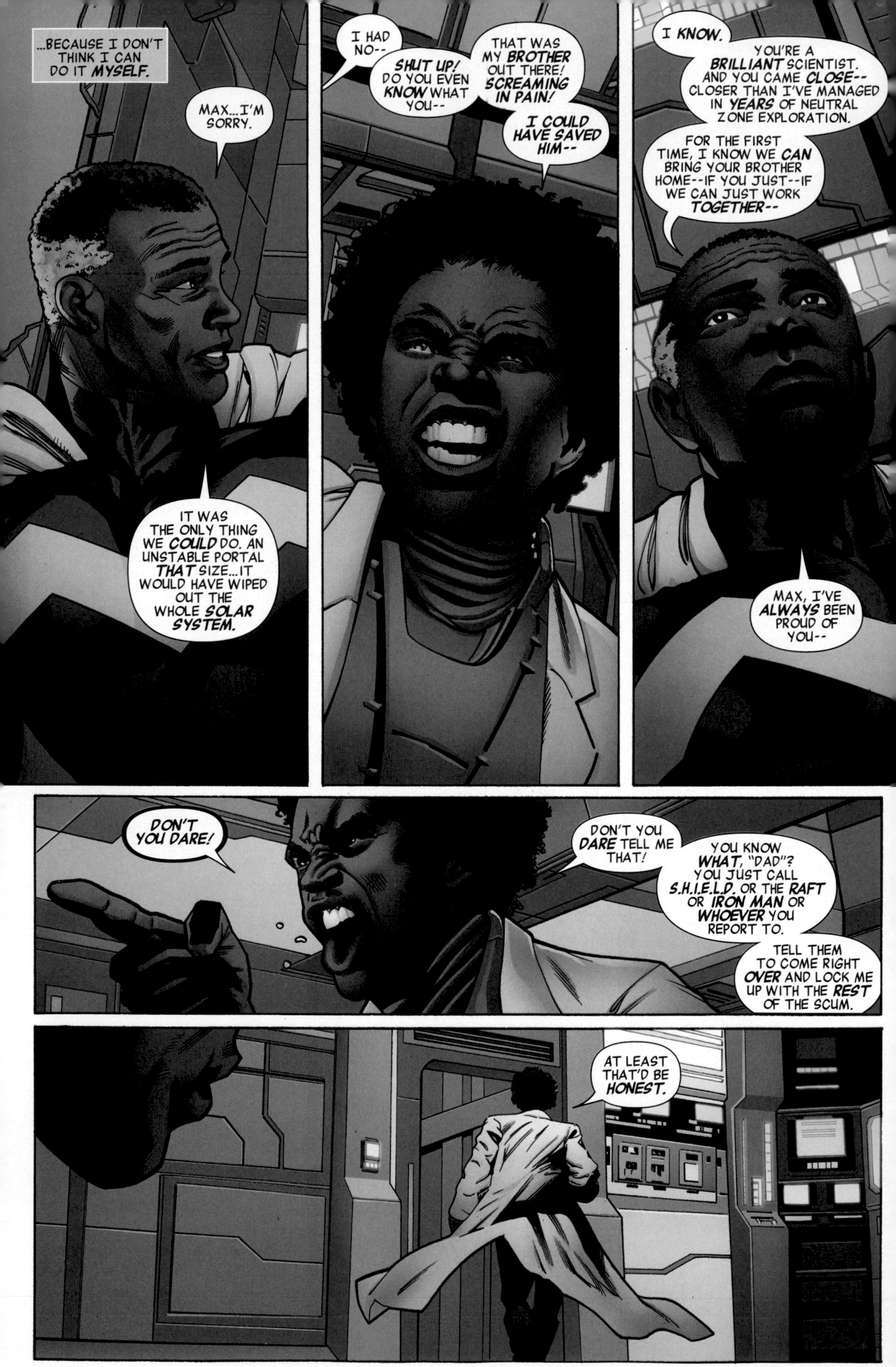
...BECAUSE I DON'T THINK I CAN DO IT MYSELF.
MAX...I'M SORRY.
IT WAS THE ONLY THING WE COULD DO. AN UNSTABLE PORTAL THAT SIZE...IT WOULD HAVE WIPED OUT THE WHOLE SOLAR SYSTEM.
I HAD NO--
SHUT UP! DO YOU EVEN KNOW WHAT YOU--
THAT WAS MY BROTHER OUT THERE! SCREAMING IN PAIN!
I COULD HAVE SAVED HIM--
I KNOW.
YOU'RE A BRILLIANT SCIENTIST. AND YOU CAME CLOSE-- CLOSER THAN I'VE MANAGED IN YEARS OF NEUTRAL ZONE EXPLORATION.
FOR THE FIRST TIME, I KNOW WE CAN BRING YOUR BROTHER HOME--IF YOU JUST--IF WE CAN JUST WORK TOGETHER--
MAX, I'VE ALWAYS BEEN PROUD OF YOU--
DON'T YOU DARE!
DON'T YOU DARE TELL ME THAT!
YOU KNOW WHAT, "DAD"? YOU JUST CALL S.H.I.E.L.D. OR THE RAFT OR IRON MAN OR WHOEVER YOU REPORT TO.
TELL THEM TO COME RIGHT OVER AND LOCK ME UP WITH THE REST OF THE SCUM.
AT LEAST THAT'D BE HONEST.

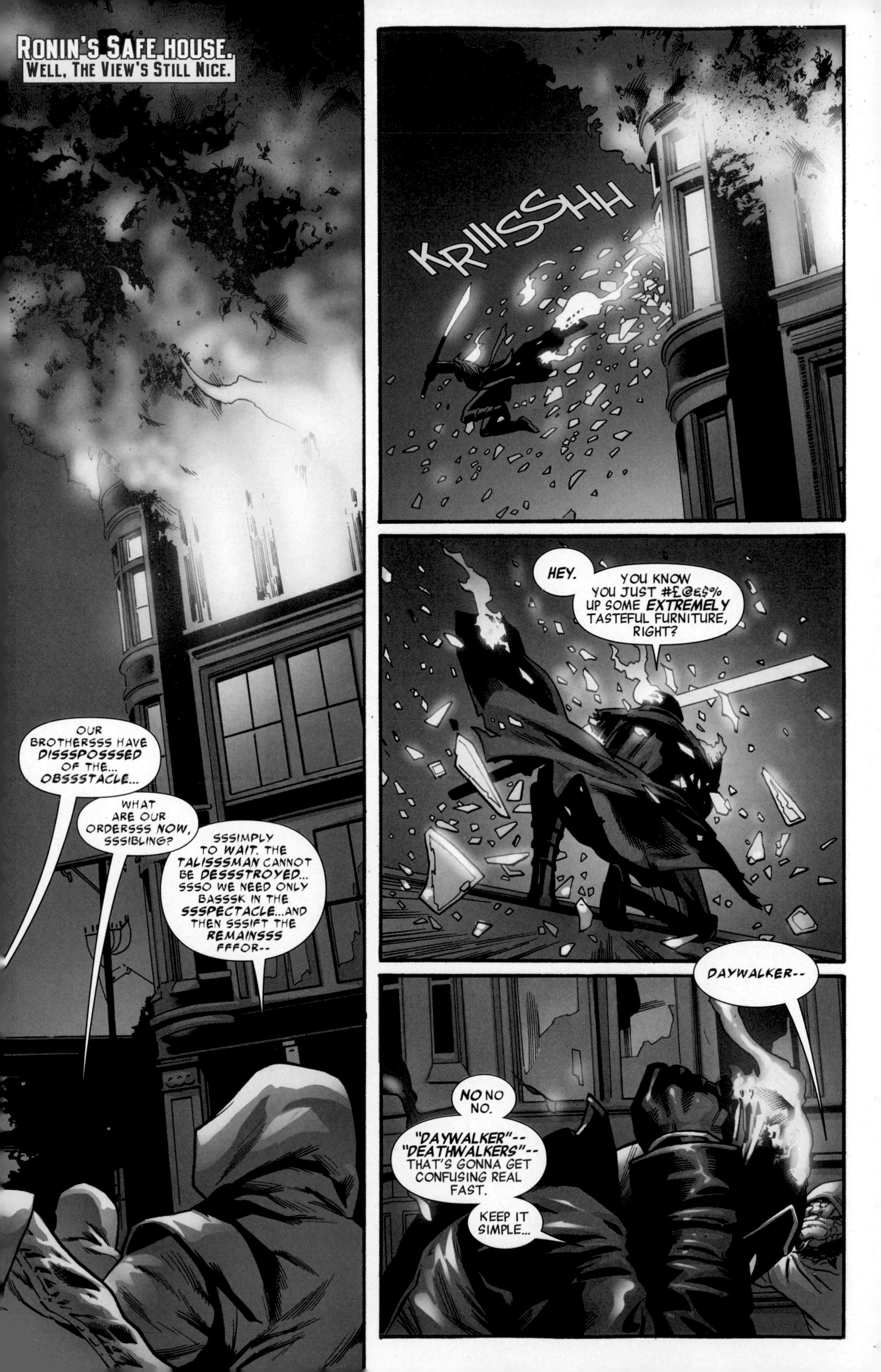
RONIN'S SAFE HOUSE.
WELL, THE VIEW'S STILL NICE.
OUR BROTHERSSS HAVE DISSSPOSSSED OF THE... OBSSSTACLE...
WHAT ARE OUR ORDERSSS NOW, SSSIBLING?
SSSIMPLY TO WAIT. THE TALISSSMAN CANNOT BE DESSSTROYED... SSSO WE NEED ONLY BASSSK IN THE SSSPECTACLE...AND THEN SSSIFT THE REMAINSSS FFFOR--
KRIIISSHH
HEY.
YOU KNOW YOU JUST #£@&$% UP SOME EXTREMELY TASTEFUL FURNITURE, RIGHT?
DAYWALKER--
NO NO NO.
"DAYWALKER"-- "DEATHWALKERS"-- THAT'S GONNA GET CONFUSING REAL FAST.
KEEP IT SIMPLE...

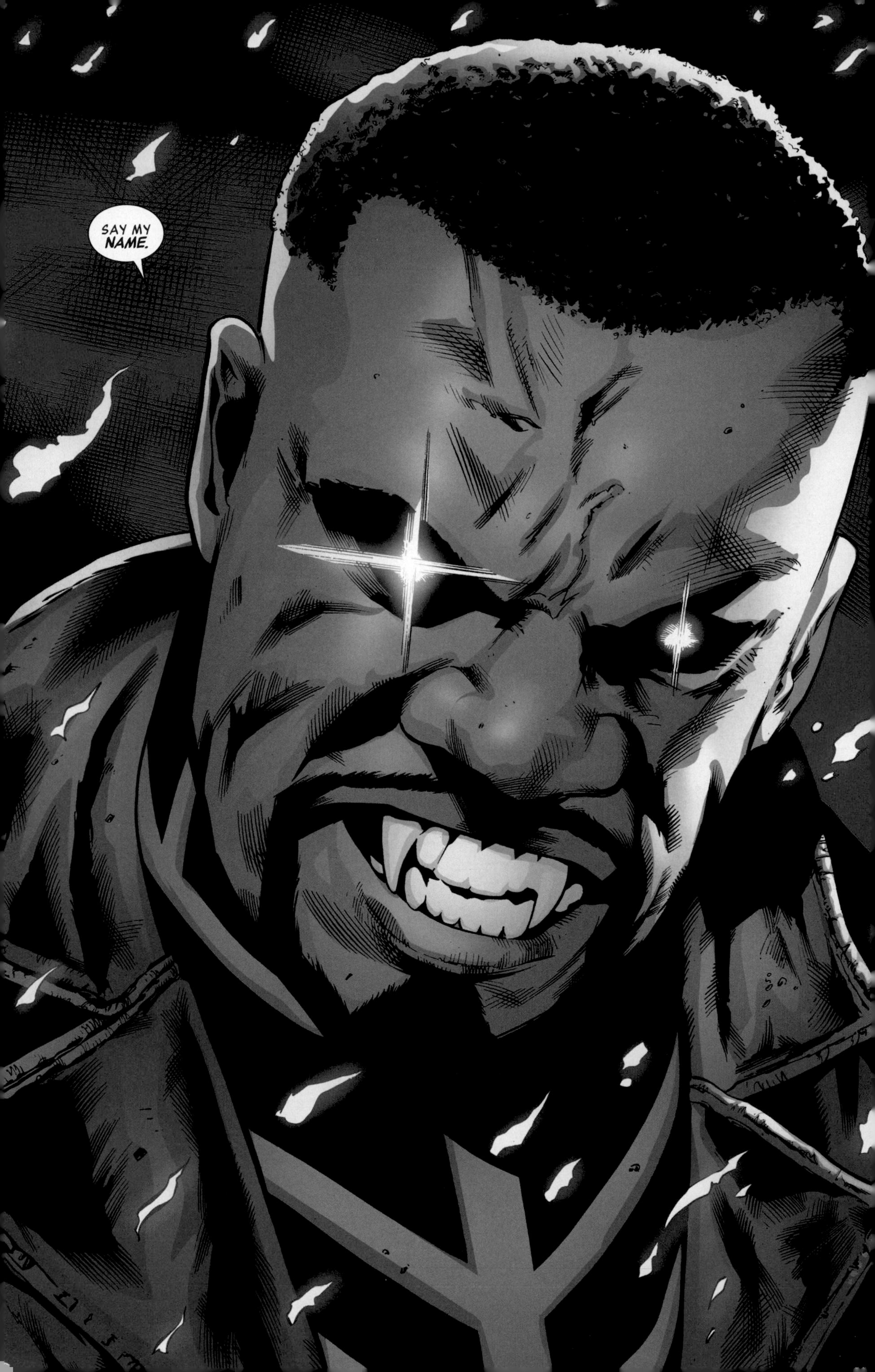
SAY MY NAME.

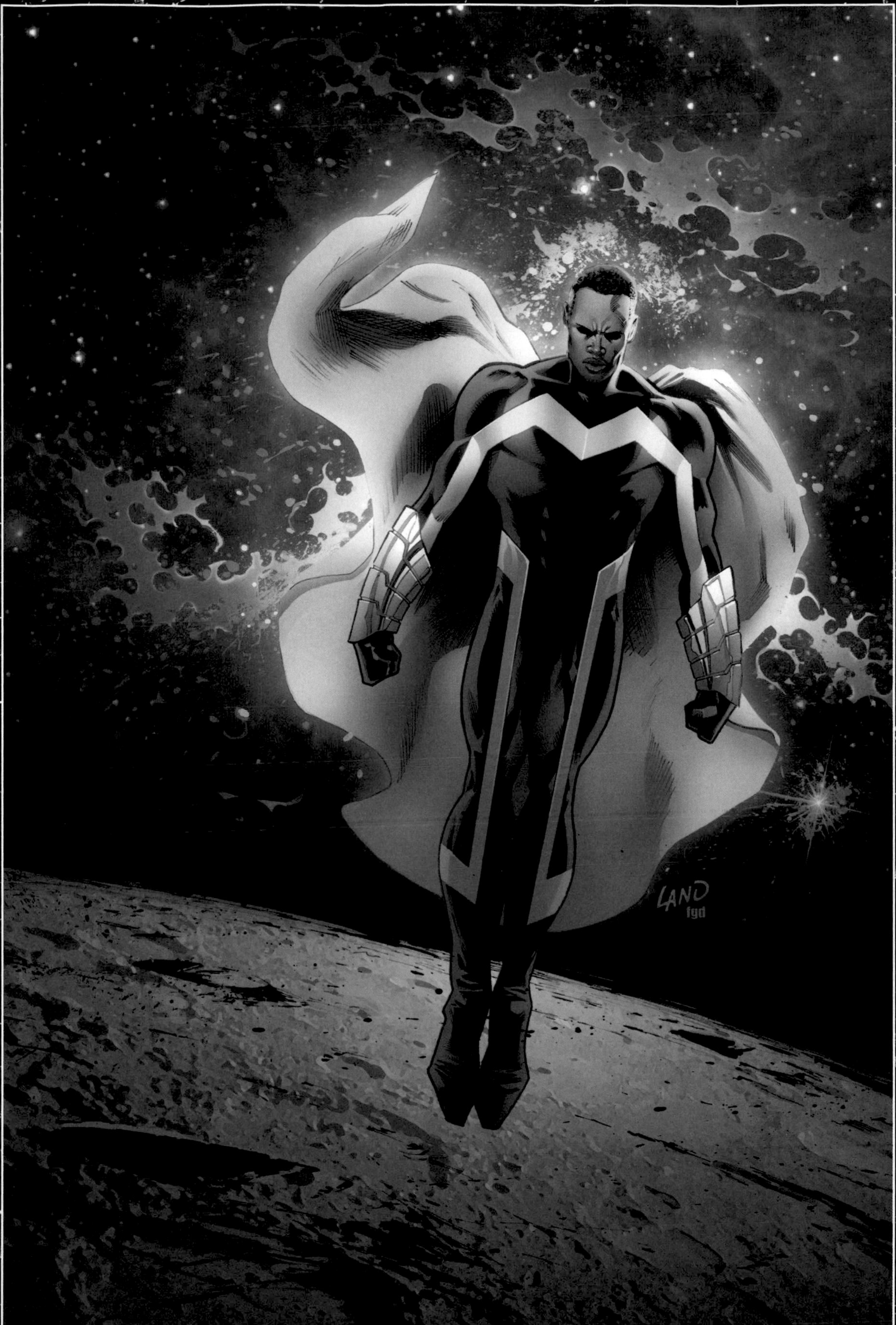
LAND
fgd

The Mighty Avengers have announced that they want to hear feedback from the people they serve, so they're answering letters from you, the public, at www.marvel.com/letterspages. And they're encouraging anyone and everyone to write in and let them know how you think they're doing. Email them at **MHEROES@marvel.com**, and make sure to mark your letters "Okay to print"!

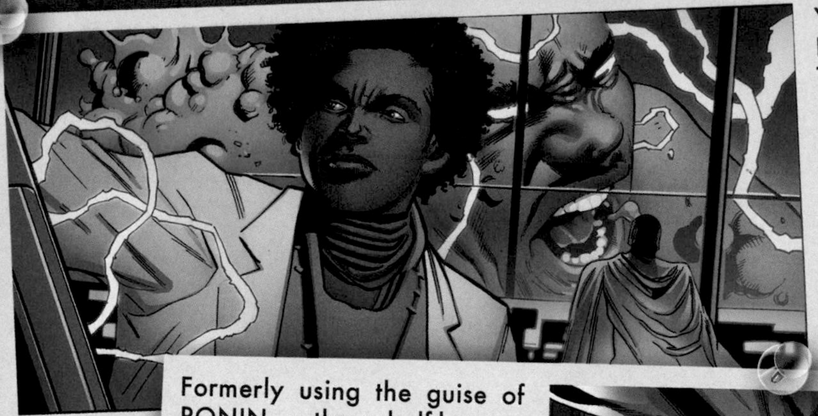

Years ago, ADAM BRASHEAR, also known as THE BLUE MARVEL, lost his son KEVIN in the NEUTRAL ZONE. His younger son MAX recently allied with villains to attempt to bring Kevin back, with disastrous results. Kevin remains in the Neutral Zone, and Max's animosity towards his father has only grown.

Formerly using the guise of RONIN, the half-human, half-vampire BLADE has been working with the mysterious KALUU to stop the DEATHWALKERS from using the TALISMAN OF KAMAR-TAJ to destroy the human world. For his troubles, a gang of WERE-SNAKES attacked him and destroyed his safe house!

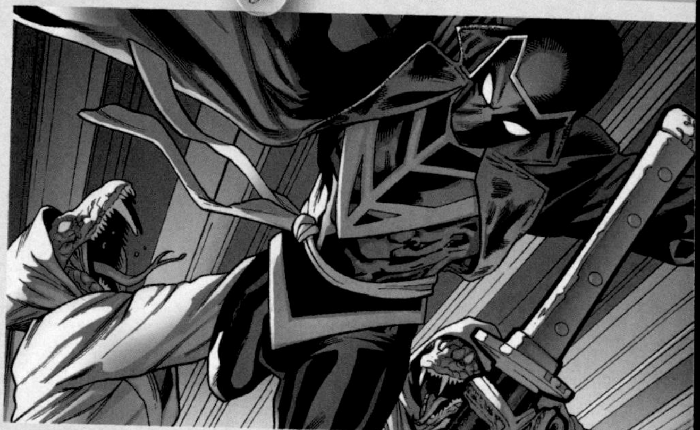

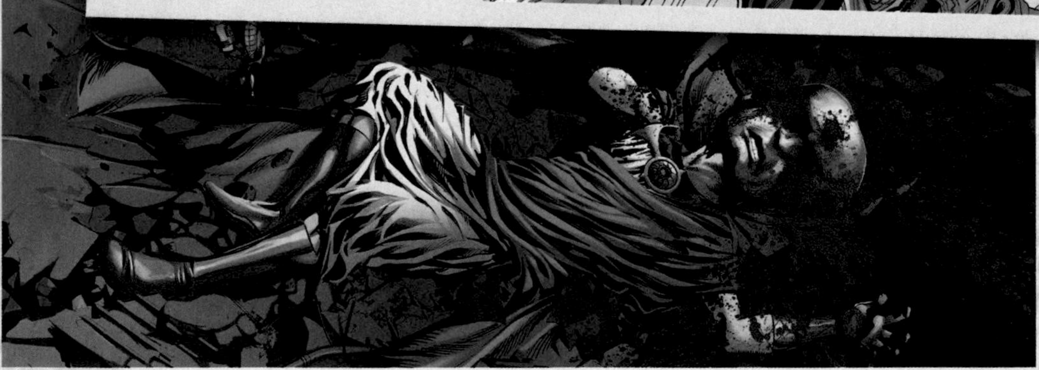

NEWS FLASH! **UATU, a WATCHER tasked to observe every action on the Earth from his base on the moon (but forbidden to intervene) has been found MURDERED and his home RANSACKED! The perpetrator or perpetrators remain unknown and at large. The Watcher is survived by his spouse ULANA and their newborn child.**

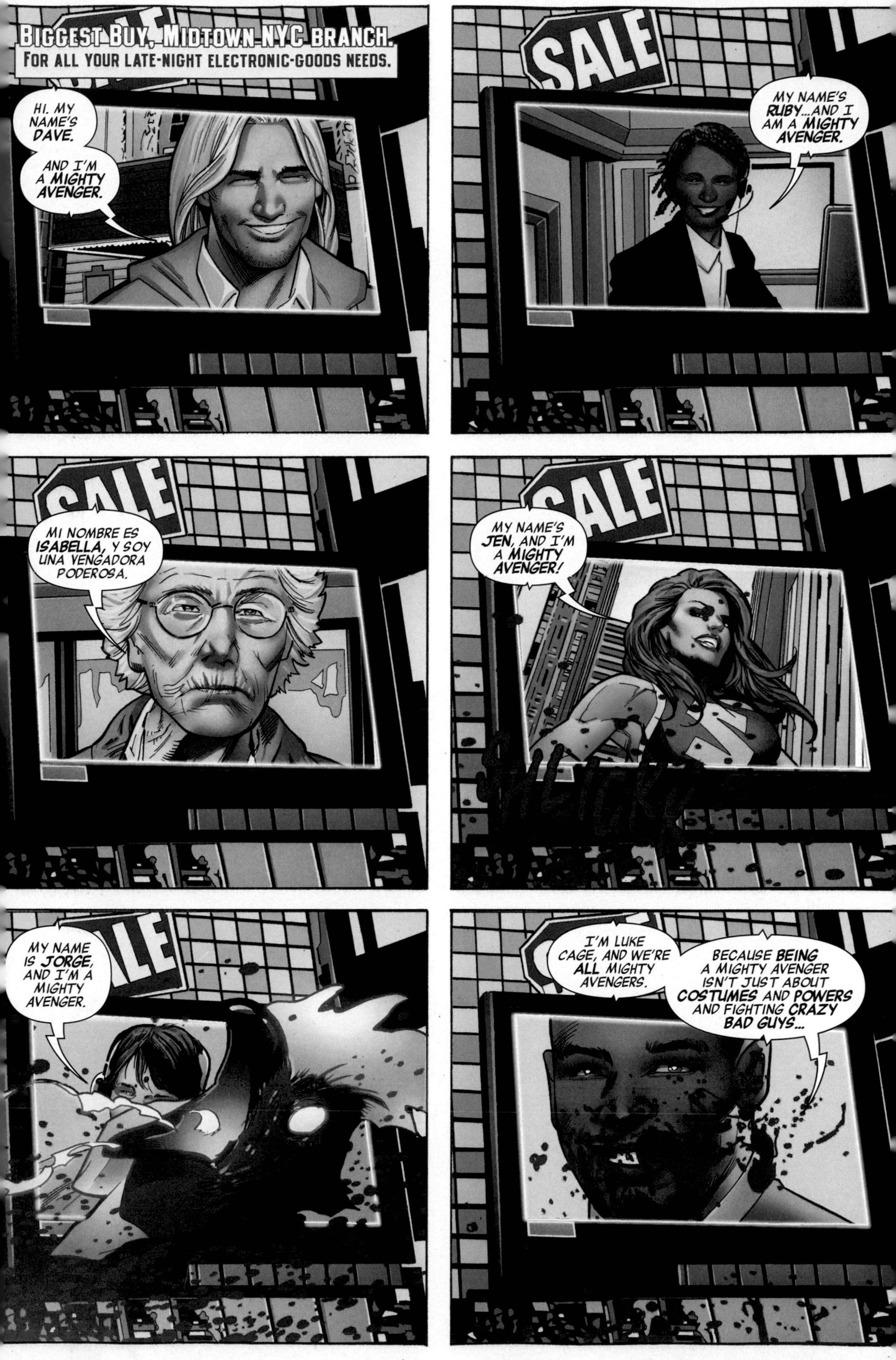
BIGGEST BUY, MIDTOWN NYC BRANCH.
FOR ALL YOUR LATE-NIGHT ELECTRONIC-GOODS NEEDS.
HI. MY NAME'S DAVE.
AND I'M A MIGHTY AVENGER.
SALE
MY NAME'S RUBY...AND I AM A MIGHTY AVENGER.
SALE
MI NOMBRE ES ISABELLA, Y SOY UNA VENGADORA PODEROSA.
SALE
MY NAME'S JEN, AND I'M A MIGHTY AVENGER!
MY NAME IS JORGE, AND I'M A MIGHTY AVENGER.
I'M LUKE CAGE, AND WE'RE ALL MIGHTY AVENGERS.
BECAUSE BEING A MIGHTY AVENGER ISN'T JUST ABOUT COSTUMES AND POWERS AND FIGHTING CRAZY BAD GUYS...

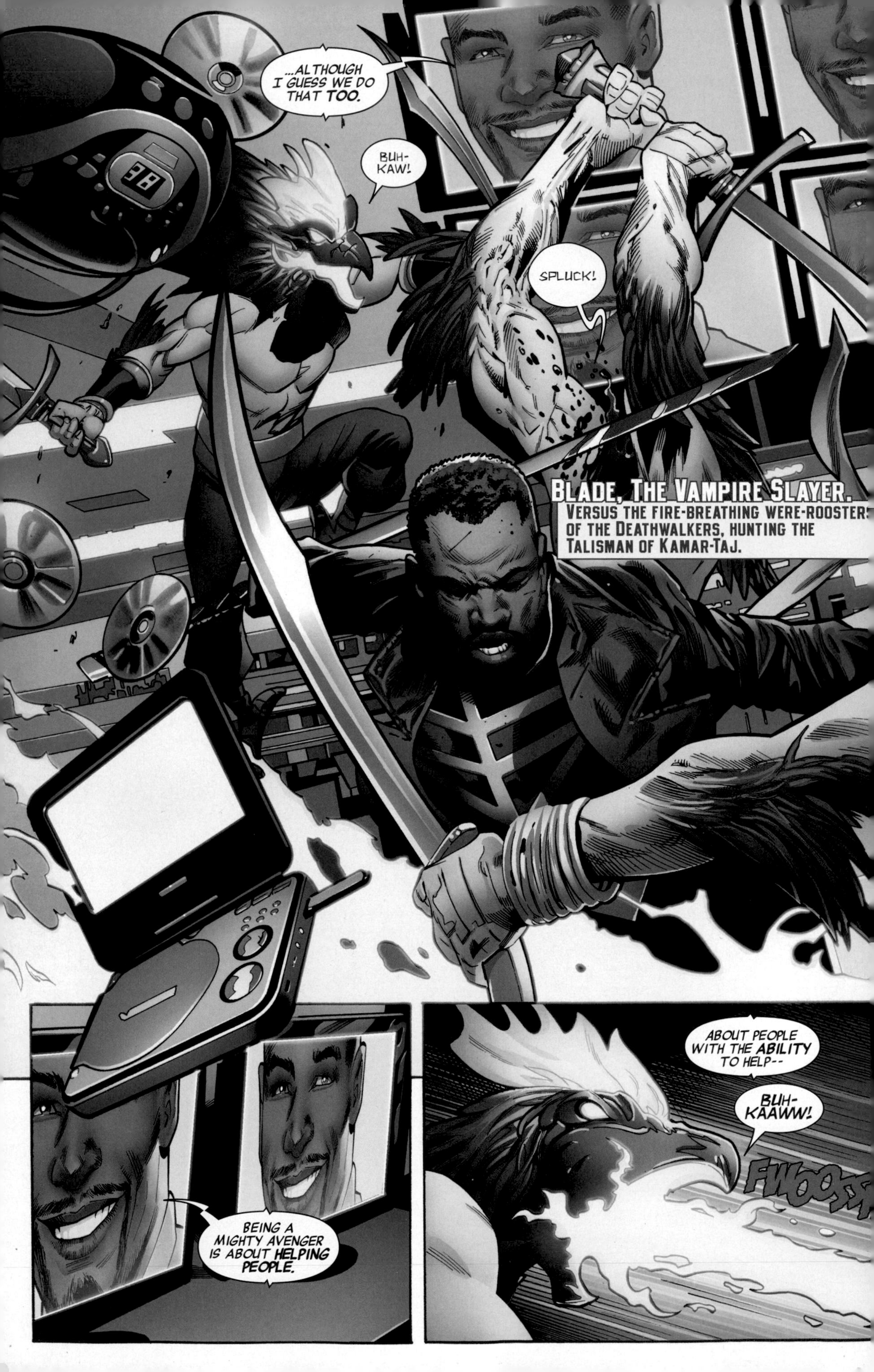
...ALTHOUGH I GUESS WE DO THAT TOO.
BUH-KAW!
SPLUCK!
BLADE, THE VAMPIRE SLAYER.
VERSUS THE FIRE-BREATHING WERE-ROOSTERS OF THE DEATHWALKERS, HUNTING THE TALISMAN OF KAMAR-TAJ.
BEING A MIGHTY AVENGER IS ABOUT HELPING PEOPLE.
ABOUT PEOPLE WITH THE ABILITY TO HELP--
BUH-KAAWW!
FWOOSH

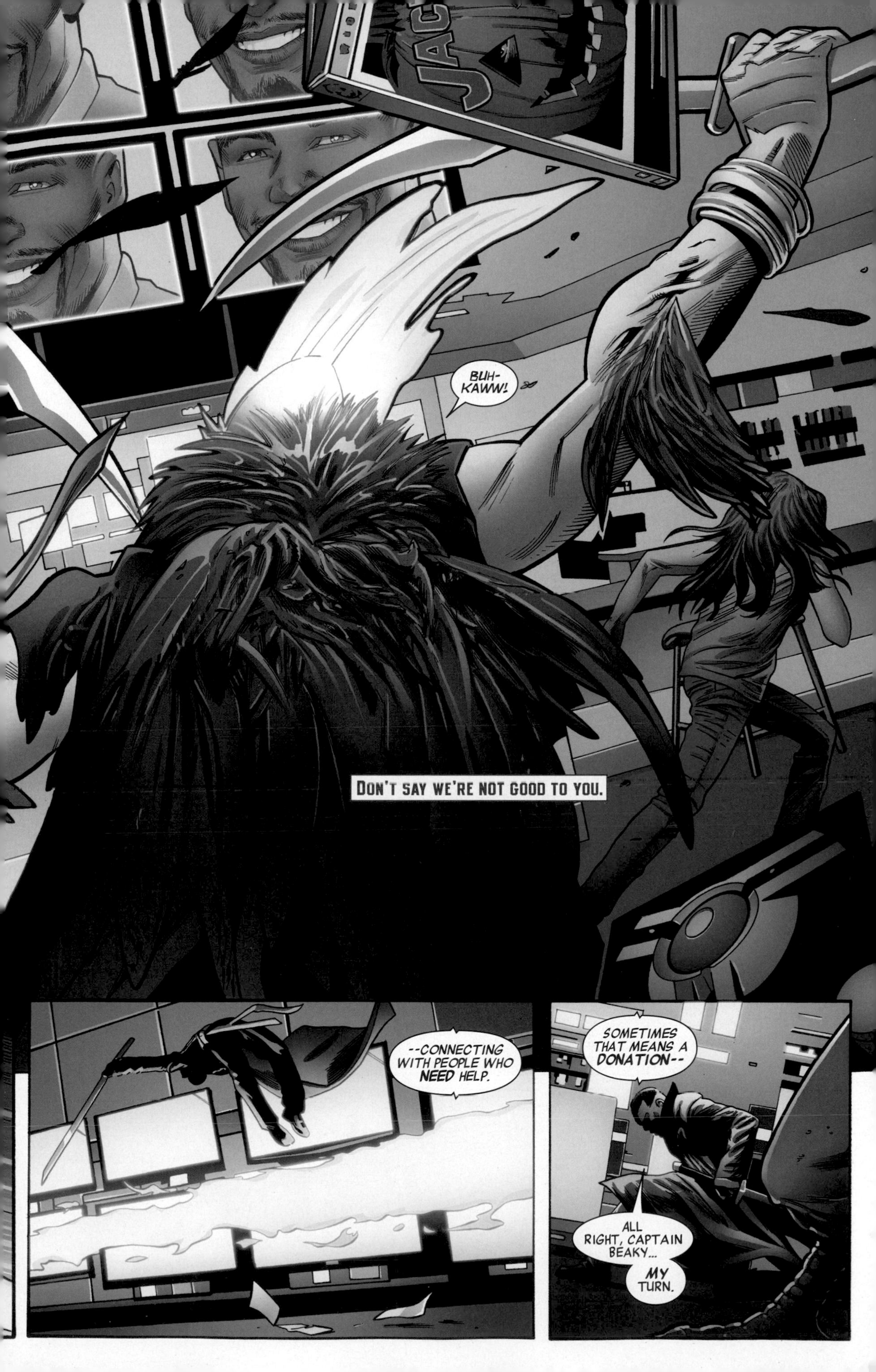
BUH-KAWW!
DON'T SAY WE'RE NOT GOOD TO YOU.
--CONNECTING WITH PEOPLE WHO NEED HELP.
SOMETIMES THAT MEANS A DONATION--
ALL RIGHT, CAPTAIN BEAKY...
MY TURN.

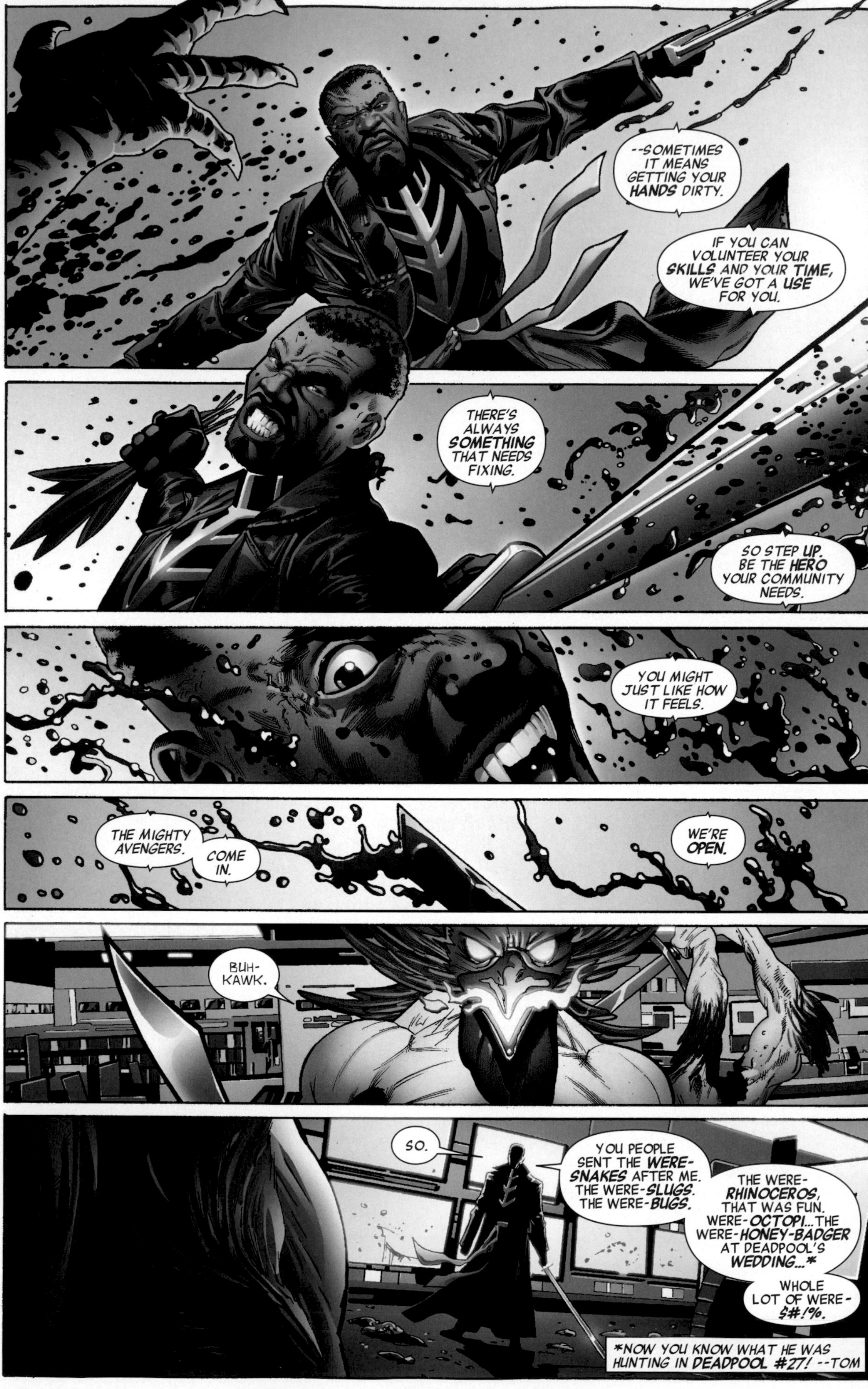
--SOMETIMES IT MEANS GETTING YOUR HANDS DIRTY.
IF YOU CAN VOLUNTEER YOUR SKILLS AND YOUR TIME, WE'VE GOT A USE FOR YOU.
THERE'S ALWAYS SOMETHING THAT NEEDS FIXING.
SO STEP UP. BE THE HERO YOUR COMMUNITY NEEDS.
YOU MIGHT JUST LIKE HOW IT FEELS.
THE MIGHTY AVENGERS.
COME IN.
WE'RE OPEN.
BUH-KAWK.
SO.
YOU PEOPLE SENT THE WERE-SNAKES AFTER ME. THE WERE-SLUGS. THE WERE-BUGS.
THE WERE-RHINOCEROS, THAT WAS FUN. WERE-OCTOPI...THE WERE-HONEY-BADGER AT DEADPOOL'S WEDDING...*
WHOLE LOT OF WERE-$#!%.
*NOW YOU KNOW WHAT HE WAS HUNTING IN DEADPOOL #27! --TOM

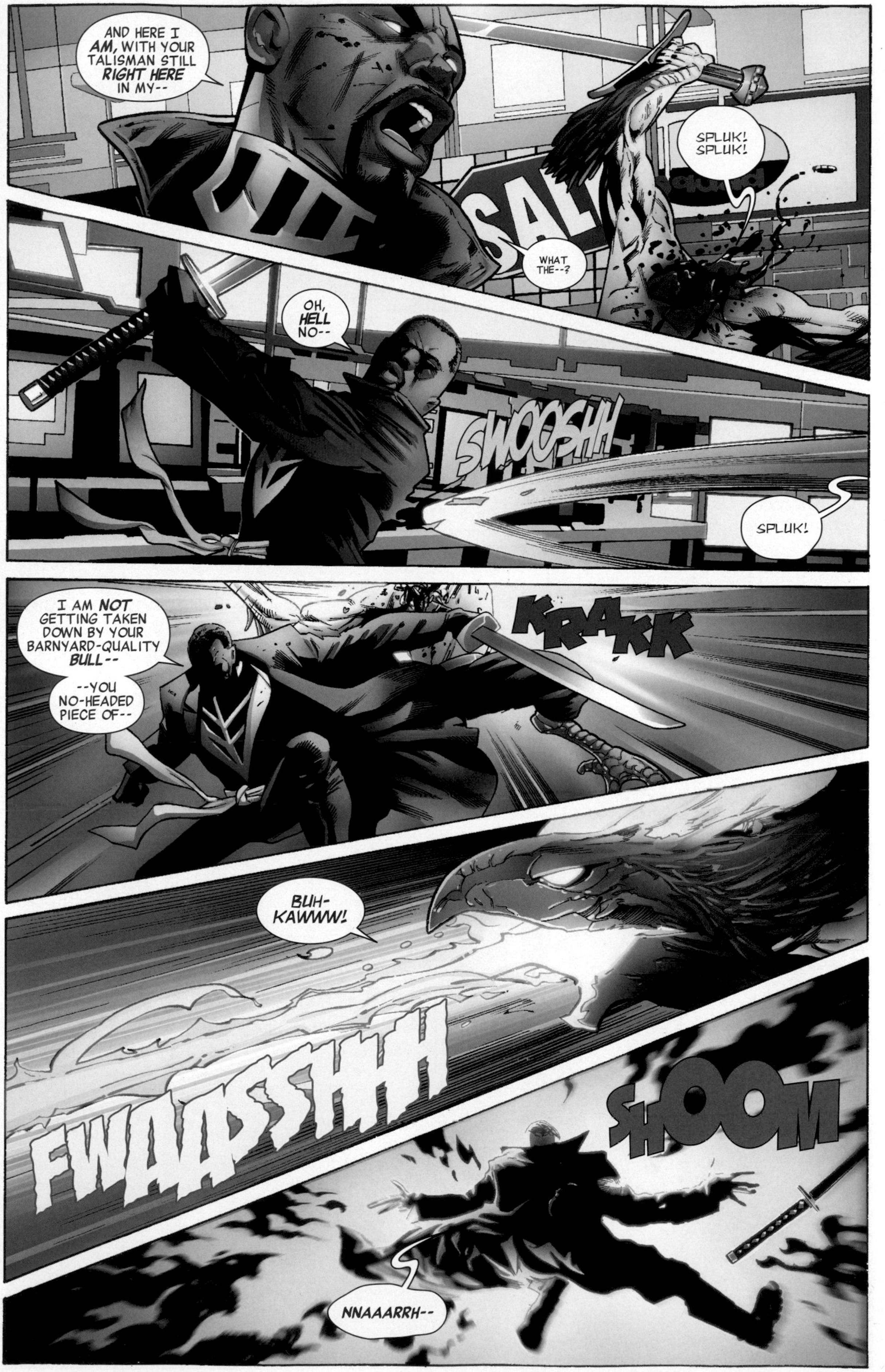
AND HERE I AM, WITH YOUR TALISMAN STILL RIGHT HERE IN MY--
SPLUK! SPLUK!
WHAT THE--?
OH, HELL NO--
SWOOSHH
SPLUK!
I AM NOT GETTING TAKEN DOWN BY YOUR BARNYARD-QUALITY BULL--
--YOU NO-HEADED PIECE OF--
KRAKK
BUH-KAWWW!
FWAASSHHH
SHOOM
NNAAARRH--

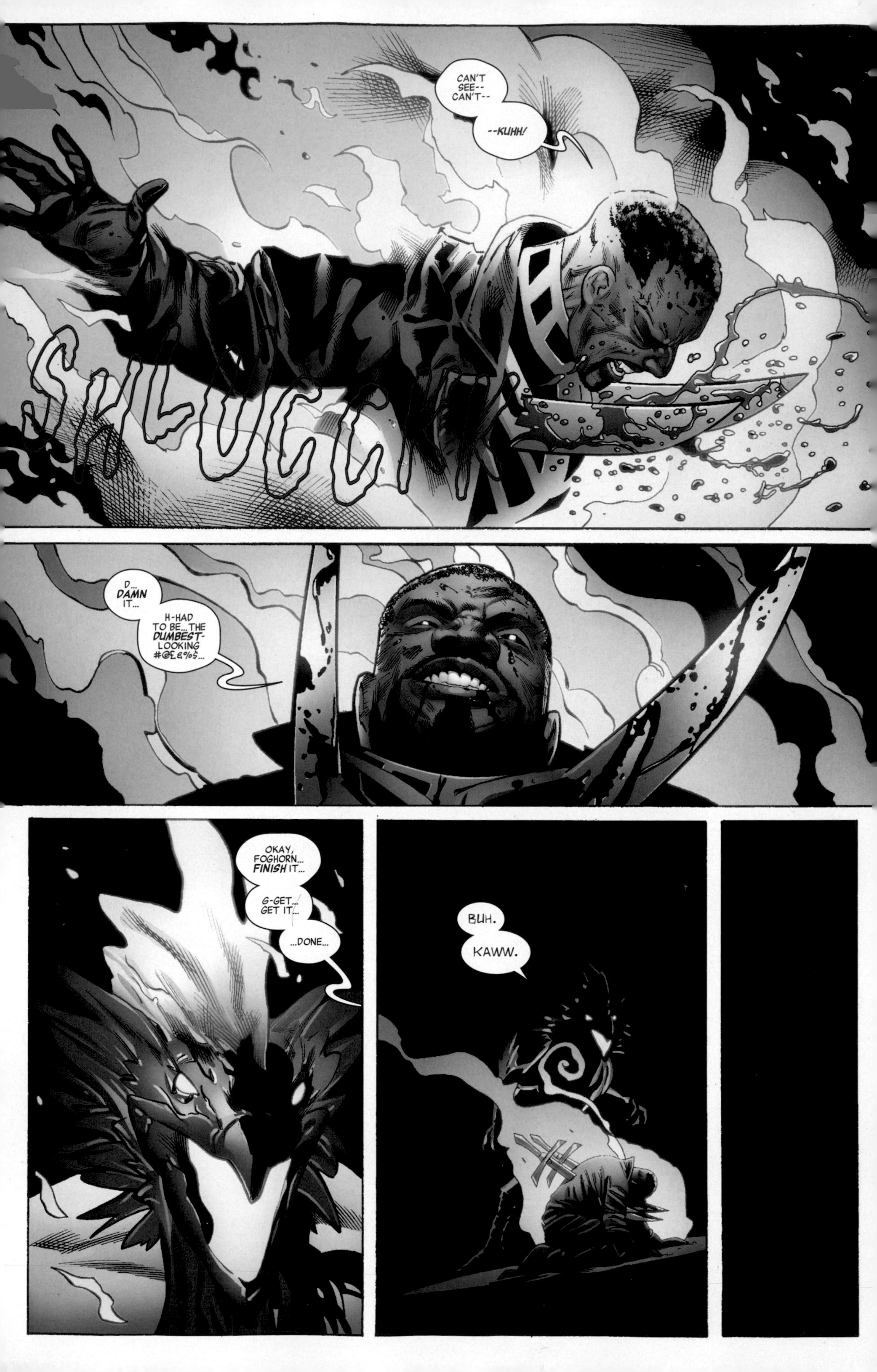
CAN'T SEE-- CAN'T--
--KUHH!
SHLUCCK
D... DAMN IT...
H-HAD TO BE... THE DUMBEST-LOOKING #@£€%$...
OKAY, FOGHORN... FINISH IT...
G-GET... GET IT...
...DONE...
BUH.
KAWW.

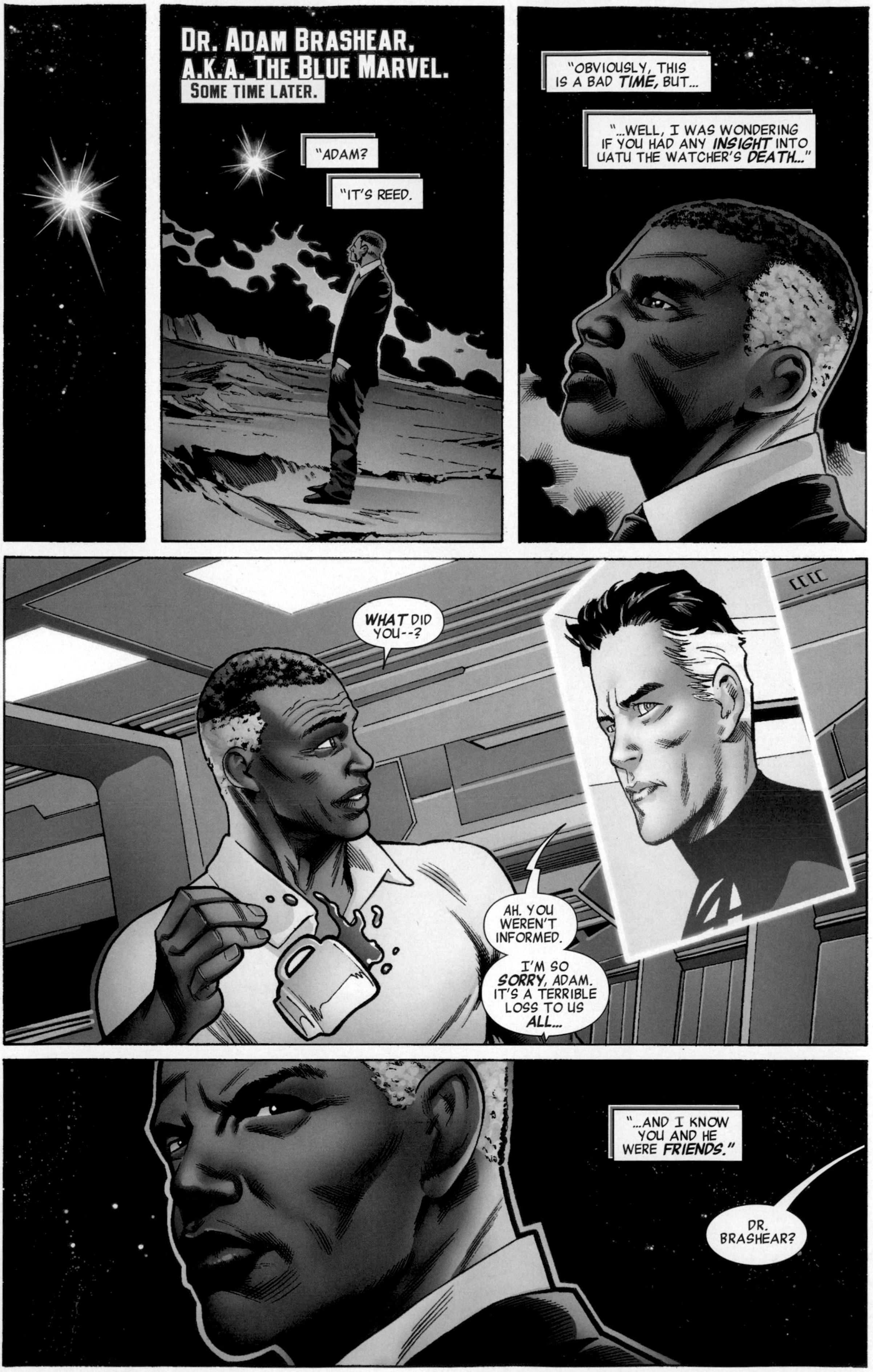
DR. ADAM BRASHEAR, A.K.A. THE BLUE MARVEL.
SOME TIME LATER.
"ADAM?
"IT'S REED.
"OBVIOUSLY, THIS IS A BAD TIME, BUT...
"...WELL, I WAS WONDERING IF YOU HAD ANY INSIGHT INTO UATU THE WATCHER'S DEATH..."
WHAT DID YOU--?
AH. YOU WEREN'T INFORMED.
I'M SO SORRY, ADAM. IT'S A TERRIBLE LOSS TO US ALL...
"...AND I KNOW YOU AND HE WERE FRIENDS."
DR. BRASHEAR?

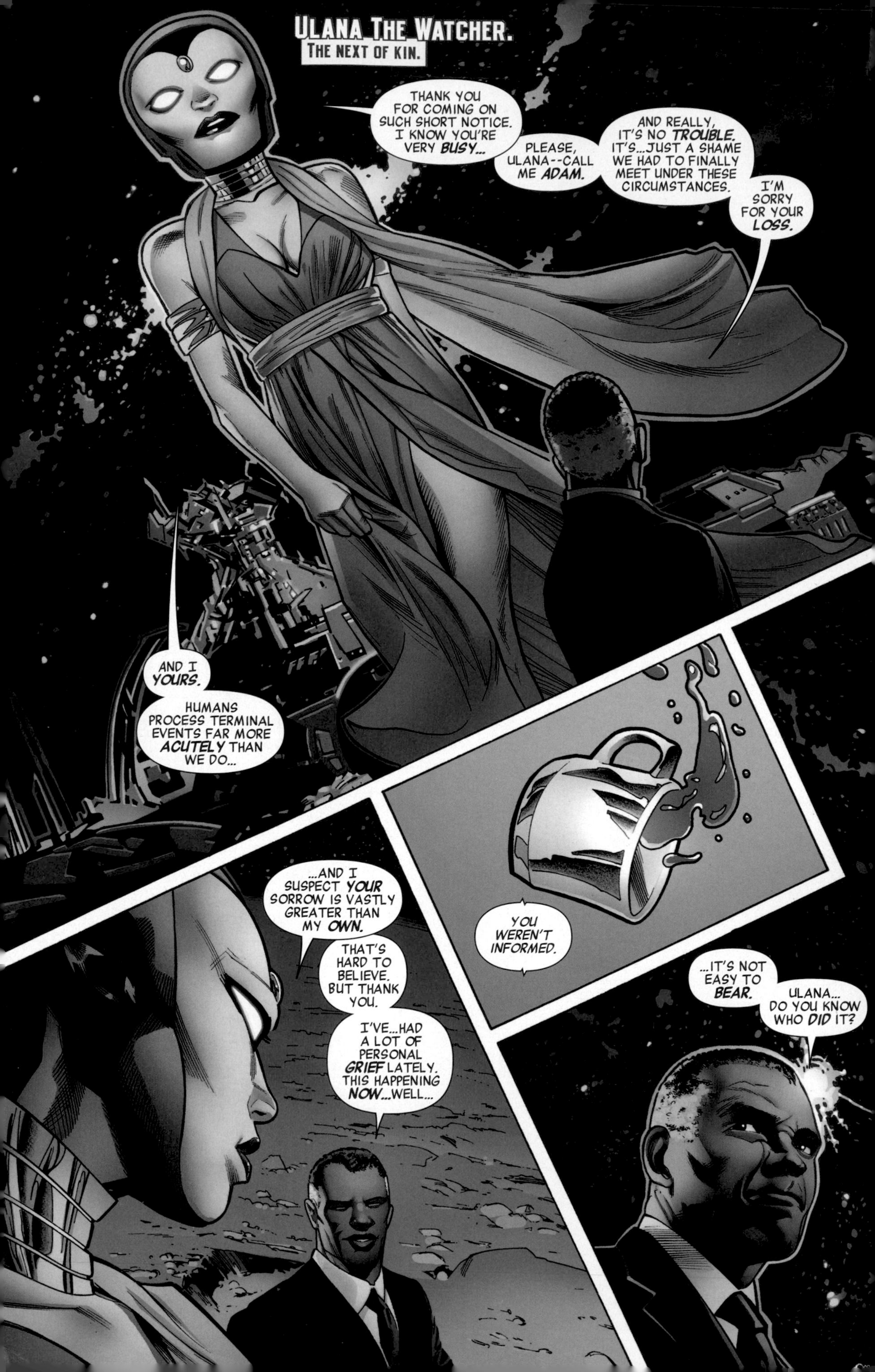
ULANA THE WATCHER.
THE NEXT OF KIN.
THANK YOU FOR COMING ON SUCH SHORT NOTICE. I KNOW YOU'RE VERY BUSY...
PLEASE, ULANA--CALL ME ADAM.
AND REALLY, IT'S NO TROUBLE. IT'S...JUST A SHAME WE HAD TO FINALLY MEET UNDER THESE CIRCUMSTANCES.
I'M SORRY FOR YOUR LOSS.
AND I YOURS.
HUMANS PROCESS TERMINAL EVENTS FAR MORE ACUTELY THAN WE DO...
...AND I SUSPECT YOUR SORROW IS VASTLY GREATER THAN MY OWN.
THAT'S HARD TO BELIEVE. BUT THANK YOU.
I'VE...HAD A LOT OF PERSONAL GRIEF LATELY. THIS HAPPENING NOW...WELL...
...IT'S NOT EASY TO BEAR.
YOU WEREN'T INFORMED.
ULANA... DO YOU KNOW WHO DID IT?

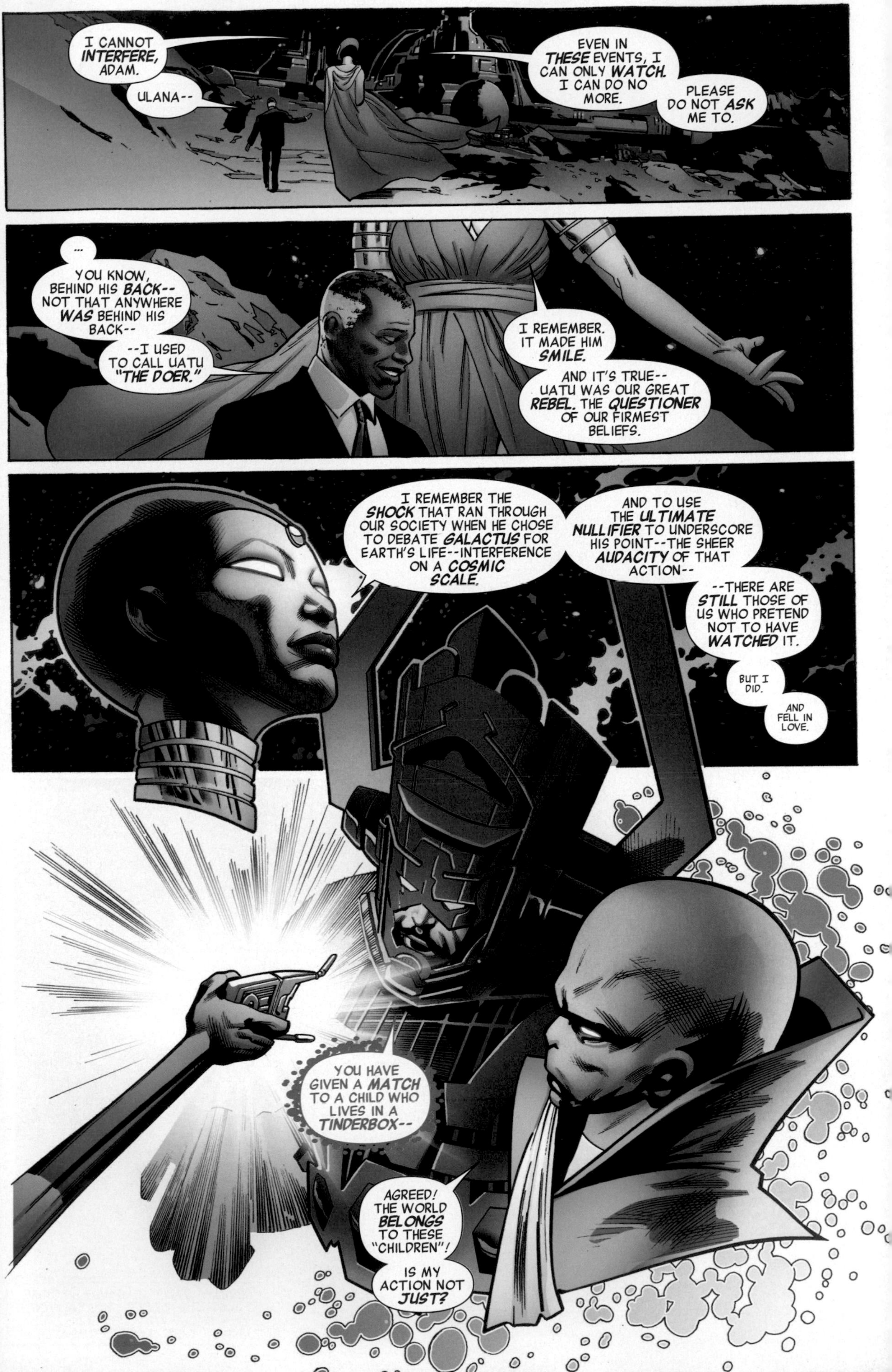

I CANNOT INTERFERE, ADAM.
ULANA--
EVEN IN THESE EVENTS, I CAN ONLY WATCH. I CAN DO NO MORE.
PLEASE DO NOT ASK ME TO.
...
YOU KNOW, BEHIND HIS BACK-- NOT THAT ANYWHERE WAS BEHIND HIS BACK--
--I USED TO CALL UATU "THE DOER."
I REMEMBER. IT MADE HIM SMILE.
AND IT'S TRUE-- UATU WAS OUR GREAT REBEL. THE QUESTIONER OF OUR FIRMEST BELIEFS.
I REMEMBER THE SHOCK THAT RAN THROUGH OUR SOCIETY WHEN HE CHOSE TO DEBATE GALACTUS FOR EARTH'S LIFE--INTERFERENCE ON A COSMIC SCALE.
AND TO USE THE ULTIMATE NULLIFIER TO UNDERSCORE HIS POINT--THE SHEER AUDACITY OF THAT ACTION--
--THERE ARE STILL THOSE OF US WHO PRETEND NOT TO HAVE WATCHED IT.
BUT I DID.
AND FELL IN LOVE.
YOU HAVE GIVEN A MATCH TO A CHILD WHO LIVES IN A TINDERBOX--
AGREED! THE WORLD BELONGS TO THESE "CHILDREN"!
IS MY ACTION NOT JUST?

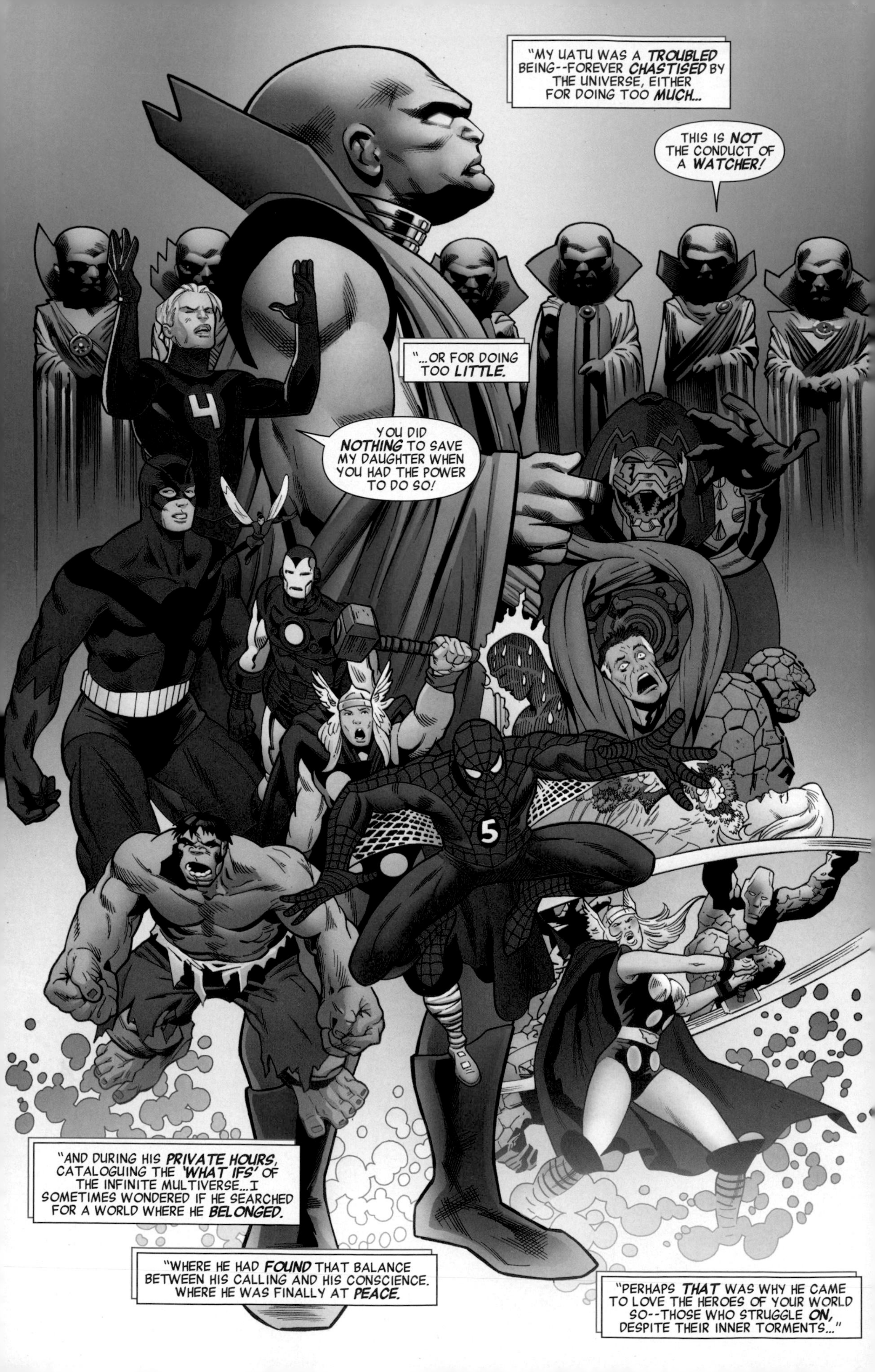
"MY UATU WAS A TROUBLED BEING--FOREVER CHASTISED BY THE UNIVERSE, EITHER FOR DOING TOO MUCH...
THIS IS NOT THE CONDUCT OF A WATCHER!
"...OR FOR DOING TOO LITTLE.
YOU DID NOTHING TO SAVE MY DAUGHTER WHEN YOU HAD THE POWER TO DO SO!
"AND DURING HIS PRIVATE HOURS, CATALOGUING THE 'WHAT IFS' OF THE INFINITE MULTIVERSE...I SOMETIMES WONDERED IF HE SEARCHED FOR A WORLD WHERE HE BELONGED.
"WHERE HE HAD FOUND THAT BALANCE BETWEEN HIS CALLING AND HIS CONSCIENCE. WHERE HE WAS FINALLY AT PEACE.
"PERHAPS THAT WAS WHY HE CAME TO LOVE THE HEROES OF YOUR WORLD SO--THOSE WHO STRUGGLE ON, DESPITE THEIR INNER TORMENTS..."

PERHAPS IN *YOU*, ADAM... HE RECOGNIZED A *FRIEND*.

A *FRIEND*...

I REMEMBER THE LAST TIME I *SAW* HIM--WHEN HE CAME TO WARN ME ABOUT *THANOS* AND *SHUMA-GORATH*.

ALL WITHOUT SAYING A *WORD*, OF COURSE. HE COULDN'T...COULDN'T *INTERFERE*.

IF I'D *KNOWN* THAT HE'D...I...

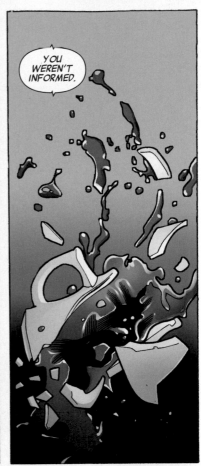

YOU WEREN'T INFORMED.

...I SHOULD HAVE *BEEN* THERE FOR HIM.

BUT I'M HERE *NOW*.

AND WHILE I *RESPECT* YOU AND YOUR PEOPLE...

...I *CAN* INTERFERE.

I'M GOING TO *FIND* UATU'S KILLER, ULANA.

AND *WHOEVER* IT IS--I'M GOING TO MAKE SURE THEY *PAY* FOR WHAT THEY DID TO MY FRIEND.

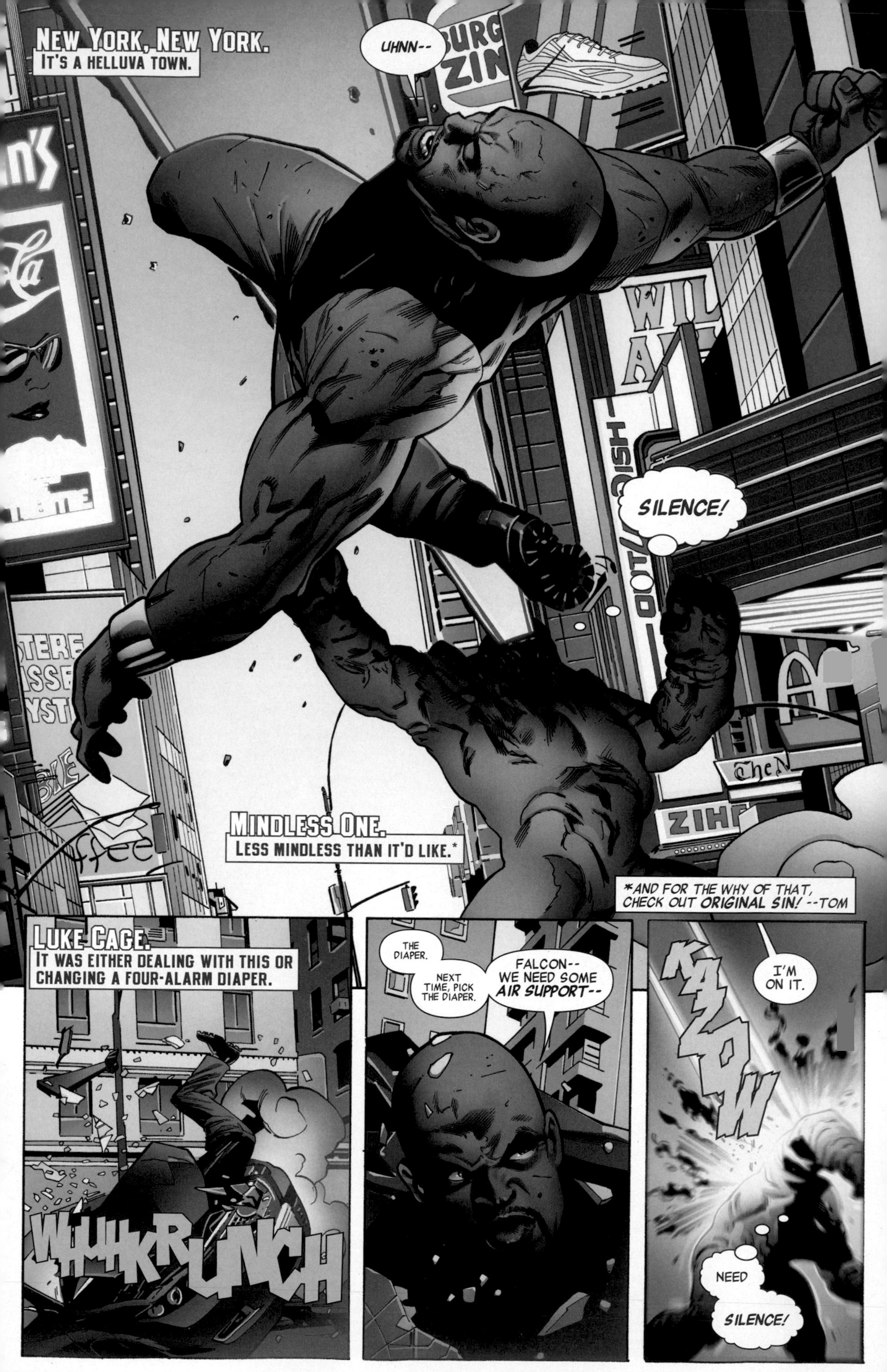

NEW YORK, NEW YORK.
IT'S A HELLUVA TOWN.
UHNN--
SILENCE!
MINDLESS ONE.
LESS MINDLESS THAN IT'D LIKE.*
*AND FOR THE WHY OF THAT, CHECK OUT ORIGINAL SIN! --TOM
LUKE CAGE.
IT WAS EITHER DEALING WITH THIS OR CHANGING A FOUR-ALARM DIAPER.
WHHKRUNCH
THE DIAPER.
NEXT TIME, PICK THE DIAPER.
FALCON-- WE NEED SOME AIR SUPPORT--
KAZOW
I'M ON IT.
NEED
SILENCE!

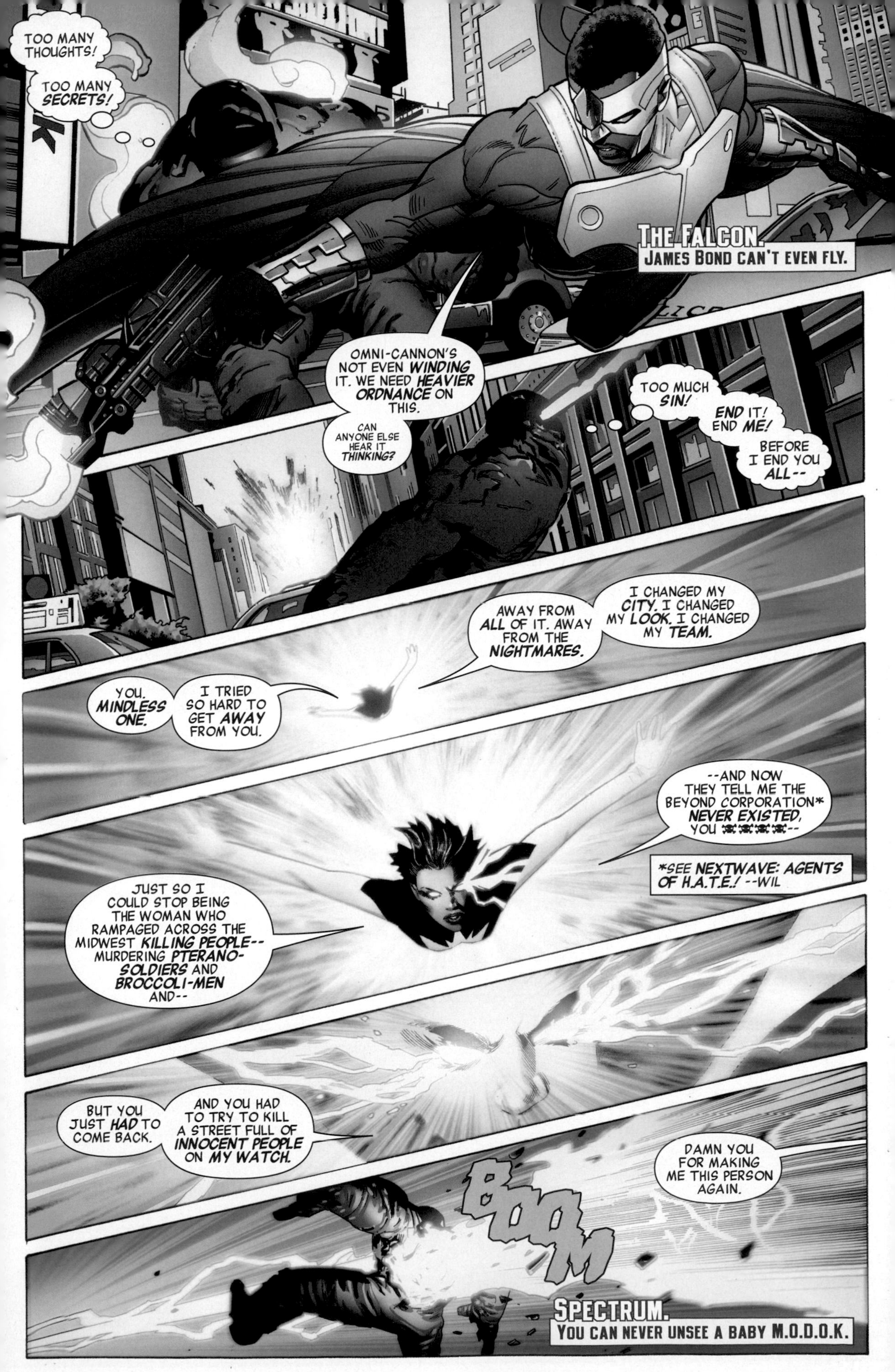

TOO MANY THOUGHTS!
TOO MANY SECRETS!
THE FALCON.
JAMES BOND CAN'T EVEN FLY.
OMNI-CANNON'S NOT EVEN WINDING IT. WE NEED HEAVIER ORDNANCE ON THIS.
CAN ANYONE ELSE HEAR IT THINKING?
TOO MUCH SIN!
END IT! END ME!
BEFORE I END YOU ALL--
I CHANGED MY CITY. I CHANGED MY LOOK. I CHANGED MY TEAM.
AWAY FROM ALL OF IT. AWAY FROM THE NIGHTMARES.
YOU. MINDLESS ONE.
I TRIED SO HARD TO GET AWAY FROM YOU.
--AND NOW THEY TELL ME THE BEYOND CORPORATION* NEVER EXISTED, YOU ☠☠☠☠--
*SEE NEXTWAVE: AGENTS OF H.A.T.E.! --WIL
JUST SO I COULD STOP BEING THE WOMAN WHO RAMPAGED ACROSS THE MIDWEST KILLING PEOPLE-- MURDERING PTERANO-SOLDIERS AND BROCCOLI-MEN AND--
BUT YOU JUST HAD TO COME BACK.
AND YOU HAD TO TRY TO KILL A STREET FULL OF INNOCENT PEOPLE ON MY WATCH.
DAMN YOU FOR MAKING ME THIS PERSON AGAIN.
BOOM
SPECTRUM.
YOU CAN NEVER UNSEE A BABY M.O.D.O.K.

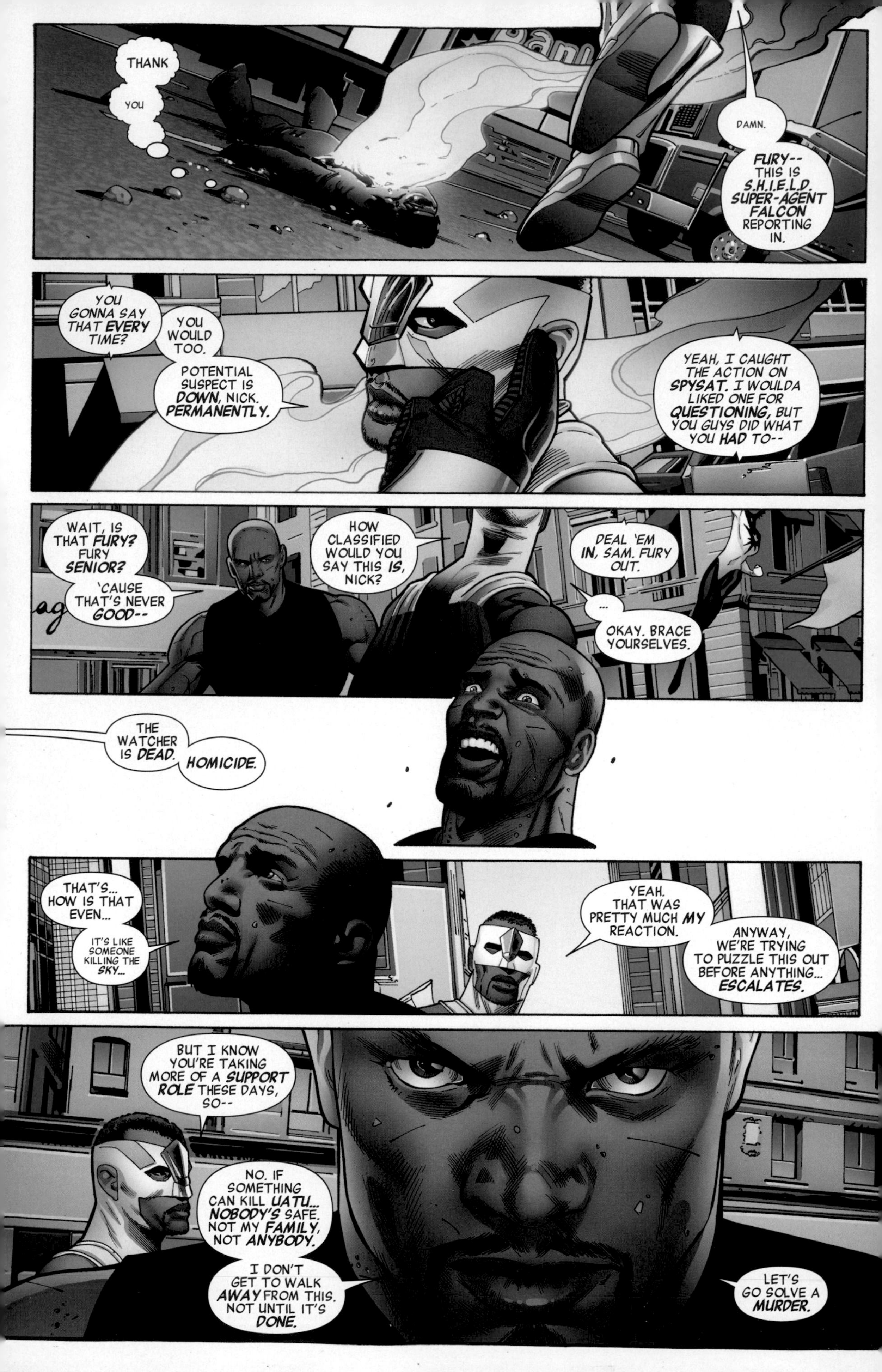

THANK
YOU
DAMN.
FURY-- THIS IS S.H.I.E.L.D. SUPER-AGENT FALCON REPORTING IN.
YOU GONNA SAY THAT EVERY TIME?
YOU WOULD TOO.
POTENTIAL SUSPECT IS DOWN, NICK. PERMANENTLY.
YEAH, I CAUGHT THE ACTION ON SPYSAT. I WOULDA LIKED ONE FOR QUESTIONING, BUT YOU GUYS DID WHAT YOU HAD TO--
WAIT, IS THAT FURY? FURY SENIOR?
'CAUSE THAT'S NEVER GOOD--
HOW CLASSIFIED WOULD YOU SAY THIS IS, NICK?
DEAL 'EM IN, SAM. FURY OUT.
...
OKAY. BRACE YOURSELVES.
THE WATCHER IS DEAD.
HOMICIDE.
THAT'S... HOW IS THAT EVEN...
IT'S LIKE SOMEONE KILLING THE SKY...
YEAH. THAT WAS PRETTY MUCH MY REACTION.
ANYWAY, WE'RE TRYING TO PUZZLE THIS OUT BEFORE ANYTHING... ESCALATES.
BUT I KNOW YOU'RE TAKING MORE OF A SUPPORT ROLE THESE DAYS, SO--
NO. IF SOMETHING CAN KILL UATU... NOBODY'S SAFE. NOT MY FAMILY, NOT ANYBODY.
I DON'T GET TO WALK AWAY FROM THIS. NOT UNTIL IT'S DONE.
LET'S GO SOLVE A MURDER.

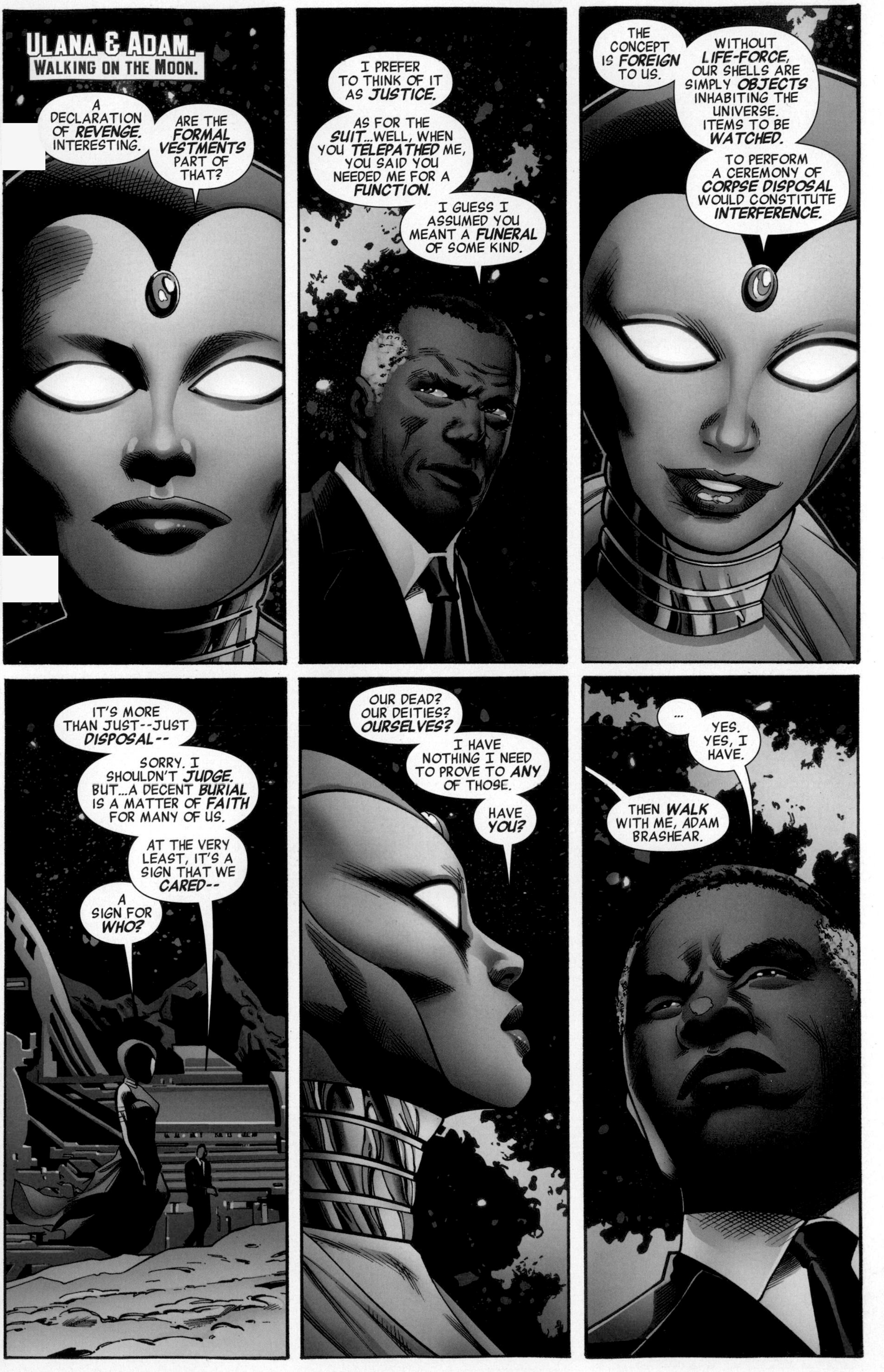
ULANA & ADAM.
WALKING ON THE MOON.
A DECLARATION OF REVENGE. INTERESTING.
ARE THE FORMAL VESTMENTS PART OF THAT?
I PREFER TO THINK OF IT AS JUSTICE.
AS FOR THE SUIT...WELL, WHEN YOU TELEPATHED ME, YOU SAID YOU NEEDED ME FOR A FUNCTION.
I GUESS I ASSUMED YOU MEANT A FUNERAL OF SOME KIND.
THE CONCEPT IS FOREIGN TO US.
WITHOUT LIFE-FORCE, OUR SHELLS ARE SIMPLY OBJECTS INHABITING THE UNIVERSE. ITEMS TO BE WATCHED.
TO PERFORM A CEREMONY OF CORPSE DISPOSAL WOULD CONSTITUTE INTERFERENCE.
IT'S MORE THAN JUST--JUST DISPOSAL--
SORRY. I SHOULDN'T JUDGE. BUT...A DECENT BURIAL IS A MATTER OF FAITH FOR MANY OF US.
AT THE VERY LEAST, IT'S A SIGN THAT WE CARED--
A SIGN FOR WHO?
OUR DEAD? OUR DEITIES? OURSELVES?
I HAVE NOTHING I NEED TO PROVE TO ANY OF THOSE.
HAVE YOU?
...
YES. YES, I HAVE.
THEN WALK WITH ME, ADAM BRASHEAR.

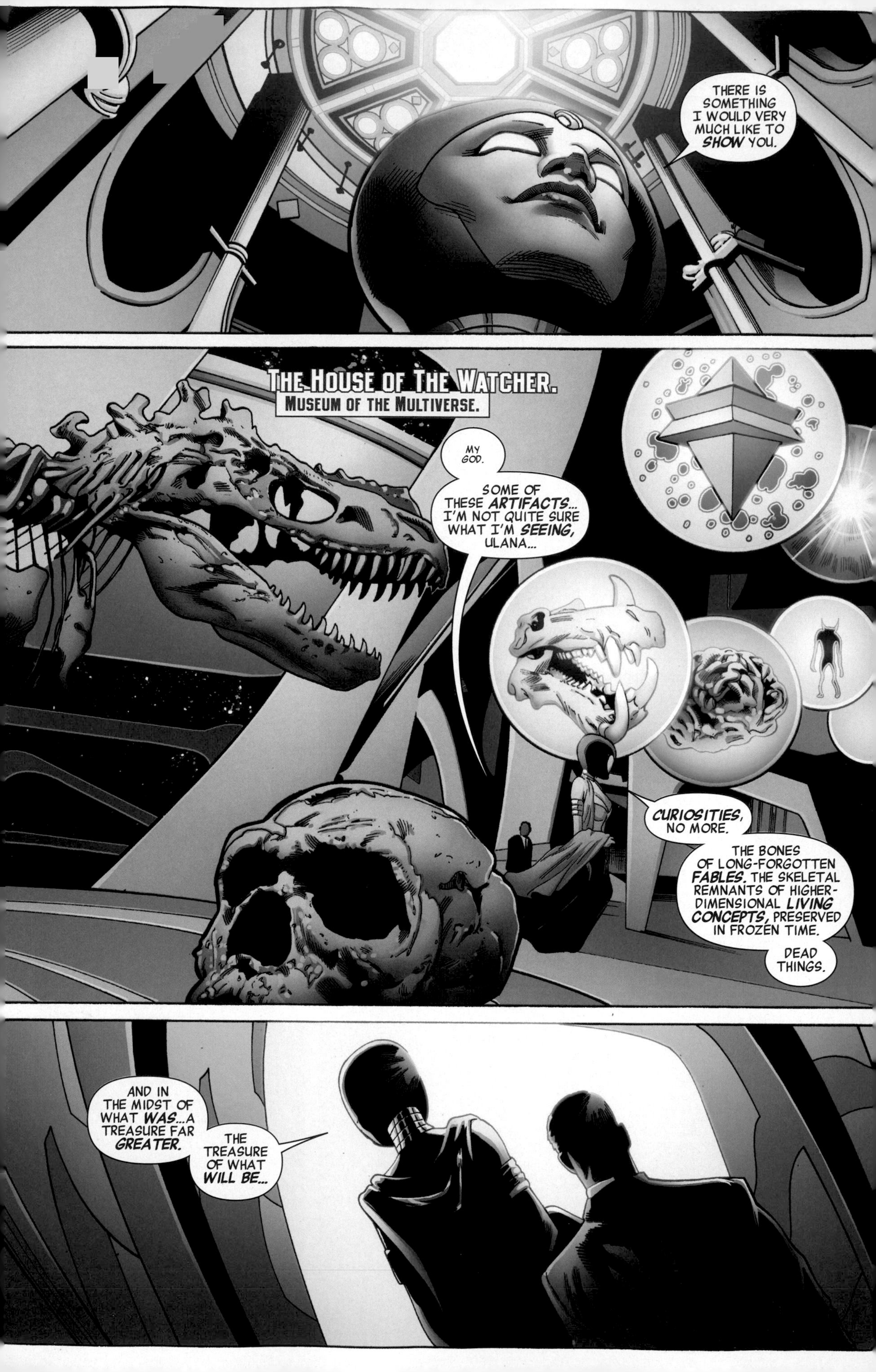
THERE IS SOMETHING I WOULD VERY MUCH LIKE TO SHOW YOU.
THE HOUSE OF THE WATCHER.
MUSEUM OF THE MULTIVERSE.
MY GOD.
SOME OF THESE ARTIFACTS... I'M NOT QUITE SURE WHAT I'M SEEING, ULANA...
CURIOSITIES, NO MORE.
THE BONES OF LONG-FORGOTTEN FABLES. THE SKELETAL REMNANTS OF HIGHER-DIMENSIONAL LIVING CONCEPTS, PRESERVED IN FROZEN TIME.
DEAD THINGS.
AND IN THE MIDST OF WHAT WAS...A TREASURE FAR GREATER.
THE TREASURE OF WHAT WILL BE...

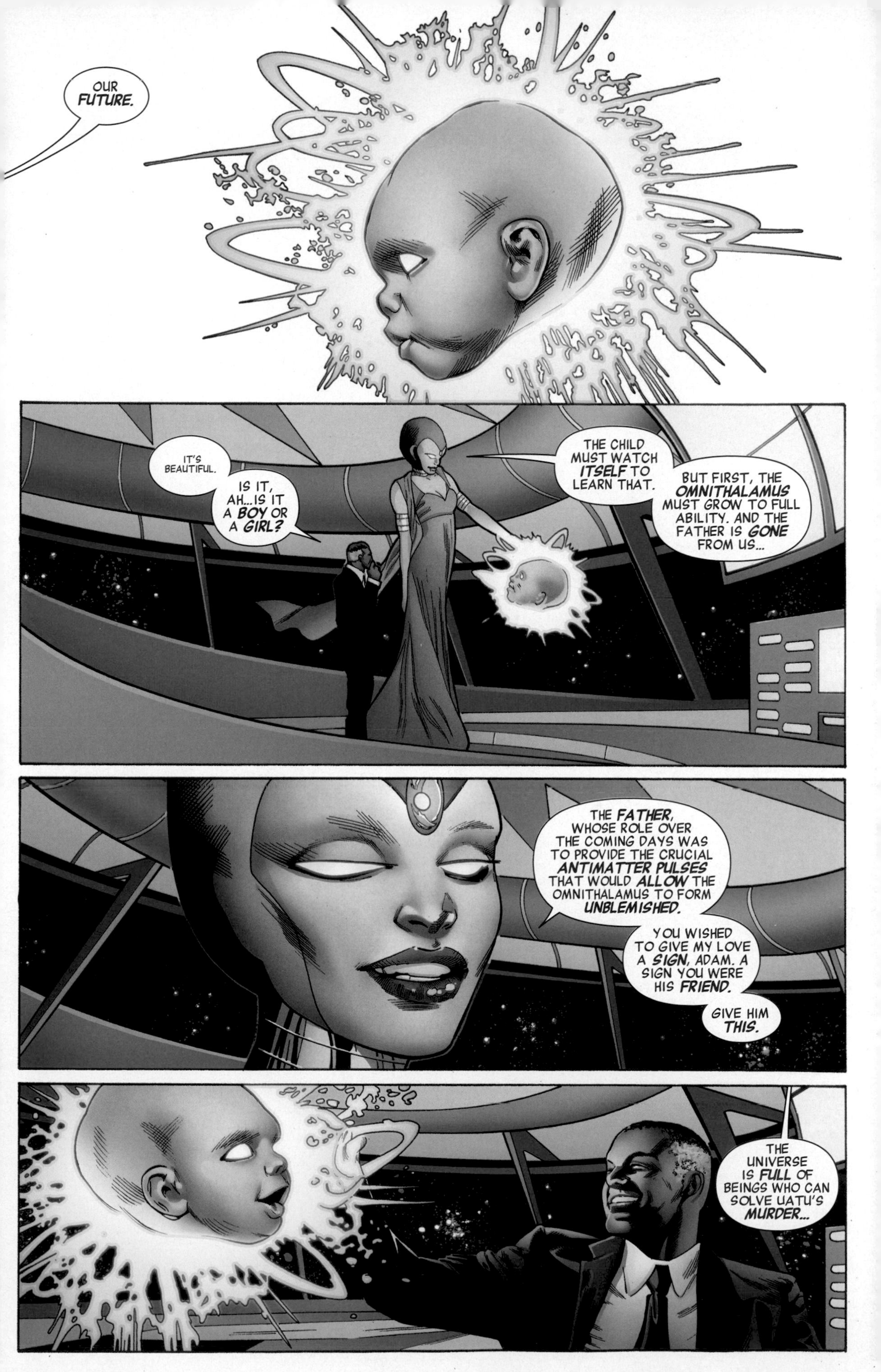
OUR FUTURE.
IT'S BEAUTIFUL.
IS IT, AH...IS IT A BOY OR A GIRL?
THE CHILD MUST WATCH ITSELF TO LEARN THAT.
BUT FIRST, THE OMNITHALAMUS MUST GROW TO FULL ABILITY. AND THE FATHER IS GONE FROM US...
THE FATHER, WHOSE ROLE OVER THE COMING DAYS WAS TO PROVIDE THE CRUCIAL ANTIMATTER PULSES THAT WOULD ALLOW THE OMNITHALAMUS TO FORM UNBLEMISHED.
YOU WISHED TO GIVE MY LOVE A SIGN, ADAM. A SIGN YOU WERE HIS FRIEND.
GIVE HIM THIS.
THE UNIVERSE IS FULL OF BEINGS WHO CAN SOLVE UATU'S MURDER...

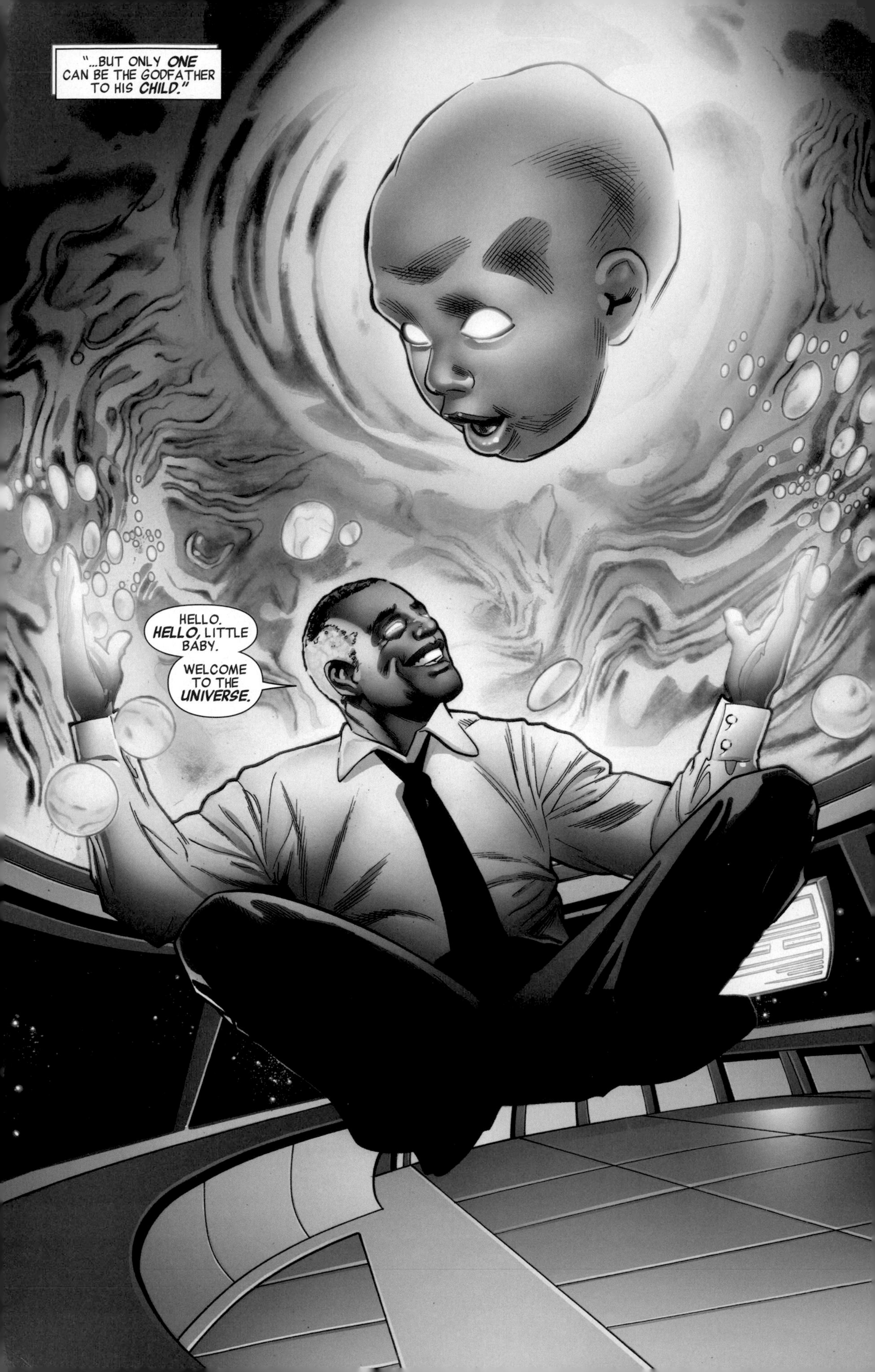
"...BUT ONLY ONE CAN BE THE GODFATHER TO HIS CHILD."
HELLO. HELLO, LITTLE BABY.
WELCOME TO THE UNIVERSE.

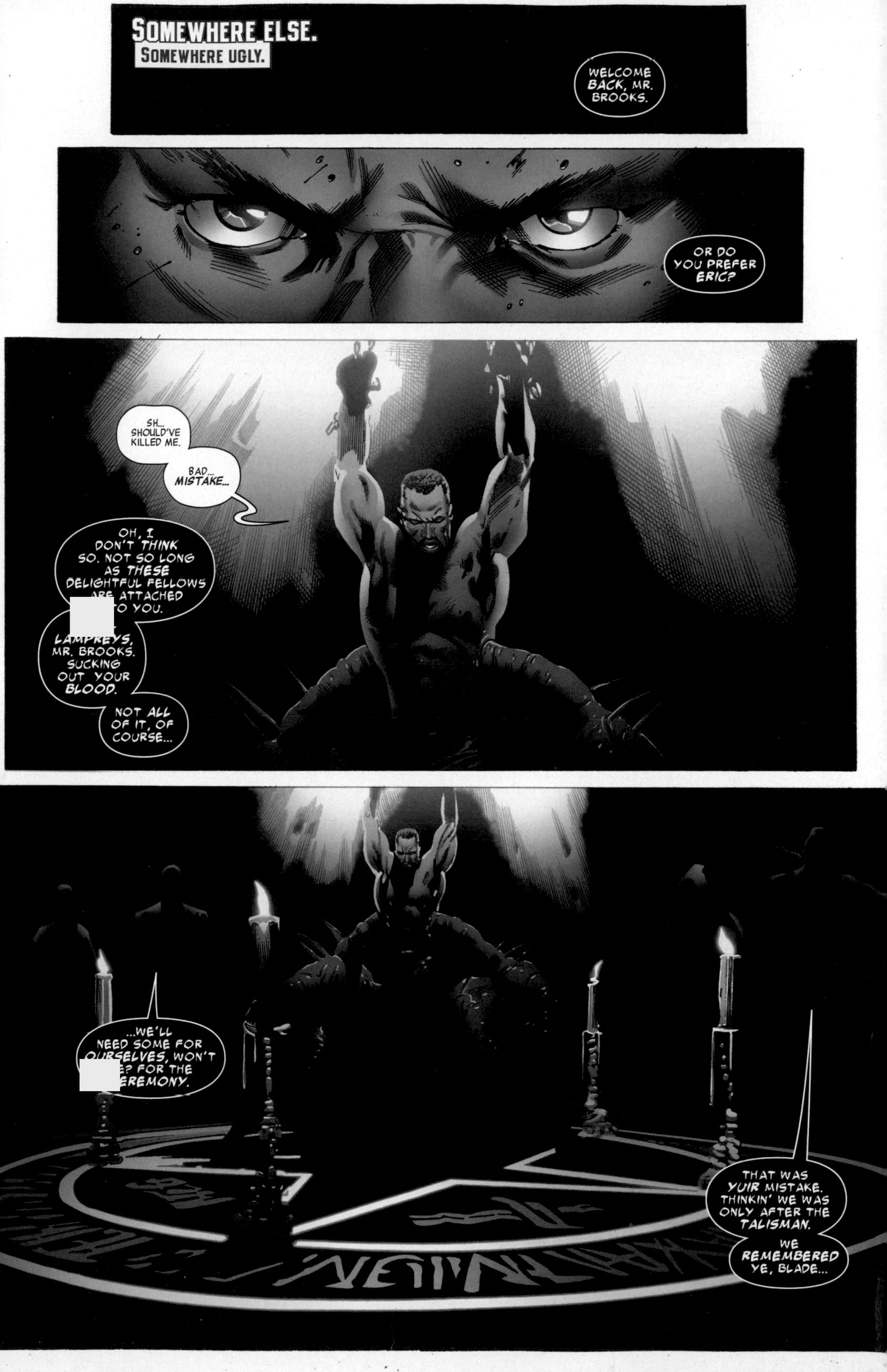
SOMEWHERE ELSE.
SOMEWHERE UGLY.
WELCOME BACK, MR. BROOKS.
OR DO YOU PREFER ERIC?
SH... SHOULD'VE KILLED ME.
BAD... MISTAKE...
OH, I DON'T THINK SO. NOT SO LONG AS THESE DELIGHTFUL FELLOWS ARE ATTACHED TO YOU.
LAMPREYS, MR. BROOKS. SUCKING OUT YOUR BLOOD.
NOT ALL OF IT, OF COURSE...
...WE'LL NEED SOME FOR OURSELVES, WON'T
E? FOR THE
EREMONY.
THAT WAS YUIR MISTAKE. THINKIN' WE WAS ONLY AFTER THE TALISMAN.
WE REMEMBERED YE, BLADE...

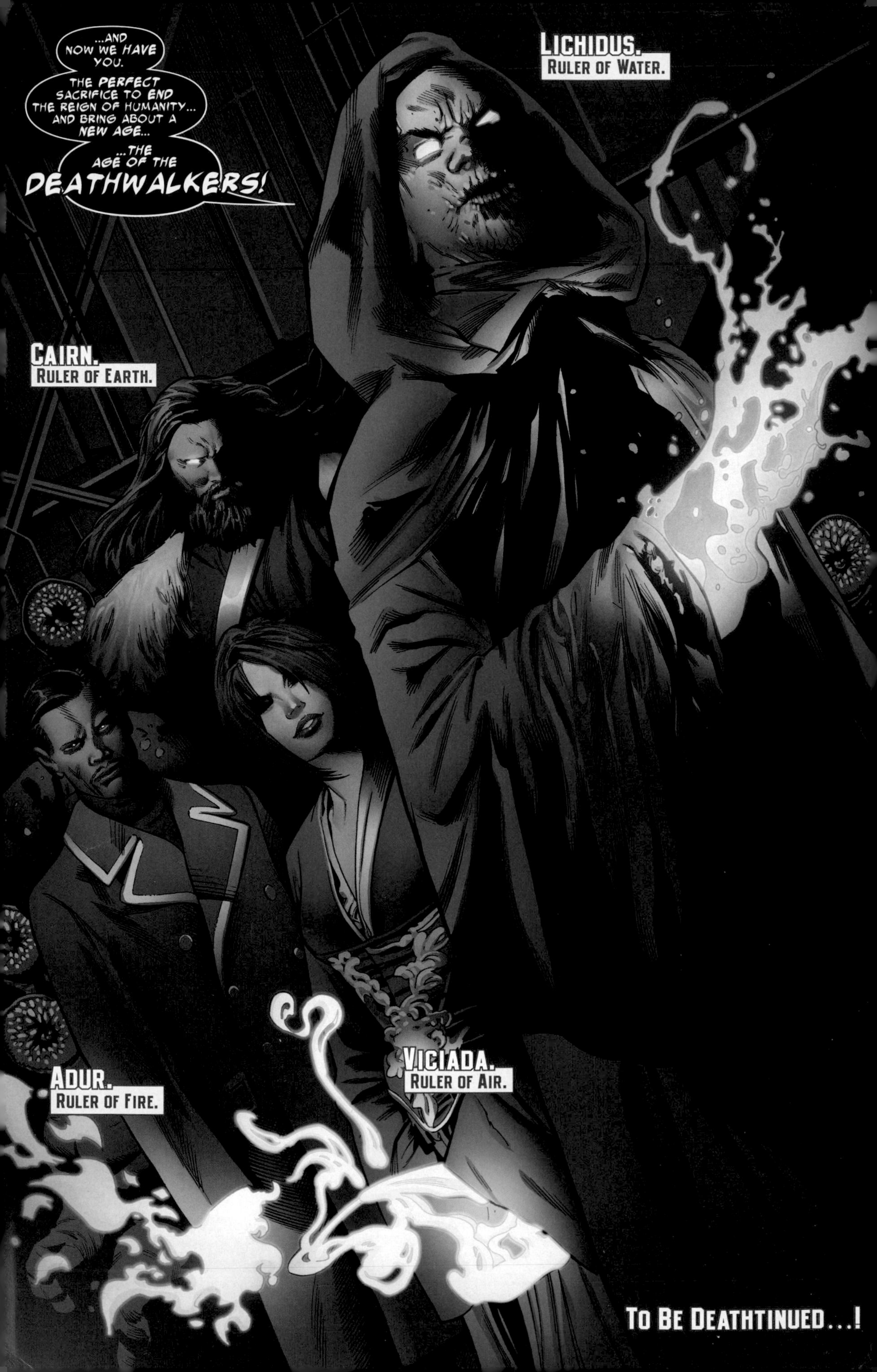
...AND NOW WE HAVE YOU.
THE PERFECT SACRIFICE TO END THE REIGN OF HUMANITY... AND BRING ABOUT A NEW AGE...
...THE AGE OF THE DEATHWALKERS!
LICHIDUS. RULER OF WATER.
CAIRN. RULER OF EARTH.
ADUR. RULER OF FIRE.
VICIADA. RULER OF AIR.
TO BE DEATHTINUED...!

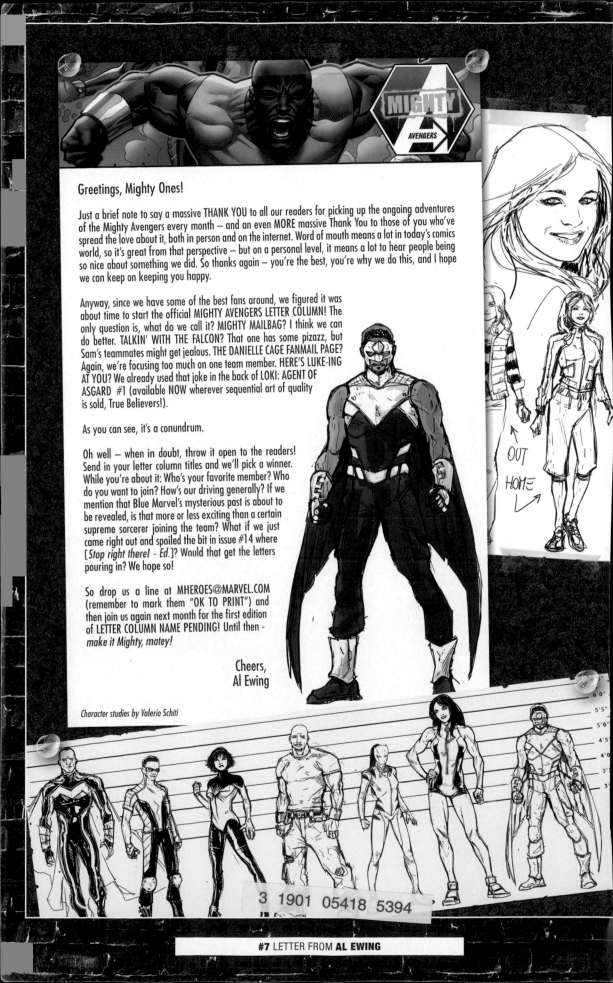

Greetings, Mighty Ones!

Just a brief note to say a massive THANK YOU to all our readers for picking up the ongoing adventures of the Mighty Avengers every month — and an even MORE massive Thank You to those of you who've spread the love about it, both in person and on the internet. Word of mouth means a lot in today's comics world, so it's great from that perspective — but on a personal level, it means a lot to hear people being so nice about something we did. So thanks again — you're the best, you're why we do this, and I hope we can keep on keeping you happy.

Anyway, since we have some of the best fans around, we figured it was about time to start the official MIGHTY AVENGERS LETTER COLUMN! The only question is, what do we call it? MIGHTY MAILBAG? I think we can do better. TALKIN' WITH THE FALCON? That one has some pizazz, but Sam's teammates might get jealous. THE DANIELLE CAGE FANMAIL PAGE? Again, we're focusing too much on one team member. HERE'S LUKE-ING AT YOU? We already used that joke in the back of LOKI: AGENT OF ASGARD #1 (available NOW wherever sequential art of quality is sold, True Believers!).

As you can see, it's a conundrum.

Oh well — when in doubt, throw it open to the readers! Send in your letter column titles and we'll pick a winner. While you're about it: Who's your favorite member? Who do you want to join? How's our driving generally? If we mention that Blue Marvel's mysterious past is about to be revealed, is that more or less exciting than a certain supreme sorcerer joining the team? What if we just came right out and spoiled the bit in issue #14 where [*Stop right there! - Ed.*]? Would that get the letters pouring in? We hope so!

So drop us a line at MHEROES@MARVEL.COM (remember to mark them "OK TO PRINT") and then join us again next month for the first edition of LETTER COLUMN NAME PENDING! Until then - *make it Mighty, matey!*

Cheers,
Al Ewing

Character studies by Valerio Schiti

OUT
HOME

3 1901 05418 5394

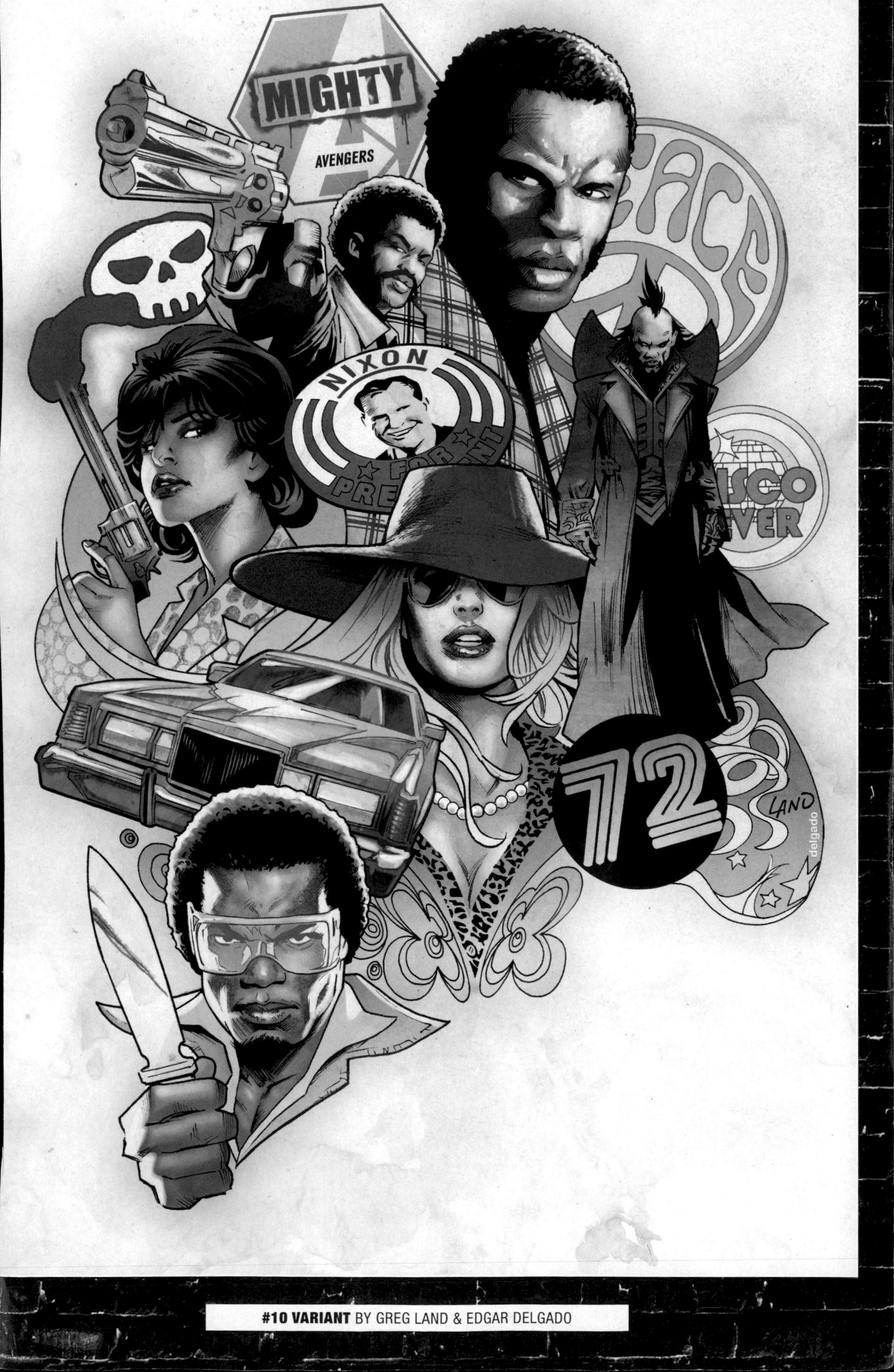
MIGHTY
AVENGERS
NIXON
FOR PRESIDENT
72
LAND
delgado

#10 VARIANT BY GREG LAND & EDGAR DELGADO